I0990411

Critical Essays on Jorge Luis Borges

*Critical Essays on
World Literature*

Robert Lecker, General Editor
McGill University

PQ 7797 .B635 Z6645 1987

Critical essays on Jorge
Luis Borges

Critical Essays on Jorge Luis Borges

Jaime Alazraki

G. K. Hall & Co. • Boston, Massachusetts

RITTER LIBRARY
BALDWIN-WALLACE COLLEGE
WITHDRAWN

Copyright © 1987 by Jaime Alazraki
All Rights Reserved

Library of Congress Cataloging in Publication Data

Alazraki, Jaime.
    Critical essays on Jorge Luis Borges.

    (Critical essays on world literature)
    Bibliography: p. 193
    Includes index.
    1. Borges, Jorge Luis, 1899-   —Criticism and interpretation.
I. Title. II. Series.
PQ7797.B635Z56 1987   868   86-14973
ISBN 0-8161-8829-7

This publication is printed on permanent/durable acid-free paper
MANUFACTURED IN THE UNITED STATES OF AMERICA

CONTENTS

INTRODUCTION   1
    Jaime Alazraki

ARTICLES AND REVIEWS
    An Autobiographical Essay   21
        Jorge Luis Borges
    A Modern Master   55
        Paul de Man
    The Author as Librarian   62
        John Updike
    Borges and the Fictive Narrative   77
        Pierre Macherey
    The Literature of Exhaustion   83
        John Barth
    A Game with Shifting Mirrors   93
        John Ashbery
    The Politics of Self-Parody   96
        Richard Poirier
    Imaginary Borges and His Books   108
        William H. Gass
    Tigers in the Mirror   116
        George Steiner
    [Review of *The Aleph and Other Stories 1933–1969*]   125
        Geoffrey H. Hartman
    Meeting Borges   127
        Alfred Kazin
    The Reality of Borges   130
        Robert Scholes

COMPARATIVE ESSAYS
    The Flaunting of Artifice in Vladimir Nabokov
      and Jorge Luis Borges   141
        Patricia Merivale

Borges and Thomas De Quincey   153
    Ronald Christ

Borges and American Fiction 1950–70   165
    Tony Tanner

From Amhoretz to Exegete: The Swerve from
    Kafka by Borges   173
    Margaret Boegeman

SELECTED BIBLIOGRAPHY OF WORKS IN ENGLISH   193
INDEX   195

INTRODUCTION

Strange destiny that of Borges. This is a line from a 1963 poem, "Elegy," in which the paradoxical nature of his life is pondered and ruminated over. Subsequent variations on the same paradox will be reformulated in forthcoming poems. The line also encapsulates the paradoxical fate of Borges's writings in the fluctuating tide of criticism. Since its beginning, Borges's texts invited controversy when not outright quarrel, particularly in his native Argentina. As early as 1924 (Borges was barely twenty-five) a literary feud divided Argentine writers with social and political concerns from those who viewed literature solely as an aesthetic artifact. This chapter of local literary history is known as the "Boedo-Florida Polemic." Each group adopted the name of the territory in Buenos Aires that represented its political affinities: Boedo was the quarter of the working class and the political left, and Florida, on the other hand, was the downtown heart of the elite. Although there were personal references to writers from both groups, the actual conflict was confined to the perception of literature defended or attacked by each group: Florida propagated and aped the experiments and prescriptions of avant-garde trends, and Boedo defended the need for social commitment in art. In spite of his early poems in praise of the Bolshevik Revolution, Borges sided with the first group.

Ten years later, in 1933, the polemic continued, but now it focused on a single writer: Borges. The Buenos Aires journal *Megáfono* devoted its eleventh issue to a poll in which fellow writers were asked to comment on the quality and value of his writings and on his place in the national literary scene. By then he had published three books of poetry and five collections of essays. He was considered the most prominent member of the so-called new generation and the most influential force among young writers. Reactions were mixed. Some praised his work as the most important ever produced in the country, others castigated him for his convoluted prose. Most expressed their preference for the poet. A few were able to detect a change from his early inflated prose into a more exact tool. One referred to his essay books as being born dead, and another characterized his style as that of "a Spaniard in the 16th-century trying to imitate a

1

Buenos Aires *compadrito* in 1900."[1] As harsh as the last assertion may sound, it was confirmed by Borges himself: in a de facto manner by refusing republication of the first three collections of essays (*Inquisitions*, 1925, *The Extent of My Hope*, 1926, and *The Language of Argentines*, 1928), and in a more explicit form when thirty-five years later he commented on those distant volumes:

> I began writing in a very self-conscious, baroque style. It was probably due to youthful timidity. The young often suspect that their plots and poems aren't very interesting, so they try to conceal them or elaborate on them by other means. When I began to write I tried to adopt the style of classical Spanish seventeenth-century writers, such as Quevedo or Saavedra Fajardo. Then I reasoned that it was my duty as an Argentine to write like an Argentine. I bought a dictionary of Argentinisms, and managed to become so Argentine in my style and vocabulary that people couldn't understand me and I couldn't even remember very well myself what the words meant. Words passed directly from the dictionary to my manuscript without corresponding to any experience.[2]

The Boedo-Florida polemic first, and the *Megáfono* poll later, colored from the outset the controversial quality of Borges criticism in Argentina. The line separating the two sides amounted to the following: his supporters and devotees hailed his sophistication and experimentalist audacity; his critics and detractors censured his cosmopolitism, his lack of commitment to Argentine realities, his contorted style. Borges's later acknowledgment of the mannerist quality of his early prose clearly indicates that some of the objections leveled by his critics were justified. Amado Alonso summarized the extent of this change in his prose when, commenting on the recent publication of the stories included in *A Universal History of Infamy*, he wrote back in 1935: "His youthful phraseology and vocabulary which lent to his prose a bumpy and squeaky course have almost completely disappeared."[3] But by then critics were deeply polarized and the antagonisms remained the staple of Borges criticism in Argentina.

In 1942, Victoria Ocampo found it necessary to devote an entire issue of her journal *Sur* to apologize to Borges for his having been denied the National Prize in Literature for *The Garden of Forking Paths* (1941). To offset the iniquity, twenty-one writers, intellectuals, critics, and friends wrote notes of protest to the jury and hymns of commendation to Borges. The *Sur* issue completely eclipsed the value of the prize and became a sort of apotheosis of Borges's work rendered by the Argentine literary establishment. It emphasized his literary accomplishments and asserted his position as a leading figure in Argentine letters, but it was not a unified chorus. Between the superlatives, there were dissonant voices that managed to express their reservations. Enrique Anderson-Imbert, for example, wrote about the narrowness of Borges's interests and the self-confined nature of his fiction, to conclude: "Those of us who devotedly accompany him in his descents to buried temples suffer at times the suffocation of so much rarified air. I doubt if we could endure to live there for too long should Borges persist in inhabiting them forever. Perhaps we will kill ourselves or die as did his Babel's librarians. Fortunately, in spite of his limitations, Borges remains sufficiently human so that his fiction could be nurtured by life."[4]

In this ambivalence, restated by Ernesto Sábato and others, lie the thrust of most objections he received in Argentina. His undeniable literary genius — it was felt — was couched in hyperintellectual assumptions and mythological perceptions of disappeared indigenous types: *gauchos* and *compadres*. Argentine reality was left out. A journal that defended the jury's decision put it bluntly: "Those who would venture through the pages of this book [*The Garden of Forking Paths*] would find an explanation to the jury's decision in the dehumanized nature of its pages, in its preciosity, in the obscure and arbitrary cerebral game which cannot even be compared to chessgame combinations since these respond to precise and rigorous relationships and not to a sheer whim often bordering on mystification."[5]

The outcry was not against the lack of social or political involvement in his writings, but, as Sábato put it, against the geometric nature of his fiction holding the perfection of a mathematical theorem and lacking at the same time the adventure and passion of life and death.[6] Borges knew and accepted his limitations. Almost echoing some of his critics, he wrote in the preface to *Discusión* of 1932: "My life has been devoid of life and death. From this poverty stems my laborious love for these minutiae."[7] Many years later, in his "Autobiographical Essay" of 1970, he reiterated his loyalty to the world of books: "If I were asked to name the chief event of my life, I should say my father's library. In fact, I sometimes think I never strayed outside that library."[8] Like Asterion, the Minotaur of his fiction, who when confronted with the chaos of the world chooses the orderly space he has found in a human construction — Daedalus's Labyrinth —, Borges has made a similar choice: confronted with the chaos of the world, he chose the order of the library, the safety of a decipherable labyrinth. His books grew out of other books. He wrote fiction based on theologies and philosophies, literature founded in literature. He knew that the hard face of reality lingers on every corner of life, but he renounced reality because, he said, of its impenetrable nature. Instead, he anchored his writings in the order of the intellect, in the chartable waters of the library. What he wrote about Paul Valéry is applicable to himself: "In a century that adores the *chaotic* idols of blood, earth, and passion, he always preferred the lucid pleasures of thought and the secret adventures of order."[9] For Borges, the intellect is the true adventure, the mind is the true passion, and life is but a dream (at least in literary terms). He has, consequently, avoided human experience in favor of intellectual knowledge. In his aloofness toward things too human, he has denounced "the tendency of modern literature to reveal men's weaknesses and to delight in their unhappiness and guilt."[10] For a writer like him, who was born in a generation characterized as "the last one of happy men," the question of unhappiness was anathema. Should Borges's readers be surprised by his indictments against forms of literature and intellectual endeavours that deal with the miseries of human unhappiness? Any form of knowledge that challenged his skeptical understanding of the world met with his strong disapproval and even condemnation. In his paraphrasis of Valéry, he attacked romanticism, Marxism, psychoanalysis and surrealism as manifestations of the savage and irrational in human life: "The meritorious mission that Valéry performed (and continues to perform) is that he proposed lucidity to men in a basely *romantic* age, in the melancholy age of *dialectical materialism*, the age of the augurs of *Freud's* sect and the traffickers in *surrealism*."[11] The derogatory tinge of these epithets is evident. Any human effort addressed at confronting life as a passionate, unjust, instinctive, or irrational force met with his stark resistance. Borges's answer was his fiction in which, like in the classical traditional of idealist philosophy that feeds much of his narrative outlook, "the world has been constructed by means of logic, with little or no appeal to concrete experience, and while it liberates imagination as to what the world *may be*, it refuses to legislate as to what the world *is*."[12]

This answer couldn't possibly please those who view literature as an effort to change life. The first two book-length studies published in Argentina and elsewhere in the mid-fifties reflected this early bifurcation in Borges criticism: Adolfo Prieto's *Borges and the New Generation* (1954) and Marcial Tamayo and Adolf Ruiz Díaz's *Borges: Enigma and Clue* (1955). The first book voiced the dissatisfaction of the young generation with Borges as a possible model for Argentine literature. It aired the complaints of the young against a writer they considered too individualistic when not solipsistic: "Borges has sharpened the singularity of his work to such a degree that it appears alien to its time and place, as if the work and the environment in which it was conceived were totally divorced. . . . The young preoccupied by the social problems of their time cannot possibly identify with him. Borges was born in a world very different from ours."[13] The excellence of his prose was acknowledged, but his lack of commitment toward the problems facing the people and the country was condemned. The book rejected Borges as a gratuitous and merely ludic writer. The second book was a more academic study of major themes and motifs in his fiction. The two prolonged and broadened the conflictive terms under which Borges criticism evolved since its inception in his native Argentina. The intellectual substratum of his work alienated some and fascinated others.

Borges might have chosen to ignore and even deny reality in his fiction, but as he himself wrote so memorably reality *is irreversible and iron bound.* Latin America is a continent besieged by economic and social turmoil and threatened by poverty, hunger, illiteracy, political manipulation, military extortion and foreign intervention. Argentina is not exempted from those ills. Just before the Falklands War, the generals who ruled the country with a fascist iron fist spoke in international forums of Western values and of Argentina as being a part *not* of the Third World but of the West. A few weeks later the catastrophe of the war ensued, bringing to an end the blackest period in Argentine history: the six horrendous years of the so-called "Dirty War" during which ten thousand innocent people were savagely murdered and many more were illegally incarcerated and brutally tortured. The generals used their pretended allegiance to the West as a mask to cover up their crimes and atrocities. The naive intellectuals who believed that "the Argentine tradition is all Western culture" — Borges dixit — and that "we Argentines, we South Americans in general, can handle all European themes, handle them without superstition,"[14] lent themselves to the monstrous game of the generals. So much so that the generals grabbed the flag of the "Western tradition" with much delight to turn the inferno they had created into a cultural crusade. Borges — it is painful to utter it — supported the generals — "those gentlemen who will save the country" — , became their intellectual in residence, and by so doing joined that satanic game. A recent book — Pedro Orgambide's *Borges y su pensamiento político* (México, 1978) examines this issue at great length and with painful detail.

Can literature make a difference? Probably not. Those few writers who spoke out were either assassinated (Rodolfo Walsh, Haroldo Conti, Paco Urondo), imprisoned and tortured (Antonio di Benedetto, Daniel Moyano), or forced into exile. Yet, in the light of those recent tragic events which have changed so radically the course of Argentina, the frowning of the young upon Borges's lack of national roots, his being out of touch with the *real* country, and his standoffish attitude toward human experience, acquire a new dimension and an added urgency. The protestations of the young were echoed by the not so young. Gabriel García Márquez, whose work epitomizes the hopes and fears of Latin America at large, has reformulated the essential ambivalence found in the early decades of Argentine criticism on Borges. In a 1967 interview conducted by Mario Vargas Llosa, the subject of Borges came up:

Vargas Llosa: . . . I have always had problems in justifying my admiration for Borges.

García Márquez: I have no problem at all. I have a great admiration for him. I read him every night. I just came from Buenos Aires and the only thing I bought there was Borges's *Complete Works*. I carry them in my suitcase; I am going to read them every day, and he is a writer I detest. His is a literature of evasion. Something strange happens to me with Borges. He is one of the writers I read the most and whom I have read most, and yet he is perhaps the one I like least. I read him because of his extraordinary ability for verbal artifice. I am fascinated by the violin he uses to express his things. He teaches you how to tune up your literary instrument. I think Borges writes about mental realities, he is sheer evasion. Cortázar, on the other hand, is profoundly Latin American.[15]

This dichotomy between Borges's verbal virtuosity and his imperviousness to the world of experience is going to remain the watershed separating those who praise him unreservedly and those who condemn his cosmopolitism and sophistry; between those who admire his limpid style but cannot condone the intellectual substance of his work, and those who accept him as both a prose master and a riveting fabulist. The dispute found its way into one of the most ambitious and widely read novels in Argentina, Ernesto Sábato's *On Heroes and Tombs*. Chapter 13 of part 2 is entirely devoted to discussing the merits and demerits of Borges's work. Borges actually appears in the novel walking through the streets of Buenos Aires and stopping casually to chat, as no doubt has occurred many times in the life of the town. The discussion that follows this scene is a tight summary of the criticism around his work. It goes like this:

> Martin asked: "Do you think he's a great writer?"
> Bruno pondered the question for some time. "I don't know. What I am certain of is that his prose is the most remarkable of any being written in Spanish today. But his style is too precious for him to be a great writer. Can you imagine Tolstoy trying to dazzle his readers with an adverb when it's a question of the life or death of one of his characters? But not everything in Borges's works is Bizantine: far from it. There's something Argentine in his best things: a certain nostalgia, a certain metaphysical sadness. . . .
> "When we read Dickens or Faulkner or Tolstoy we feel that total understanding of the human soul. When we read Borges, on the other hand, we feel his inability to understand and sense the whole of the country, including all its deep-rooted, complex rottenness."[16]

Julio Cortázar, sometimes mistakenly associated with Borges for his attraction toward the fantastic — mistakenly, since for Borges the fantastic is an intellectual exercise whereas for Cortázar it is an effort to overcome the shortcomings of language and rational order — has most succinctly summarized the extent of his debt and that of the writers of his generation with Borges: "Borges's great lesson — he said in an interview — was neither a lesson of themes or contents nor of technique. It was a lesson in writing. The attitude of a man who, facing each sentence, has studiously thought not which adjective he would add, but which one he would remove in a manner reminiscent of Mallarmé's attitude of extreme rigor toward the written page."[17]

Carlos Fuentes, the Mexican novelist and author of a very fine essay on Latin-American fiction, has written in it that "without Borges's prose there simply would not be a modern Spanish-American novel." But he has also added: "The big vacuum in Borges is, we all know it, his lack of a critical perception of society and the imagination."[18] Other Latin American writers and intellectuals have made similar statements.[19] Borges has contributed to reinforce that sense of remoteness his Spanish-American readers find in his writings. When asked about his fellow writers in Latin America, either from his generation or a younger one, his answer has been invariably the same: "I cannot give an opinion on a writer I haven't read." His blindness is no excuse. He has olympically ignored his own tradition and, at the same time, he has found time (and sight) to continue his study of Old English and Old Norse. In a very oblique way, Borges has either scolded or discarded the tremendous accomplishments of Latin American writers of the last fifty years with the exception of some of his own friends.

For Argentines, first, and for Latin Americans at large afterward, Borges has become a sort of father figure: the progenitor of a language out of which, like from a seed, contemporary Spanish-American fiction evolved and reached maturity. At the same time, he has come to represent also the denial of everything Latin-American, the glorification of the West and the mutilation of that part of the continent alien to or different from what the West has sanctioned as acceptable or civilized. If to be civilized meant to be like a European or an American, culture thus understood amounted to the rejection of precisely that part which by dint of its idiosyncratic differences defined what was unique and *real* among Latin Americans. When the presence of the father becomes a repressive hindrance in our psychological growth—Freud tells us—he needs to be "killed." The Polish writer Witold Gombrowicz lived in Argentina between 1939 and 1963. In his *Argentine Diaries* he left a testimony of those long twenty-four years. He describes the country as a "chimpanzee" but also as a youthful country with which he was or wanted to be passionately in love. When he left Buenos Aires for Europe never to return he shouted from the deck of the ship to a handful of friends and fellow writers who came to say good-bye to him and were standing on the wharf: "*Maten a Borges*" (Kill Borges).

Borges's fate outside Latin America was different. Across the Atlantic or in North America he was read either as a European or as a North American. He was so familiar with both literary traditions that his readers there thought of him as a fellow countryman. The drawback of his not being the spokesman for his country was overcome. He was finally a citizen of the world and he could consequently be read as the brilliant writer and sophisticated mind he truly was. The reactions of his readers matched the caliber of his writings, and Borges criticism reached unexpected heights precisely outside Argentina. Let us trace a brief account of the highlights of this criticism.

Outside Latin America, Borges was first known in France for very specific and even circumstantial reasons. During World War II many French intellectuals either moved or emigrated to Argentina. Roger

Caillois was one of them. He lived four years in Buenos Aires and during that time he was the editor of *Lettres Françaises*, which was published in exile during the German occupation of France and sponsored by *Sur*, the magazine in whose pages Borges published essays, stories, and book and film reviews from its first issue in 1931 until its last one in 1984. The French translations of Borges's short stories first appeared in *Lettres Françaises*. The fourteenth issue (October 1944) included "The Lottery in Babylon" and "The Library of Babel" translated into French by Nestor Ibarra. It was through this issue of *Lettres Françaises* that French readers first came in contact with Borges's fiction. Upon his return to Paris in 1946, Caillois asked Paul Verdevoye for the translation of *Ficciones*, but its publications, including the pieces translated by Ibarra, was postponed until 1951 when it appeared in Editions Gallimard.[20] The same publisher issued *Labyrinthes* two years later. It included four stories from *The Aleph* translated and prefaced by Roger Caillois. *Other Inquisitions*, his best collection of essays, was translated into French by Paul and Sylvia Bénichou and it was published by Gallimard also in 1957. The next year *A Universal History of Infamy* and *A History of Eternity* appeared together translated into French by Caillois in Editions du Rocher.

This bibliographic chronology readily shows that by the time Borges was first published in English in 1961 he had already been widely read in France. It also helps to explain the delay with which Borges criticism began appearing in English when compared with French. By 1964, the mammoth *Cahiers de L' Herne* devoted to Borges appeared in Paris: 516 large pages with crowded typography containing notes, essays, comments, interviews, articles and twenty unpublished translations into French of texts by Borges. But even before this heavy vade mecum appeared, Borges had been the subject of critical scrutiny in France through magazines such as *Les Temps Modernes*, *Hygiene des lettres*, *Le Monde*, *Le Figaro Litteraire*, *Lettres Francaises*, *Tel Quel*, *Nouvelle Revue Francaise*, *Les Nouvelles Littéraires*, *L' Observateur*, *Cahiers du Sud*, *La Revue Euro-péenne*.

The International Publishers' Prize shared by Borges and Samuel Beckett in 1961, the publications in the United States of *Labyrinths* (a selection of his fiction and essays) and *Ficciones* the year after, and of *Dreamtigers* and *Other Inquisitions* two years later turned Borges into one of the most visible major writers in the English-speaking world, particularly in the United States. Two additional factors contributed considerably to Borges's recognition in the United States. In 1961 he was invited to the University of Texas at Austin where he gave a series of lectures, and in 1967 he was the Charles Eliot Norton Lecturer at Harvard. Borges turned into a familiar presence in the Anglo-Saxon world. By 1970, George Steiner could say: "There is a sense in which the Director of the Biblioteca Nacional of Argentina is now the most original of Anglo-American writers." More important, however, was the fact that during the sixties and seventies he became a frequent contributor to American journals of massive circulation such as the *New Yorker, Harper's Bazaar, Atlantic Monthly,* the *New York Review of Books, Salmagundi,* the *Antioch Review, Esquire, New York, TriQuarterly, Encounter,* and others. *Vogue* and the *Times Literary Supplement* of London completed the task of making Borges accessible for the English reader.

Critical reaction to the English translations of his major works published between 1962 and 1964 followed immediately. The sixties were the turning point for Borges's recognition in the Anglo-Saxon world. It first occurred at the academic level, understandably so, since university inquiry does not depend on translations. Isolated articles appeared in professional journals since 1958, and increased in number after 1962. By 1963 and 1964, two Ph.D. dissertations were written in English in the United States. Until then — as George Steiner put it — "the splendor of Borges was clandestine, signaled to the happy few, bartered in undertones of mutual recognitions. Only ten years ago [by 1960], it was a mark of arcane erudition and a wink to the initiate to realize that H. Bustos Domecq was the joint pseudonym of Borges and his close collaborator Adolfo Bioy Casares. Such information was close-guarded, parsimoniously dispensed, often nearly impossible to come by, as were Borges's poems, stories, and essays themselves, scattered, out of print, pseudonymous." All this changed after the publication of the first English translations. Critics as well as writers in the United States began reading Borges voraciously. The response to that larger reading was recorded in sporadic and circum-stantial reviews by critics who — as Paul de Man wrote — "have called him one of the greatest writers alive today, but who have not as yet made substantial contributions to the interpretation of his work." This was in 1964 when Paul de Man published his seminal essay "A Modern Master" in the *New York Review of Books.* This early piece became the first serious attempt at understanding not so much the message of his work as the relationships between that message and its code. The controversial sides of his writings were left south of the Río Grande. North-American readers approached Borges without the social and political concerns (others may say bias) that afflicted his compatriots and were able to focus more poignantly on the intricacies of his art. De Man acknowledged as a sort of truism the very fact that so strongly offended a good deal of the Argentine critics, that the world of his stories "is the representation, not of an actual experience, but of an intellectual proposition." Once this was recognized not as a handicap but as a choice and even as a virtue, the next point de Man raised was the question of the narrative genre of these *ficciones:* "One does not expect the same kind of psychological insight or the same immediacy of personal experience from *Candide* as from *Madame Bovary,* and Borges should be read with expectations closer to those one brings to Voltaire's tale than to a nineteenth-century novel." Having removed the expectation of reading Borges as one reads Flaubert or Tolstoy (an expectation that persistently haunted Sábato, as we have seen) de Man touched the core of Borges's artifice: if his *ficciones* are closer to Voltaire's, he reasoned, "he differs, however, from his eighteenth-century antecedents in that the subject of the stories is the creation of style itself. . . . His main characters are prototypes for the writer, and his worlds, are prototypes for a highly stylized kind of poetry or fiction. For all their variety of tone and setting, the different stories all have a similar point of departure, a similar structure, a similar climax, and a similar outcome; the inner cogency that links these four moments constitutes Borges's distinctive style, as well as his comment upon this style. His stories are about the style in which they are written." De Man's essay is the demonstration of this tenet.

If deconstruction — as de Man himself defined it in his *Allegories of Reading* — "always has for its target to reveal the existence of hidden articulations and fragmentations within assumedly monadic totalities," his "Modern Master" can be viewed as a deconstructionist reading of Borges with admirable results. His point of departure is thematic: *infamy*, as a motif throughout his fiction and as a central theme in the first collection on that subject. But the infamous character is, in turn, a mirror-image of the writer: the creation of beauty begins as an act of duplicity. "The duplicity of the artist, the grandeur as well as the misery of his calling, is a recurrent theme closely linked with the theme of infamy." Duplicity as strategy is then linked with duplicity as outlook: "The writer's particular duplicity stems from the fact that he presents the invented form as if it possessed the attributes of reality." This articulation between theme, strategy and outlook is then ingeniously extended to the level of structure: "All the stories have a similar mirror-like structure, although the devices vary with diabolical ingenuity." Finally, duplicity as a deliberate infamous act is also seen as the criterion for evaluating art: "This mirror-like proliferation constitutes, for Borges, an indication of poetic success. The works of literature he most admires contain this element: *Hamlet, Don Quijote,* and *One Thousand and One Nights.* For each mirrored image is stylistically superior to the preceding one, as the dyed cloth is more beautiful than the plain, the distorted translation richer than the original, Ménard's *Quijote* aesthetically more complex than Cervantes's." Borges is more concerned with the poet's irrepressible urge for order than with the implications of that fictive order in historic reality, as if the very gap separating the two — the real and the imaginary — were the ultimate test of all art forms. De Man confirms this paradoxical chasm: "By carrying this process to its limits, the poet can achieve ultimate success — an ordered picture of reality that contains the totality of all things, subtly transformed and enriched by the imaginative process that engendered them." But he also offers us a glimpse of the leprous face hidden underneath the beautiful gold mask worn by Hakim, the masked dyer of the early story with that title. "In this," he comments, "Hakim resembles the artist who confers irresistibly attractive qualities upon something that does not necessarily possess them." Borges, according to de Man, accomplishes a similar feat: "Probably because Borges is such a brilliant writer, his mirror world is also profoundly though always ironically, sinister. The shades of terror vary from the criminal gusto of the *History of Infamy* to the darker and shabbier world of the later *Ficciones*, and in *Dreamtigers* the violence is even starker and more somber, closer, I suppose, to the atmosphere of Borges's native Argentina." This conclusion amounts to defining art as an inevitable evasion of reality, but now that "evasion," far from being the sin some Argentine critics accused Borges of committing, has become "the necessary condition of art."

Paul de Man's article represents, within the Anglo-Saxon world, the first serious effort aimed at exploring the meanderings and iridescences of Borges's texts. It also marks a switch in focus, from the paraphrases and gloss of his themes to the close examination of his art's performance. A year later, John Updike's essay "The Author as Librarian" appeared in the *New Yorker*. If the first opened a new direction in Borges scholarship, the second advanced a new perception of his work as a possible catalyst for American fiction: "The question is"—Updike asks—"whether or not Borges's work can serve, in its gravely considered oddity, as any kind of clue to the way out of the dead-end narcissism and downright trashiness of present American fiction." His article is a thorough examination of the way Borges writes, of his paradoxical reasoning, of his interests in the obscure and forgotten. It is also an attempt to answer that central question he posed at the beginning of his inquisition. Like de Man, Updike underlines from the outset the strong intellectual bent of Borges's stories: "His fables are written from a height of intelligence less rare in philosophy and physics than in fiction." He also noticed his consistent bookishness, his tendency to reduce everything to a condition of mystery, the feeling of confinement one is induced to accept by his handling of ideas: "Borges's essays as a whole do not open outward into enlightenment. . . . They have a quality I can only called *sealed*. They are what Borges terms Quevedo's poems— 'verbal objects.' They are structured like mazes and, like mirrors, they reflect back and forth on one another. His ideas border on delusions; the dark hints—of a cult of books, of a cabalistic unity hidden in history—that he so studiously develops are special to the corrupt light of libraries and might vanish, one fears, outdoors."

As much as Updike recognizes that "his stories have the close texture of argument and his critical articles have the suspense and tension of fiction," it is in the examination of his stories where he comes to grips with the question of Borges's role in American fiction. He was one of the first readers to point out not so much the similarities in Borges's and Kafka's narratives as their differences, and in discriminating between the two he reached a more conclusive and exact assessment of what is singular in Borges's narrative world. In discussing "The Library of Babel," he concludes:

This kind of comedy and desperation, these themes of vindication and unattainability, suggest Kafka. But *The Castle* is a more human work, more personal and neurotic; the fantastic realities of Kafka's fiction are projections of the narrator-hero's anxieties, and have no communion, no interlocking structure, without him. The "Library of Babel" instead has an adamant solidity. Built of mathematics and science, it will certainly survive the weary voice describing it, and outlast all its librarians, already decimated (we learn in a footnote) by "suicide and pulmonary disease." We move, with Borges, beyond psychology, beyond the human, and confront, in his work, the world atomized and vacant. Perhaps not since Lucretius has a poet so definitely felt men as incidents in space.

With a strong sense of awe for the beauty of his prose and the geometric perfection of his arguments and plots, Updike corroborates some of the reservations and disclaimers expressed early on by his Argentine critics: not Borges's lack of social and national commitments, nor the alleged gratuitousness of his work, but the absence of human experience in favor of aseptic intellectualizations. In summing up what he regards as Borges's superior strengths and perplexing shortcomings, Updike writes not without puzzlement: "What are we to make of him? The economy of his prose, the tact of his imagery, the courage of his thought are there to be admired and emulated. In resounding the note of the marvelous last struck in English by Wells and Chesterton, in permitting infinity to enter and distort his imagination, he has lifted fiction away from the flat earth where most of our novels and short stories still take place. Yet discouragingly large areas of truth seem excluded from his vision." In a more explicit and cohesive way, Updike reiterates the same conclusion drawn by Paul de Man, namely that Borges's main characters and his worlds are prototypes and that the subject of his stories "is the creation of style itself: the stories are about the style in which they are written." This was a very keen conclusion for a critic, and a very decisive one for a writer. Borges may not offer anything tangible or relevant about the human condition and about man interacting with his social environment, but his lesson on the ins and outs of the craft, his notion that "one literature differs from another, either before or after it, not so much because of the text as for *the manner in which it is read*" (italics mine), were felt as literary events after which literature cannot be the same, or rather, cannot be written in quite the same way. This is how Updike formulated his conclusion:

> I feel in Borges a curious implication: the unrealities of physical science and the senseless repetitions of history have made the world outside the library an uninhabitable vacuum. Literature is now the only world capable of housing and sustaining new literature. Is this too curious? Did not Eliot recommend forty years ago, in reviewing *Ulysses* that new novels be retellings of old myths? Is not the greatest of modern

novels, *Remembrance of Things Past*, about the writing of itself? Have not many books already been written from within Homer and the Bible? Did not Cervantes write from within Ariosto and Shakespeare from within Holinshed? Borges, by predilection and by program, carries these inklings toward a logical extreme: the view of books as, in sum, an alternate creation, vast, accessible, highly colored, rich in arcana, possibly sacred. Just as physical man, in his cities, has manufactured an environment whose scope and challenge and hostility eclipse that of the natural world, so literate man has heaped up a counterfeit universe capable of supporting life.

It is the latter that Updike sees as the most valuable and enduring lesson given by Borges: literature as the subject of literature, artifice as its main character, writing as the rewriting of the already written. This teaching arrived when American fiction needed it most, if one is to believe Updike's own definition of it quoted earlier ("flat earth," "dead-end narcissism," "trashiness"). In the end, Updike's appraisal of Borges's work does not differ in substance from that of García Márquez's. Márquez is more blunt and opinionated; Updike is more meticulously analytical and inquisitive, but both coincide in disclosing his flaws and virtues. Márquez refers to Borges's fiction as "a literature of evasion whose subjects are mental realities"; Updike speaks of Borges's bookishness, of his "*sealed* essays whose ideas border on delusions," of his fiction which is "beyond the human." On the positive pole, Márquez praises "the violin of his style," and Updike hails the magic of his artifice as the ultimate lesson for North Americans. In the closing sentence of his essay, Updike writes: "Ironic and blasphemous as Borges's hidden message may seem, the texture and method of his creations, though strictly inimitable, answer to a deep need in contemporary fiction — the need to confess the fact of artifice."

In the same way that Márquez was not alone in acknowledging Borges's contribution of new linguistic habits that made possible, at least partly, the rise of the new Latin-American novel, Updike was not alone in viewing Borges as a possible answer to a deep need for artifice in contemporary fiction. Two years after Updike published his long piece in the *New Yorker*, John Barth wrote an essay, by now famous, that not only subscribed to and expanded on Updike's basic prognosis, but also named the phenomenon with an unequivocal and fortunate term: "the literature of exhaustion." One may say that Barth's article is an explanation if not a demonstration of Updike's dictum — "the need in contemporary fiction to confess the fact of artifice." We need artifice — Barth would retort — because if "the number of metaphors literature is capable of *has been exhausted, the ways of stating them* are, in fact, limitless" (italics mine). I have deliberately quoted Borges instead of Barth to point out that if Barth's notion is implicit in Updike's essay, it appears already in an explicit way in Borges's note "The Metaphor" of 1952. Although Barth speaks of themes and Borges of metaphors, it is clear that the word *metaphor* should be understood literally as well as figuratively to mean theme. Once again Borges has anticipated his critics. Yet, the urgency of Barth's concept stems from his own work and from the context of American fiction in which it is inserted. Barth comes to his focal point in his comments on "Pierre Menard, Author of the *Quixote*": "The important thing to observe is that Borges *doesn't* attribute the *Quixote* to himself, much less recompose it, like Pierre Menard; instead, he writes a remarkable and original work of literature, the implicit theme of which is the difficulty, perhaps the unnecessity, of writing original works of literature. His artistic victory, if you like, is that he confronts an intellectual dead end and employs it against itself to accomplish new human work."

Barth's insights promoted a feverish output of scholarship around this topic: John Stark's *The Literature of Exhaustion: Borges, Nabokov, Barth* (Duke University Press, 1974) and Tony Tanner's *City of Words: American Fiction 1950–1970* (Harper & Row, 1971) are two distinct specimens at hand. They both attribute to Borges and Nabokov the status of champions in the race against exhaustion. In addition, Tony Tanner views Nabokov and Borges as "two writers whose work is exerting a strong influence on the American fiction of the present" and his book is devoted to probing the extent of that influence. In the introductory chapter included here, he writes: "A part of the appeal that Borges has for American writers is his sense that 'reality' is an infinitely plural affair, that there are many different worlds and that the intersection points might not be so fixed as some people think, that the established ways in which we classify and order reality are as much 'fictions' as his stories."

Robert Scholes addresses his essay to the question of the relationship between fiction and reality. If Ana María Barrenechea concluded her pioneer study *The Expression of Irreality in Borges's Work* — as the original Spanish edition of 1957 was entitled, — with the assertion that "Borges is an admirable writer pledged to destroy reality and convert Man into a shadow,"[21] Scholes sets out to demonstrate precisely the opposite. He opens his article "The Reality of Borges" with the declaration: "My argument here is simple. I submit that we have missed the reality of Borges because we have misunderstood his view of reality and of the relationship between words and the world." To further explain: "Poems are made of words, and reality is not. . . . These fictions or inventions, then, move language *toward* reality, not away from it. Artful writing offers a key that can open the doors of the prison-house of language. . . . The mirrorings and mappings of Borges's fiction take us deeply into reality, though the images are obviously fabulations rather than descriptions. And this is a major point. Reality is too subtle for realism to catch it. It cannot be transcribed directly. But by invention, by fabulation, we may open a way toward reality that will come as close to it as human ingenuity may come."

Scholes does not explain to what type of reality Borges's fiction brings us closer. Perhaps to a poetic vision of reality, but then that vision is not—

Borges would reply—"a mirror of the world, but rather one thing more added to the world."[22] If by means of the word we come closer to the world, as Scholes suggests, it is because the word, fiction, has managed to color, to fictionalize the world so that we can "read" it according to the language coined by fiction. If the world is shaped by the images and fabulations of fiction, we have no choice but to understand and explain it by means of those images and fables. This is the gist of William Gass's answer to Scholes in his piece "Imaginary Borges and His Books" published ten years before Scholes's: "If, Wittgenstein thought, 'philosophy is a battle against the bewitchment of our intelligence by means of language,' then Borges's prose, at least, performs a precisely similar function, for there is scarcely a story which is not built upon a sophistry, a sophistry so fanatically embraced, so pedantically developed, so soberly defended, it becomes the principal truth in *the world his parables create* (puzzles, paradoxes, equivocations, and obscure and idle symmetries which appear as menacing laws); and we are compelled to wonder again whether we are awake or asleep, whether we are a dreamer or ourselves a dream, *whether art imitates nature or nature mirrors art instead . . .*" (italics mine).

Most current criticism on Borges in English tends to see his fictions independently from the dichotomy art / nature, and this is the point dramatized by Gass: those opposites are much too old and much too worn out to warrant revival. The questions dealt with in his stories—he seems to be saying—resemble, in their condition of refined verbal objects, beautiful and precise clockworks. Set to measure natural time, they end up setting their own artificial time. It is this "necessity for artifice" that remains, among most American critics, Borges's terra firma. It is also this intercourse between wakefulness and dream, reality and fiction, nature and art, so deeply at work throughout his writings, that generates the by now broadly accepted Borgesian dimension.

Back in the sixties, the film critic for the *New Yorker* felt that in order to define the uncanny quality of Nicholas Roeg's movie *Don't Look Now* the use of that sole modifier (*Borgesian*) was sufficient. If, as George Steiner wrote, "the concentrated strangeness of Borges's repertoire makes for a certain preciousness, a rococo elaboration that can be spellbinding but also airless," it is also true that his "dreams of wit and elegance" satisfy a need for artifice to counteract the suffocating drabness of daily existence, particularly when that existence has been blessed (or cursed) by indulgence and wasteful prosperity. Borges becomes a commodity, a consumer's item, a diversion ("a metaphysical Fabergé," John Ashbery calls him). Woody Allen's film *The Purple Rose of Cairo*, with all its clever charm and double play of fictionality is, at its core, an adaptation bordering on trivialization of Borges's artifice. Those who saw the picture will recognize immediately in Allen's manipulation of the "play within the play" or "the screen within the screen" technique the hallmark of Borges's art or, in Steiner's rendition, "the process whereby a fantastically private picture of the world leaps beyond the wall of mirrors [read 'screen'] behind which it was created, and reaches out to change the general landscape of awareness." Via Woody Allen, Borges has become popular entertainment. But even before that, when Borges was the surreptitious password of a few, the weight of his work rested on the rococo lightness of his intellectual contortions: serious enough to cause perplexity and light enough to provide enjoyment. This is the conclusion offered by John Ashbery as early as 1967 in his review of *A Personal Anthology.* "One always ends up" — says he — "comparing Borges to Kafka," to encounter, in the end, deeper oppositions than affinities between the two. This one, among the former: "We read Kafka from something like necessity; we read Borges for enjoyment, our own indifference taking pleasure in the frightful but robust spectacle of a disinherited cosmos."

Not much different is Alfred Kazin's judgment. In his profile of Borges written in 1971, he writes: "Borges's Buenos Aires, which is his whole world, is ineffably far-flung, a multitude, yet strangely empty of everything except place names, anecdotes, and a few friends. The great city seems as vague as the endless pampas. . . . He certainly does not put us in close touch with his own country. His Argentina remains a place of dreams. Borges's mind is the realest thing in it."

Paralleling the writing of articles by recognized writers and critics in journals of massive circulation and others of literary prestige, the academic world mounted a true industry on Borges scholarship. "Critical commentaries on Borges, interviews with, memoirs about, special issues of quarterlies devoted to, editions of, pullulate. The air is gray with theses: on 'Borges and Beowulf,' on 'The Influence of the Western on the Narrative Pace of the Later Borges,' on 'Borges's Enigmatic Concern with *West Side Story*' ('I have seen it many times'), on 'The Real Origins of the Words *Tlön* and *Uqbar* in Borges's Stories,' on 'Borges and the Zohar.' A journal of Borgesian studies is being founded. Its first issue will deal with the function of the mirror and the labyrinth in Borges's art, and with the dreamtigers that wait behind the mirror or, rather, in its silent crystal maze." Steiner's put-on is a caricature, but it illustrates quite accurately the frenzy. Each of those theses (actually written, although not exactly on those topics) became a book, and each of those books provoked reviews, articles and counter-theses, bibliographies and biographies, symposia and new interviews, prizes (some invented for the occasion) and honorary degrees.

The first Symposium to be held in the United States took place in 1969 in Norman, Oklahoma, under the auspices of the University of Oklahoma Conference on Writers of the Hispanic World. The papers were gathered in a handsome volume entitled *The Cardinal Points of Borges* (1971), edited by L. Dunham and I. Ivask. It was the first attempt to produce in English something similar to what *L'Herne* had been for French readers. Slimmer, more modest, less intimidating, it offers a good introduction to specific aspects of his work. The actual equivalent of *L'Herne* in English was the twenty-fifth issue of *TriQuarterly*. Its gestation began during the breaks of the Oklahoma Conference in 1969, and it was completed in 1972 when it was published. It includes twenty original studies touching on a variety of subjects and using different approaches, an anthology of twenty-one texts by Borges translated into English for the first time, one interview, a photo album with captions by Borges himself, a transcription of a question-and-answer session at N.Y.U., and a rather brief bibliography: 467 crowded pages that represent a tribute to Borges and a solid effort of academe to struggle with him.

Countless symposia followed, and with them new volumes collecting their papers, new interviews seeking to pin Borges down, new quarterlies trying to leave their mark in scholarship. It will be too prolix to list them here, but it is clear from this bibliographic flood that Borges criticism is rapidly approaching a state of saturation. Not that the possibilities for research and commentary have been exhausted. They will never be, simply because as Borges says, in closing his "Pierre Menard," "thinking, analyzing, inventing are not anomalous acts; they are the normal respiration of the intelligence."[23] Universities will continue searching for some untouched image, for some baroque pearl, and, in sum, for the unattainable philosophers' stone. This is in the nature of that institution; its raison d'être hangs on that endeavor. But the feverish outpouring of printing ink that characterized the sixties and seventies in major journals of wide circulation is over.

Before Tony Tanner published his book on American fiction from 1950 to 1970, stressing the role of Borges and Nabokov during those two decades, Morris Dickstein wrote in the *New York Times Book Review* of 26 April 1970: "In the last three years, an important segment of American fiction has entered a new and more unexpected phase, a more deliberately experimental one. Call this the *Borgesian phase*, though Borges has not been the only model." At that time American fiction was facing a "technical crisis," in Updike's mind. By the eighties the situation changed considerably, and in the same way that Borges's example served to release the influence of writers such as Kafka and Beckett in American letters, he was also displaced as an influential force by later writers and by the accomplishments of his American counterparts. This may account for the diminishment or even absence of commentary on Borges in that type of journal during the eighties. It is also self-evident that the last two collections of short stories (*Doctor Brodies' Report* of 1970 and *The Book of Sand* of 1975) did not attract the same kind of enthralling attention created by his earlier collections: Borges himself was quitting Borges, although not completely.

Rehash won't do it. The same Updike that greeted the earlier work (in an earlier time) with such fascination, treated more recently a new anthology in English of Borges's work (*Borges: A Reader*, ed. R. Monegal and A. Reid [Dutton, 1982]) as "a superfluous recycling."[24] The terse judgment is also indicative of a relentless process that has gradually put Borges on the wane, at least as an active and influential voice. It could also be applied to Borges criticism where the redundancy of glossing and reglossing him has reached proportions of abuse. In selecting the pieces here included, I have tried to avoid — in so far as this is possible when it comes to an author so fiercely studied — tautology. More important, still, was my effort to avoid a smorgasbord, a neutral catalog of innocuous samplings. I opted for including those articles that in my belief contributed a new facet to our understanding of Borges. I couldn't comment on all of them because of space limitation, but I do hope that by placing them in the context of certain factors and circumstances of literary history I have defined a critical space in whose surface some of the major directions in Borges criticism become recognizable.

I should also warn the reader about another criterion accountable for this selection. With the exception of Pierre Macherey's essay, all others were written by critics writing in English and from an American vantage point. The reason is not technical. Quite the opposite. Since Borges's impact was particularly resounding in the United States, as I think some of the articles clearly show, I felt it was pertinent to restrict my choice to the American perspective. This far from limiting their value adds to their relevance. First, because they are among the best pieces of critical commentary written in any language. And second, because by concentrating on a single perspective I have been able to articulate what I think constitutes an image of the reception of Borges in the United States. Ten years ago, I compiled a similar anthology in Spanish. Naturally, the principle of selection was different then. Although addressed to Spanish readers, it aimed at offering a more cosmopolitan picture of Borges criticism — a less parochial one would be more accurate. In the present case that purpose is no longer needed. The need is now, I feel, to go beyond the array of collective volumes and single-penned books and offer patterns of criticism, a kaleidoscopic figure in which the differences of the parts do not hinder the unity of the whole. Not an inventory but the articulation of a statement that underlies a critical process. In this sense, Borges's "Autobiographical Essay" belongs to this whole. It was originally written in English and intended for American readers. Published in the *New Yorker* on 19 September 1970, it dramatizes the time and thrust of that critical process. Besides, having let others present *their* readings of Borges, it is only fair to give the floor to the author as a reader of his own work.

Jaime Alazraki

Harvard University

Notes

1. Ramón Doll, "Discusiones con Borges, una encuesta," *Letras* (Buenos Aires), no. 1 (September 1933):3–13.

2. Rita Guibert, *Seven Voices* (New York: Random House / Vintage, 1973), 100.

3. Amado Alonso, "Borges, narrador," in *Materia y forma en poesía* (Madrid, Gredos, 1960), 345.

4. Enrique Anderson-Imbert, "Desagravio a Borges," *Sur* (Buenos Aires), no. 94 (July 1942), 24–25.

5. Anonymous, "Los premios nacionales de literatura," *Nosotros* (Buenos Aires), no. 76, (July 1924), 117–18.

6. See Ernesto Sábato, "Borges" (*Uno y el universo*, 1945), *El escritor y sus fantasmas* ("Interrogatorio preliminar," and "Borges y el destino de nuestra ficción"). All included in *Ensayos* (Buenos Aires, Losada, 1970).

7. Jorge Luis Borges, *Discusión* (Buenos Aires: Emecé, 1957), 10.

8. Jorge Luis Borges, "An Autobiographical Essay," in *The Aleph and Other Stories 1933–1969* (Bantam Books, 1971), 140.

9. Jorge Luis Borges, *Other Inquisitions 1937–1952* (New York: Washington Square Press, 1966), 78.

10. Guibert, *Seven Voices*, 97–98.

11. Borges, *Other Inquisitions*, p. 78.

12. I am quoting from Bertrand Russell, *Our Knowledge of the External World* (The New American Library. A Mentor Book, 1960), 15.

13. Adolfo Prieto, *Borges y la nueva generación* (Buenos Aires: Letras Universitarias, 1954), 16, 21.

14. Jorge Luis Borges, "The Argentine Writer and Tradition," in *Labyrinths; Selected Stories and Other Writings*, ed D. A. Yates and J. E. Irby (New York: New Directions, 1964), 184.

15. Gabriel García Márquez and Mario Vargas Llosa, *La novela en América Latina: diálogo* (Lima: Universidad Nacional de Ingeniería, 1967), 36, 40.

16. Ernesto Sábato, *On Heroes and Tombs*, trans. Helen R. Lane (Boston: David R. Godine, 1981), 172–73.

17. Ernesto Gonzalez Bermejo, *Conversaciones con Cortázar* (Barcelona: Edhasa, 1978), 21.

18. Carlos Fuentes, *La nueva novela hispanoamericana* (México City: Joaquín Mortiz, 1969), 26.

19. On this subject, see my article "Borges and the New Latin American Novel," in *Prose for Borges*, ed. Charles Newman and Mary Kinzie (Evanston: Northwestern University Press, 1974), 331–50.

20. See María Luisa Bastos, *Borges ante la crítica argentina* (Buenos Aires: Ediciones Hispamerica, 1974), 135.

21. Ana María Barrenechea, *Borges the Labyrinth Maker* (New York: New York University Press, 1965), 144.

22. Jorge Luis Borges, *Dreamtigers*, trans. Mildred Boyer and Harold Moreland (Austin: University of Texas Press, 1964), 38.

23. Jorge Luis Borges, *Ficciones*, trans. Anthony Kerrigan et al. (New York: Grove Press, 1962), 44.

24. John Updike, "Borges Warmed Over," in *Hugging the Shore: Essays and Criticis* (New York: Knopf, 1983), 784.

ARTICLES AND REVIEWS

An Autobiographical Essay Jorge Luis Borges*

FAMILY AND CHILDHOOD

I cannot tell whether my first memories go back to the eastern or to the western bank of the muddy, slow-moving Río de la Plata — to Montevideo, where we spent long, lazy holidays in the villa of my uncle Francisco Haedo, or to Buenos Aires. I was born there, in the very heart of that city, in 1899, on Tucumán Street, between Suipacha and Esmeralda, in a small, unassuming house belonging to my maternal grandparents. Like most of the houses of that day, it had a flat roof; a long, arched entranceway, called a *zaguán*; a cistern, where we got our water; and two patios. We must have moved out to the suburb of Palermo quite soon, because there I have my first memories of another house with two patios, a garden with a tall windmill pump, and, on the other side of the garden, an empty lot. Palermo at that time — the Palermo where we lived, Serrano and Guatemala — was on the shabby northern outskirts of town, and many people, ashamed of saying they lived there, spoke in a dim way of living on the Northside. We lived in one of the few two-story homes on our street; the rest of the neighborhood was made up of low houses and vacant lots. I have often spoken of this area as a slum, but I do not quite mean that in the American sense of the word. In Palermo lived shabby, genteel people as well as more undesirable sorts. There was also a Palermo of hoodlums, called *compadritos*, famed for their knife fights, but this Palermo was only later to capture my imagination, since we did our best — our successful best — to ignore it. Unlike our neighbor Evaristo Carriego, however, who was the first Argentine poet to explore the literary possibilities that lay there at hand. As for myself, I was hardly aware of the existence of *compadritos*, since I lived essentially indoors.

*From *The Aleph and Other Stories 1933–1969*, ed. and trans. Norman Thomas di Giovanni (New York: E. P. Dutton, 1970). English translation © 1968, 1969, 1970 by Emecé Editores, S. A., and N. T. di Giovanni; © 1970 by Jorge Luis Borges, Adolfo Bioy-Casares and N. T. di Giovanni. Reprinted by permission of the publisher, E. P. Dutton, Inc.

My father, Jorge Guillermo Borges, worked as a lawyer. He was a philosophical anarchist — a disciple of Spencer — and also a teacher of psychology at the Normal School for Modern Languages, where he gave his course in English, using as his text William James's shorter book of psychology. My father's English came from the fact that his mother, Frances Haslam, was born in Staffordshire of Northumbrian stock. A rather unlikely set of circumstances brought her to South America. Fanny Haslam's elder sister married an Italian-Jewish engineer named Jorge Suárez, who brought the first horse-drawn tramcars to Argentina, where he and his wife settled and sent for Fanny. I remember an anecdote concerning this venture. Suárez was a guest at General Urquiza's "palace" in Entre Ríos, and very improvidently won his first game of cards with the General, who was the stern dictator of that province and not above throat-cutting. When the game was over, Suárez was told by alarmed fellow-guests that if he wanted the license to run his tramcars in the province, it was expected of him to lose a certain amount of gold coins each night. Urquiza was such a poor player that Suárez had a great deal of trouble losing the appointed sums.

It was in Paraná, the capital city of Entre Ríos, that Fanny Haslam met Colonel Francisco Borges. This was in 1870 or 1871, during the siege of the city by the *montoneros*, or gaucho militia, of Ricardo López Jordán. Borges, riding at the head of his regiment, commanded the troops defending the city. Fanny Haslam saw him from the flat roof of her house; that very night a ball was given to celebrate the arrival of the government relief forces. Fanny and the Colonel met, danced, fell in love, and eventually married.

My father was the younger of two sons. He had been born in Entre Ríos and used to explain to my grandmother, a respectable English lady, that he wasn't really an Entrerriano, since "I was begotten on the pampa." My grandmother would say, with English reserve, "I'm sure I don't know what you mean." My father's words, of course, were true, since my grandfather was, in the early 1870's, Commander-in-Chief of the northern and western frontiers of the Province of Buenos Aires. As a child, I heard many stories from Fanny Haslam about frontier life in those days. One of these I set down in my "Story of the Warrior and the Captive." My grandmother had spoken with a number of Indian chieftains, whose rather uncouth names were, I think, Simón Coliqueo, Catriel, Pincén, and Namuncurá. In 1874, during one of our civil wars, my grandfather, Colonel Borges, met his death. He was forty-one at the time. In the complicated circumstances surrounding his defeat at the battle of La Verde, he rode out slowly on horseback, wearing a white poncho and followed by ten or twelve of his men, toward the enemy lines, where he was struck by two Remington bullets. This was the first time Remington rifles were used in the Argentine, and it tickles my fancy to think that the firm that shaves me every morning bears the same name as the one that killed my grandfather.

Fanny Haslam was a great reader. When she was over eighty, people used to say, in order to be nice to her, that nowadays there were no writers who could vie with Dickens and Thackeray. My grandmother would answer, "On the whole, I rather prefer Arnold Bennett, Galsworthy, and Wells." When she died, at the age of ninety, in 1935, she called us to her side and said, in English (her Spanish was fluent but poor), in her thin voice, "I am only an old woman dying very, very slowly. There is nothing remarkable or interesting about this." She could see no reason whatever why the whole household should be upset, and she apologized for taking so long to die.

My father was very intelligent and, like all intelligent men, very kind. Once, he told me that I should take a good look at soldiers, uniforms, barracks, flags, churches, priests, and butcher shops, since all these things were about to disappear, and I could tell my children that I had actually seen them. The prophecy has not yet come true, unfortunately. My father was such a modest man that he would have liked being invisible. Though he was very proud of his English ancestry, he used to joke about it, saying with feigned perplexity, "After all, what are the English? Just a pack of German agricultural laborers." His idols were Shelley, Keats, and Swinburne. As a reader, he had two interests. First, books on metaphysics and psychology (Berkeley, Hume, Royce, and William James). Second, literature and books about the East (Lane, Burton, and Payne). It was he who revealed the power of poetry to me—the fact that words are not only a means of communication but also magic symbols and music. When I recite poetry in English now, my mother tells me I take on his very voice. He also, without my being aware of it, gave me my first lessons in philosophy. When I was still quite young, he showed me, with the aid of a chessboard, the paradoxes of Zeno—Achilles and the tortoise, the unmoving flight of the arrow, the impossibility of motion. Later, without mentioning Berkeley's name, he did his best to teach me the rudiments of idealism.

My mother, Leonor Acevedo de Borges, comes of old Argentine and Uruguayan stock, and at ninety-four is still hale and hearty and a good Catholic. When I was growing up, religion belonged to women and children; most men in Buenos Aires were freethinkers—though, had they been asked, they might have called themselves Catholics. I think I inherited from my mother her quality of thinking the best of people and also her strong sense of friendship. My mother has always had a hospitable mind. From the time she learned English, through my father, she has done most of her reading in that language. After my father's death, finding that she was unable to keep her mind on the printed page, she tried her hand at translating William Saroyan's *The Human Comedy* in order to compel herself to concentrate. The translation found its way into print, and she was honored for this by a society of Buenos Aires Armenians. Later on, she translated some of Hawthorne's stories and one of Herbert Read's books on art, and she also produced some of the translations of Melville, Virginia Woolf, and Faulkner that are considered mine. She has always been a companion to me — especially in later years, when I went blind — and an understanding and forgiving friend. For years, until recently, she handled all my secretarial work, answering letters, reading to me, taking down my dictation, and also traveling with me on many occasions both at home and abroad. It was she, though I never gave a thought to it at the time, who quietly and effectively fostered my literary career.

Her grandfather was Colonel Isidoro Suárez, who, in 1824, at the age of twenty-four, led a famous charge of Peruvian and Colombian cavalry, which turned the tide of the battle of Junín, in Peru. This was the next to last battle of the South American War of Independence. Although Suárez was a second cousin to Juan Manuel de Rosas, who ruled as dictator in Argentina from 1835 to 1852, he preferred exile and poverty in Montevideo to living under a tyranny in Buenos Aires. His lands were, of course, confiscated, and one of his brothers was executed. Another member of my mother's family was Francisco de Laprida, who, in 1816, in Tucumán, where he presided over the Congress, declared the independence of the Argentine Confederation, and was killed in 1829 in a civil war. My mother's father, Isidoro Acevedo, though a civilian, took part in the fighting of yet other civil wars in the 1860's and 1880's. So, on both sides of my family, I have military forebears; this may account for my yearning after that epic destiny which my gods denied me, no doubt wisely.

I have already said that I spent a great deal of my boyhood indoors. Having no childhood friends, my sister and I invented two imaginary companions, named, for some reason or other, Quilos and The Windmill. (When they finally bored us, we told our mother that they had died.) I was always very nearsighted and wore glasses, and I was rather frail. As most of my people had been soldiers — even my father's brother had been a naval officer — and I knew I would never be, I felt ashamed, quite early, to be a bookish kind of person and not a man of action. Throughout my boyhood, I thought that to be loved would have amounted to an injustice. I did not feel I deserved any particular love, and I remember my birthdays filled me with shame, because everyone heaped gifts on me when I thought that I had done nothing to deserve them — that I was a kind of fake. After the age of thirty or so, I got over the feeling.

At home, both English and Spanish were commonly used. If I were asked to name the chief event in my life, I should say my father's library. In fact, I sometimes think I have never strayed outside that library. I can still picture it. It was in a room of its own, with glass-fronted shelves, and must have contained several thousand volumes. Being so nearsighted, I have forgotten most of the faces of that time (perhaps even when I think of my grandfather Acevedo I am thinking of his photograph), and yet I vividly remember so many of the steel engravings in *Chamber's Encyclopaedia* and in the *Britannica*. The first novel I ever read through was *Huckleberry Finn*. Next came *Roughing It* and *Flush Days in California*. I also read books by Captain Marryat, Wells's *First Men in the Moon*, Poe, a one-volume edition of Longfellow, *Treasure Island*, Dickens, *Don Quixote*, *Tom Brown's School Days*, Grimms' *Fairy Tales*, Lewis Carroll, *The Adventures of Mr Verdant Green* (a now forgotten book), Burton's *A Thousand Nights and a Night*. The Burton, filled with what was then considered obscenity, was forbidden, and I had to read it in hiding up on the roof. But at the time, I was so carried away with the magic that I took no notice whatever of the objectionable parts, reading the tales unaware of any other significance. All the foregoing books I read in English. When later I read *Don Quixote* in the original, it sounded like a bad translation to me. I still remember those red volumes with the gold lettering of the Garnier edition. At some point, my father's library was broken up, and when I read the *Quixote* in another edition I had the feeling that it wasn't the real *Quixote*. Later, I had a friend get me the Garnier, with the same steel engravings, the same footnotes, and also the same errata. All those things form part of the book for me; this I consider the real *Quixote*.

In Spanish, I also read many of the books by Eduardo Gutiérrez about Argentine outlaws and desperadoes — *Juan Moreira* foremost among them — as well as his *Siluetas militares*, which contains a forceful account of Colonel Borges' death. My mother forbade the reading of *Martin Fierro*, since that was a book fit only for hoodlums and schoolboys and, besides, was not about real gauchos at all. This too I read on the sly. Her feelings were based on the fact that Hernández had been an upholder of Rosas and therefore an enemy to our Unitarian ancestors. I read also Sarmiento's *Facundo*, many books on Greek mythology, and later Norse. Poetry came to me through English — Shelley, Keats, FitzGerald, and Swinburne, those great favorites of my father, who could quote them voluminously, and often did.

A tradition of literature ran through my father's family. His great-uncle Juan Crisóstomo Lafinur was one of the first Argentine poets, and he wrote an ode on the death of his friend General Manuel Belgrano, in 1820. One of my father's cousins, Alvaro Melián Lafinur, whom I knew from childhood, was a leading minor poet and later found his way into the Argentine Academy of Letters. My father's maternal grandfather, Edward Young Haslam, edited one of the first English papers in Argentina, the *Southern Cross*, and was a Doctor of Philosophy or Letters, I'm not sure which, of the University of Heidelberg. Haslam could not afford Oxford or Cambridge, so he made his way to Germany, where he got his degree, going through the whole course in Latin. Eventually, he died in Paraná. My father wrote a novel, which he published in Majorca in 1921, about the history of Entre Ríos. It was called *The Caudillo*. He also wrote (and destroyed) a book of essays, and published a translation of FitzGerald's Omar Khayyám in the same meter as the original. He destroyed a book of Oriental stories—in the manner of the Arabian Nights—and a drama, *Hacia la nada* (Toward Nothingness), about a man's disappointment in his son. He published some fine sonnets after the style of the Argentine poet Enrique Banchs. From the time I was a boy, when blindness came to him, it was tacitly understood that I had to fulfill the literary destiny that circumstances had denied my father. This was something that was taken for granted (and such things are far more important than things that are merely said). I was expected to be a writer.

I first started writing when I was six or seven. I tried to imitate classic writers of Spanish—Miguel de Cervantes, for example. I had set down in quite bad English a kind of handbook on Greek mythology, no doubt cribbed from Lemprière. This may have been my first literary venture. My first story was a rather nonsensical piece after the manner of Cervantes, an old-fashioned romance called "La visera fatal" (The Fatal Helmet). I very neatly wrote these things into copybooks. My father never interfered. He wanted me to commit all my own mistakes, and once said, "Children educate their parents, not the other way around." When I was nine or so, I translated Oscar Wilde's "The Happy Prince" into Spanish, and it was published in one of the Buenos Aires dailies, *El Pais*. Since it was signed merely "Jorges Borges," people naturally assumed the translation was my father's.

I take no pleasure whatever in recalling my early schooldays. To begin with, I did not start school until I was nine. This was because my father, as an anarchist, distrusted all enterprises run by the State. As I wore spectacles and dressed in an Eton collar and tie, I was jeered at and bullied by most of my schoolmates, who were amateur hooligans. I cannot remember the name of the school but recall that it was on Thames Street. My father used to say that Argentine history had taken the place of the catechism, so we were expected to worship all things Argentine. We were taught Argentine history, for example, before we were allowed any knowledge of the many lands and many centuries that went into its making. As far as Spanish composition goes, I was taught to write in a flowery way: *Aquellos que lucharon por una patria libre, independiente, gloriosa . . .* (Those who struggled for a free, independent, and glorious nation . . .). Later on, in Geneva, I was to be told that such writing was meaningless and that I must see things through my own eyes. My sister Norah, who was born in 1901, of course attended a girls' school.

During all these years, we usually spent our summers out in Adrogué, some ten or fifteen miles to the south of Buenos Aires, where we had a place of our own—a large one-story house with grounds, two summer-houses, a windmill, and a shaggy brown sheepdog. Adrogué then was a lost and undisturbed maze of summer homes surrounded by iron fences with masonry planters on the gateposts, of parks, of streets that radiated out of the many plazas, and of the ubiquitous smell of eucalyptus trees. We continued to visit Adrogué for decades.

My first real experience of the pampa came around 1909, on a trip we took to a place belonging to relatives near San Nicolás, to the northwest of Buenos Aires. I remember that the nearest house was a kind of blur on the horizon. This endless distance, I found out, was called the pampa, and when I learned that the farmhands were gauchos, like the characters in Eduardo Gutiérrez, that gave them a certain glamor. I have always come to things after coming to books. Once, I was allowed to accompany them on horseback, taking cattle to the river early one morning. The men were small and darkish and wore *bombachas*, a kind of wide, baggy trousers. When I asked them if they knew how to swim, they replied, "Water is meant for cattle." My mother gave a doll, in a large cardboard box, to the foreman's daughter. The next year, we went back and asked after the little girl. "What a delight the doll has been to her!" they told us. And we were shown it, still in its box, nailed to the wall like an image. Of course, the girl was allowed only to look at it, not to touch it, for it might have been soiled or broken. There it was, high up out of harm's way, worshiped from afar. Lugones has written that in Córdoba, before magazines came in, he had many times seen a playing card used as a picture and nailed to the wall in gauchos' shacks. The four of *copas*, with its small lion and two towers, was particularly coveted. I think I began writing a poem about gauchos, probably under the influence of the poet Ascasubi, before I went to Geneva. I recall trying to work in as many gaucho words as I could, but the technical difficulties were beyond me. I never got past a few stanzas.

EUROPE

In 1914, we moved to Europe. My father's eyesight had begun to fail and I remember his saying, "How on earth can I sign my name to legal papers when I am unable to read them?" Forced into early retirement, he planned our trip in exactly ten days. The world was unsuspicious then; there were no passports or other red tape. We first spent some weeks in Paris, a city that neither then nor since has particularly charmed me, as it does every other good Argentine. Perhaps, without knowing it, I was always a bit of a Britisher; in fact, I always think of Waterloo as a victory. The idea of the trip was for my sister and me to go school in Geneva; we were to live with my maternal grandmother, who traveled with us and eventually died there, while my parents toured the Continent. At the same time, my father was to be treated by a famous Genevan eye doctor. Europe in those days was cheaper than Buenos Aires, and Argentine money then stood for something. We were so ignorant of history, however, that we had no idea that the First World War would break out in August. My mother and father were in Germany when it happened, but managed to get back to us in Geneva. A year or so later, despite the war, we were able to journey across the Alps into northern Italy. I have vivid memories of Verona and Venice. In the vast and empty amphitheater of Verona I recited, loud and bold, several gaucho verses from Ascasubi.

That first fall—1914—I started school at the College of Geneva, founded by John Calvin. It was a day school. In my class there were some forty of us; a good half were foreigners. The chief subject was Latin, and I soon found out that one could let other studies slide a bit as long as one's Latin was good. All these other courses, however—algebra, chemistry, physics, mineralogy, botany, zoology—were studied in French. That year, I passed all my exams successfully, except for French itself. Without a word to me, my fellow-schoolmates sent a petition around to the headmaster, which they had all signed. They pointed out that I had had to study all of the different subjects in French, a language I also had to learn. They asked the headmaster to take this into account, and he very kindly did so. At first, I had not even understood when a teacher was calling on me, because my name was pronounced in the French manner, in a single syllable (rhyming roughly with "forge"), while we pronounce it with two syllables, the "g" sounding like a strong Scottish "h." Every time I had to answer my schoolmates would nudge me.

We lived in a flat on the southern, or old side of town. I still know Geneva far better than I know Buenos Aires, which is easily explained by the fact that in Geneva no two streetcorners are alike and one quickly learns the differences. Every day, I walked along that green and icy river, the Rhone, which runs through the very heart of the city, spanned by seven quite different-looking bridges. The Swiss are rather proud and standoffish. My two bosom friends were of Polish-Jewish origin—Simon Jichlinski and Maurice Abramowicz. One became a lawyer and the other a physician. I taught them to play *truco*, and they learned so well and fast that at the end of our first game they left me without a cent. I became a good Latin scholar, while I did most of my private reading in English. At home, we spoke Spanish, but my sister's French soon became so good she even dreamed in it. I remember my mother's coming home one day and finding Norah hidden behind a red plush curtain, crying out in fear, "*Une mouche, une mouche!*" It seems she had adopted the French notion that flies are dangerous. "You come out of there," my mother told her, somewhat unpatriotically. "You were born and bred among flies!" As a result of the war—apart from the Italian trip and journeys inside Switzerland—we did no traveling. Later on, braving German submarines and in the company of only four or five other passengers, my English grandmother joined us.

On my own, outside of school, I took up the study of German. I was sent on this adventure by Carlyle's *Sartor Resartus* (The Tailor Retailored), which dazzled and also bewildered me. The hero, Diogenes Devil'sdung, is a German professor of idealism. In German literature I was looking for something Germanic, akin to Tacitus, but I was only later to find this in

Old English and in Old Norse. German literature turned out to be romantic and sickly. At first, I tried Kant's *Critique of Pure Reason* but was defeated by it, as most people — including most Germans — are. Then I thought verse would be easier, because of its brevity. So I got hold of a copy of Heine's early poems, the *Lyrisches Intermezzo,* and a German-English dictionary. Little by little, owing to Heine's simple vocabulary, I found I could do without the dictionary. Soon I had worked my way into the loveliness of the language. I also managed to read Meyrinks' novel *Der Golem.* (In 1969, when I was in Israel, I talked over the Bohemian legend of the Golem with Gershom Scholem, a leading scholar of Jewish mysticism, whose name I had twice used as the only possible rhyming word in a poem of my own on the Golem.) I tried to be interested in Jean-Paul Richter, for Carlyle's and De Quincey's sake — this was around 1917 — but I soon discovered that I was very bored by the reading. Richter, in spite of his two British champions, seemed to me very long-winded and perhaps a passionless writer. I became, however, very interested in German expressionism and still think of it as beyond other contemporary schools, such as imagism, cubism, futurism, surrealism, and so on. A few years later, in Madrid, I was to attempt some of the first, and perhaps the only, translations of a number of expressionist poets into Spanish.

At some point while in Switzerland, I began reading Schopenhauer. Today, were I to choose a single philosopher, I would choose him. If the riddle of the universe can be stated in words, I think these words would be in his writings. I have read him many times over, both in German and, with my father and his close friend Macedonio Fernández, in translation. I still think of German as being a beautiful language — perhaps more beautiful than the literature it has produced. French, rather paradoxically, has a fine literature despite its fondness for schools and movements, but the language itself is, I think, rather ugly. Things tend to sound trivial when they are said in French. In fact, I even think of Spanish as being the better of the two languages though Spanish words are far too long and cumbersome. As an Argentine writer, I have to cope with Spanish and so am only too aware of its shortcomings. I remember that Goethe wrote that he had to deal with the worst language in the world — German. I suppose most writers think along these lines concerning the language they have to struggle with. As for Italian, I have read and reread *The Divine Comedy* in more than a dozen different editions. I've also read Ariosto, Tasso, Croce, and Gentile, but I am quite unable to speak Italian or to follow an Italian play or film.

It was also in Geneva that I first met Walt Whitman, through a German translation by Johannes Schlaf (*"Als ich in Alabama meinen Morgengang machte"* — "As I have walk'd in Alabama my morning walk"). Of course, I was struck by the absurdity of reading an American poet in German, so I ordered a copy of *Leaves of Grass* from London. I remember it still — bound in green. For a time, I thought of Whitman not only as a great poet but as the *only* poet. In fact, I thought that all poets the world over had been merely leading up to Whitman until 1855, and that not to imitate him was a proof of ignorance. This feeling had already come over me with Carlyle's prose, which is now unbearable to me, and with the poetry of Swinburne. These were phases I went through. Later on, I was to go through similar experiences of being overwhelmed by some particular writer.

We remained in Switzerland until 1919. After three or four years in Geneva, we spent a year in Lugano. I had my bachelor's degree by then, and it was now understood that I should devote myself to writing. I wanted to show my manuscripts to my father, but he told me he didn't believe in advice and that I must work my way all by myself through trial and error. I had been writing sonnets in English and in French. The English sonnets were poor imitations of Wordsworth, and the French, in their own watery way, were imitative of symbolist poetry. I still recall one line of my French experiments: *"Petite boîte noire pour le violon casse."* The whole piece was titled "Poeme pour être recité avec un accent russe." As I knew I wrote a foreigner's French, I thought a Russian accent better than an Argentine one. In my English experiments, I affected some eighteenth-century mannerisms, such as "o'er" instead of "over" and, for the sake of metrical ease, "doth sing" instead of "sings." I knew, however, that Spanish would be my unavoidable destiny.

We decided to go home, but to spend a year or so in Spain first. Spain at that time was slowly being discovered by Argentines. Until then, even eminent writers like Leopoldo Lugones and Ricardo Güiraldes deliberately left Spain out of their European travels. This was no whim. In Buenos Aires, Spaniards always held menial jobs — as domestic servants, waiters, and laborers — or were small tradesmen, and we Argentines never thought of ourselves as Spanish. We had, in fact, left off being Spaniards in 1816, when we declared our independence from Spain. When, as a boy, I read Prescott's *Conquest of Peru*, it amazed me to find that he portrayed the conquistadors in a romantic way. To me, descended from certain of these officials, they were an uninteresting lot. Through French eyes, however, Latin Americans saw the Spaniards as picturesque, thinking of them in terms of the stock in trade of García Lorca — gypsies, bullfights, and Moorish architecture. But though Spanish was our language and we came mostly of Spanish and Portuguese blood, my own family never thought of our trip in terms of going back to Spain after an absence of some three centuries.

We went to Majorca because it was cheap, beautiful, and had hardly any tourists but ourselves. We lived there nearly a whole year, in Palma and in Valldemosa, a village high up in the hills. I went on studying Latin, this time under the tutelage of a priest, who told me that since the innate was sufficient to his needs, he had never attempted reading a novel. We went over Virgil, of whom I still think highly. I remember I astonished the natives by my fine swimming, for I had learned in swift rivers, such as the Uruguay and the Rhone, while Majorcans were used only to a quiet, tideless sea. My father was writing his novel, which harked back to old times during the civil war of the 1870's in his native Entre Ríos. I recall giving him some quite bad metaphors, borrowed from the German expressionists, which he accepted out of resignation. He had some five hundred copies of the book printed, and brought them back to Buenos Aires, where he gave them away to friends. Every time the word "Paraná"—his home town—had come up in the manuscript, the printers changed it to "Panamá," thinking they were correcting a mistake. Not to give them trouble, and also seeing it was funnier that way, my father let this pass. Now I repent my youthful intrusions into his book. Seventeen years later, before he died, he told me that he would very much like me to rewrite the novel in a straightforward way, with all the fine writing and purple patches left out. I myself in those days wrote a story about a werewolf and sent it to a popular magazine in Madrid, *La Esfera*, whose editors very wisely turned it down.

The winter of 1919–20 we spent in Seville, where I saw my first poem into print. It was titled "Hymn to the Sea" and appeared in the magazine *Grecia*, in its issue of December 31, 1919. In the poem, I tried my hardest to be Walt Whitman:

> O sea! O myth! O sun! O wide resting place!
> I know why I love you. I know that we are both very old,
> that we have known each other for centuries. . . .
> O Protean, I have been born of you—
> both of us chained and wandering,
> both of us hungering for stars,
> both of us with hopes and disappointments. . . !

Today, I hardly think of the sea, or even of myself, as hungering for stars. Years after, when I came across Arnold Bennett's phrase "the third-rate grandiose," I understood at once what he meant. And yet when I arrived in Madrid a few months later, as this was the only poem I had ever printed, people there thought of me as a singer of the sea.

In Seville, I fell in with the literary group formed around *Grecia*. This group, who called themselves ultraists, had set out to renew literature, a branch of the arts of which they knew nothing whatever. One of them once told me his whole reading had been the Bible, Cervantes, Darío, and one or two of the books of the Master, Rafael Cansinos-Assens. It baffled my Argentine mind to learn that they had no French and no inkling at all that such a thing as English literature existed. I was even introduced to a local worthy popularly known as "the Humanist" and was not long in discovering that his Latin was far smaller than mine. As for

Grecia itself, the editor, Isaac del Vando Villar, had the whole corpus of his poetry written for him by one or another of his assistants. I remember one of them telling me one day, "I'm very busy—Isaac is writing a poem."

Next, we went to Madrid, and there the great event to me was my friendship with Rafael Cansinos-Assens. I still like to think of myself as his disciple. He had come from Seville, where he had studied for the priesthood, but, having found the name Cansinos in the archives of the Inquisition, he decided he was a Jew. This led him to the study of Hebrew, and later on he even had himself circumcised. Literary friends from Andalusia took me to meet him. I timidly congratulated him on a poem *he* had written about the sea. "Yes," he said, "and how I'd like to see it before I die." He was a tall man with the Andalusian contempt for all things Castilian. The most remarkable fact about Cansinos was that he lived completely for literature, without regard for money or fame. He was a fine poet and wrote a book of psalms—chiefly erotic—called *El candelabro de los siete brazos,* which was published in 1914. He also wrote novels, stories, and essays, and, when I knew him, presided over a literary circle.

Every Saturday I would go to the Café Colonial, where we met at midnight, and the conversation lasted until daybreak. Sometimes there were as many as twenty or thirty of us. The group despised all Spanish local color—*cante jondo* and bullfights. They admired American jazz, and were more interested in being Europeans than Spaniards. Cansinos would propose a subject—The Metaphor, Free Verse, The Traditional Forms of Poetry, Narrative Poetry, The Adjective, The Verb. In his own quiet way, he was a dictator, allowing no unfriendly allusions to contemporary writers and trying to keep the talk on a high plane.

Cansinos was a wide reader. He had translated De Quincey's *Opium-Eater,* the *Meditations of Marcus Aurelius* from the Greek, novels of Barbusse, and Schwob's *Vies imaginaires.* Later, he was to undertake complete translations of Goethe and Dostoevski. He also made the first Spanish version of the Arabian Nights, which is very free compared to Burton's or Lane's, but which makes, I think, for more pleasurable reading. Once, I went to see him and he took me into his library. Or, rather, I should say his whole house was a library. It was like making your way through a woods. He was too poor to have shelves, and the books were piled one on top of the other from floor to ceiling, forcing you to thread your way among the vertical columns. Cansinos seemed to me as if he were all the past of that Europe I was leaving behind—something like the symbol of all culture, Western and Eastern. But he had a perversity that made him fail to get on with his leading contemporaries. It lay in writing books that lavishly praised second- or third-rate writers. At the time, Ortega y Gasset was at the height of his fame, but Cansinos thought of him as a bad philosopher and a bad writer. What I got from him, chiefly, was the pleasure of literary conversation. Also, I was stimulated by him to far-flung reading. In writing, I began aping him. He wrote long and flowing sentences with an un-Spanish and strongly Hebrew flavor to them.

Oddly, it was Cansinos who, in 1919, invented the term "ultraism." He thought Spanish literature had always been behind the times. Under the pen name of Juan Las, he wrote some short, laconic ultraist pieces. The whole thing—I see now—was done in a spirit of mockery. But we youngsters took it very seriously. Another of the earnest followers was Guillermo de Torre, whom I met in Madrid that spring and who married my sister Norah nine years later.

In Madrid at this time, there was another group gathered around Ramón Gómez de la Serna. I went there once and didn't like the way they behaved. They had a buffoon who wore a bracelet with a rattle attached. He would be made to shake hands with people and the rattle would rattle and Gómez de la Serna would invariably say, "Where's the snake?" That was supposed to be funny. Once, he turned to me proudly and remarked, "You've never seen this kind of thing in Buenos Aires, have you?" I owned, thank God, that I hadn't.

In Spain, I wrote two books. One was a series of essays called, I now wonder why, *Los naipes del tahur* (The Sharper's Cards). They were literary and political essays (I was still an anarchist and a freethinker and in favor of pacifism), written under the influence of Pío Baroja. Their aim was to be bitter and relentless, but they were, as a matter of fact, quite tame. I went in for using such words as "fools," "harlots," "liars." Failing to find a publisher, I destroyed the manuscript on my return to Buenos Aires. The second book was titled either *The Red Psalms* or *The Red Rhythms*. It was a collection of poems—perhaps some twenty in all—in free verse and in praise of the Russian Revolution, the brotherhood of man, and pacifism. Three or four of them found their way into magazines— "Bolshevik Epic," "Trenches," "Russia." This book I destroyed in Spain on the eve of our departure. I was then ready to go home.

BUENOS AIRES

We returned to Buenos Aires on the *Reina Victoria Eugenia* toward the end of March, 1921. It came to me as a surprise, after living in so many European cities—after so many memories of Geneva, Zurich, Nîmes, Córdoba, and Lisbon—to find that my native town had grown, and that it was now a very large, sprawling, and almost endless city of low buildings with flat roofs, stretching west toward what geographers and literary hands call the pampa. It was more than a homecoming; it was a rediscovery. I was able to see Buenos Aires keenly and eagerly because I had been away from it for a long time. Had I never gone abroad, I wonder whether I would ever have seen it with the peculiar shock and glow that it now gave me. The city—not the whole city, of course, but a few places in

RITTER LIBRARY
BALDWIN-WALLACE COLLEGE

it that became emotionally significant to me—inspired the poems of my first published book, *Fervor de Buenos Aires.*

I wrote these poems in 1921 and 1922, and the volume came out early in 1923. The book was actually printed in five days; the printing had to be rushed, because it was necessary for us to return to Europe. (My father wanted to consult his Genevan doctor about his sight.) I had bargained for sixty-four pages, but the manuscript ran too long and at the last minute five poems had to be left out—mercifully. I can't remember a single thing about them. The book was produced in a somewhat boyish spirit. No proofreading was done, no table of contents was provided, and the pages were unnumbered. My sister made a woodcut for the cover, and three hundred copies were printed. In those days, publishing a book was something of a private venture. I never thought of sending copies to the booksellers or out for review. Most of them I just gave away. I recall one of my methods of distribution. Having noticed that many people who went to the offices of *Nosotros*—one of the older, more solid literary magazines of the time—left their overcoats hanging in the cloak room, I brought fifty or a hundred copies to Alfredo Bianchi, one of the editors. Bianchi stared at me in amazement and said, "Do you expect me to sell these books for you?"

"No," I answered. "Although I've written them, I'm not altogether a lunatic. I thought I might ask you to slip some of these books into the pockets of those coats hanging out there." He generously did so. When I came back after a year's absence, I found that some of the inhabitants of the overcoats had read my poems, and a few had even written about them. As a matter of fact, in this way I got myself a small reputation as a poet.

The book was essentially romantic, though it was written in a rather lean style and abounded in laconic metaphors. It celebrated sunsets, solitary places, and unfamiliar corners; it ventured into Berkeleyan metaphysics and family history; it recorded early loves. At the same time, I also mimicked the Spanish seventeenth century and cited Sir Thomas Browne's *Religio Medici* in my preface. I'm afraid the book was a plum pudding—there was just too much in it. And yet, looking back on it now, I think I have never strayed beyond that book. I feel that all my subsequent writing has only developed themes first taken up there; I feel that all during my lifetime I have been rewriting that one book.

Were the poems in *Fervor de Buenos Aires* ultraist poetry? When I came back from Europe in 1921, I came bearing the banners of ultraism. I am still known to literary historians as "the father of Argentine ultraism." When I talked things over at the time with fellow-poets Eduardo González Lanuza, Norah Lange, Francisco Piñero, my cousin Guillermo Juan (Borges), and Roberto Ortelli, we came to the conclusion that Spanish ultraism was overburdened—after the manner of futurism—with modernity and gadgets. We were unimpressed by railway trains, by propellers, by airplanes, and by electric fans. While in our manifestos we still upheld the primacy of the metaphor and the elimination of transitions and decorative adjectives, what we wanted to write was essential poetry— poems beyond the here and now, free of local color and contemporary circumstances. I think the poem "Plainness" sufficiently illustrates what I personally was after:

> The garden's grillwork gate
> opens with the ease of a page
> in a much thumbed book,
> and, once inside, our eyes
> have no need to dwell on objects
> already fixed and exact in memory.
> Here habits and minds and the private language
> all families invent
> are everyday things to me.
> What necessity is there to speak
> or pretend to be someone else?
> The whole house knows me,
> they're aware of my worries and weakness.
> This is the best that can happen—
> what heaven perhaps will grant us:
> not to be wondered at or required to succeed
> but simply to be let in
> as part of an undeniable Reality,
> like stones of the road, like trees.

I think this is a far cry from the timid extravagances of my earlier Spanish ultraist exercises, when I saw a trolley car as a man shouldering a gun, or the sunrise as a shout, or the setting sun as being crucified in the west. A sane friend to whom I later recited such absurdities remarked, "Ah, I see you held the view that poetry's chief aim is to startle." As to whether the poems in *Fervor* are ultraist or not, the answer—for me—was given by my friend and French translator Néstor Ibarra, who said, "Borges left off being an ultraist poet with the first ultraist poem he wrote." I can now only regret my early ultraist excesses. After nearly a half century, I find myself still striving to live down that awkward period of my life.

Perhaps the major event of my return was Macedonio Fernández. Of all the people I have met in my life—and I have met some quite remarkable men—no one has ever made so deep and so lasting an impression on me as Macedonio. A tiny figure in a black bowler hat, he was waiting for us on the Dársena Norte when we landed, and I came to inherit his friendship from my father. Both men had been born in 1874. Paradoxically, Macedonio was an outstanding conversationalist and at the same time a man of long silences and few words. We met on Saturday evening at a café—the Perla, in the Plaza del Once. There we would talk till daybreak, Macedonio presiding. As in Madrid Cansinos had stood for all learning, Macedonio now stood for pure thinking. At the same time, I was a great reader and went out very seldom (almost every night after dinner, I used to go to bed and read), but my whole week was lit up with the expectation that on Saturday I'd be seeing and hearing Macedonio. He lived quite near us and I could have seen him whenever I wanted, but I somehow felt that I had no right to that privilege and that in order to give Macedonio's Saturday its full value I had to forgo him throughout the week. At these meetings, Macedonio would speak perhaps three or four times, risking only a few quiet observations, which were addressed — seemingly — to his neighbor alone. These remarks were never affirmative. Macedonio was very courteous and soft-spoken and would say, for example, "Well, I suppose you've noticed. . . ." And thereupon he would let loose some striking, highly original thought. But, invariably, he attributed his remark to the hearer.

He was a frail, gray man with the kind of ash-colored hair and moustache that made him look like Mark Twain. The resemblance pleased him, but when he was reminded that he also looked like Paul Valéry, he resented it, since he had little use for Frenchmen. He always wore that black bowler, and for all I know may even have slept in it. He never undressed to go to bed, and at night, to fend off drafts that he thought might cause him toothache, he draped a towel around his head. This made him look like an Arab. Among his other eccentricities were his nationalism (he admired one Argentine president after another for the sufficient reason that the Argentine electorate could not be wrong), his fear of dentistry (this led him to tugging at his teeth, in public, behind a hand, so as to stave off the dentist's pliers), and a habit of falling sentimentally in love with streetwalkers.

As a writer, Macedonio published several rather unusual volumes, and papers of his are still being collected close to twenty years after his death. His first book, published in 1928, was called *No toda es vigilia la de los ojos abiertos* (We're Not Always Awake When Our Eyes Are Open). It was an extended essay on idealism, written in a deliberately tangled and crabbed style, in order, I suppose, to match the tangledness of reality. The next year, a miscellany of his writings appeared — *Papeles de Recienvenido* (Newcomer's Papers) — in which I myself took a hand, collecting and ordering the chapters. This was a sort of miscellany of jokes within jokes. Macedonio also wrote novels and poems, all of them startling but hardly readable. One novel of twenty chapters is prefaced by fifty-six different forewords. For all his brilliance, I don't think Macedonio is to be found in his writings at all. The real Macedonio was in his conversation.

Macedonio lived modestly in boardinghouses, which he seemed to change with frequency. This was because he was always skipping out on the rent. Every time he would move, he'd leave behind piles and piles of manuscripts. Once, his friends scolded him about this, telling him it was a shame all that work should be lost. He said to us, "Do you really think I'm rich enough to lose anything?"

Readers of Hume and Schopenhauer may find little that is new in Macedonio, but the remarkable thing about him is that he arrived at his conclusions by himself. Later on, he actually read Hume, Schopenhauer, Berkeley, and William James, but I suspect he had not done much other reading, and he always quoted the same authors. He considered Sir Walter Scott the greatest of novelists, maybe just out of loyalty to a boyhood enthusiasm. He had once exchanged letters with William James, whom he had written in a medley of English, German, and French, explaining that it was because "I knew so little in any one of those languages that I had constantly to shift tongues." I think of Macedonio as reading a page or so and then being spurred into thought. He not only argued that we are such stuff as dreams are made on, but he really believed that we are all living in a dream world. Macedonio doubted whether truth was communicable. He thought that certain philosophers had discovered it but that they had failed to communicate it completely. However, he also believed that the discovery of truth was quite easy. He once told me that if he could lie out on the pampa, forgetting the world, himself, and his quest, truth might suddenly reveal itself to him. He added that, of course, it might be impossible to put that sudden wisdom into words.

Macedonio was fond of compiling small oral catalogs of people of genius, and in one of them I was amazed to find the name of a very lovable lady of our acquaintance, Quica González Acha de Tomkinson Alvear. I stared at him open-mouthed. I somehow did not think Quica ranked with Hume and Schopenhauer. But Macedonio said, "Philosophers have had to try and explain the universe, while Quica simply feels and understands it." He would turn to her and ask, "Quica, what is Being?" Quica would answer, "I don't know what you mean, Macedonio." "You see," he would say to me, "she understands so perfectly that she cannot even grasp the fact that we are puzzled." This was his proof of Quica's being a woman of genius. When I later told him he might say the same of a child or a cat, Macedonio took it angrily.

Before Macedonio, I had always been a credulous reader. His chief gift to me was to make me read skeptically. At the outset, I plagiarized him devotedly, picking up certain stylistic mannerisms of his that I later came to regret. I look back on him now, however, as an Adam bewildered by the Garden of Eden. His genius survives in but a few of his pages; his influence was of a Socratic nature. I truly loved the man, on this side idolatry, as much as any.

This period, from 1921 to 1930, was one of great activity, but much of it was perhaps reckless and even pointless. I wrote and published no less than seven books—four of them essays and three of them verse. I also founded three magazines and contributed with fair frequency to nearly a dozen other periodicals, among them *La Prensa*, *Nosotros*, *Inicial*, *Criterio*, and *Síntesis*. This productivity now amazes me as much as the fact that I feel only the remotest kinship with the work of these years. Three of the four essay collections—whose names are best forgotten—I have never allowed to be reprinted. In fact, when in 1953 my present publisher—Emecé—proposed to bring out my "complete writings," the only reason I accepted was that it would allow me to keep those preposterous volumes suppressed. This reminds me of Mark Twain's suggestion that a fine library could be started by leaving out the works of Jane Austen, and that even if that library contained no other books it would still be a fine library, since her books were left out.

In the first of these reckless compilations, there was a quite bad essay on Sir Thomas Browne, which may have been the first ever attempted on him in the Spanish language. There was another essay that set out to classify metaphors as though other poetic elements, such as rhythm and music, could be safely ignored. There was a longish essay on the nonexistence of the ego, cribbed from Bradley or the Buddha or Macedonio Fernández. When I wrote these pieces, I was trying to play the sedulous ape to two Spanish baroque seventeenth-century writers, Quevedo and Saavedra Fajardo, who stood in their own stiff, arid, Spanish way for the same kind of writing as Sir Thomas Browne in "Urne-Buriall." I was doing my best to write Latin in Spanish, and the book collapses under the sheer weight of its involutions and sententious judgments. The next of these failures was a kind of reaction. I went to the other extreme—I tried to be as Argentine as I could. I got hold of Segovia's dictionary of Argentinisms and worked in so many local words that many of my countrymen could hardly understand it. Since I have mislaid the dictionary, I'm not sure I would any longer understand the book myself, and so have given it up as utterly hopeless. The third of these unmentionables stands for a kind of partial redemption. I was creeping out of the second book's style and slowly going back to sanity, to writing with some attempt at logic and at making things easy for the reader rather than dazzling him with purple passages. One such experiment, of dubious value, was "Hombres pelearon" (Men Fought), my first venture into the mythology of the old Northside of Buenos Aires. In it, I was trying to tell a purely Argentine story in an Argentine way. This story is one I have been retelling, with small variations, ever since. It is the tale of the motiveless, or disinterested, duel—of courage for its own sake. I insisted when I wrote it that in our sense of the language we Argentines were different from the Spaniards. Now, instead, I think we should try to stress our linguistic affinities. I was still writing, but in a milder way, so that Spaniards would not understand me—writing, it might be said, to be un-understood. The Gnostics claimed that the only way to avoid a sin was to commit it and be rid of it. In my books of these years, I seem to have committed most of the major literary sins, some of them under the influence of a great writer, Leopoldo Lugones, whom I still cannot help admiring. These sins were fine writing, local color, a quest for the unexpected, and a seventeenth-century style. Today, I no longer feel guilty over these excesses; those books were written by somebody else. Until a few years ago, if the price were not too stiff, I would buy up copies and burn them.

Of the poems of this time, I should perhaps have also suppressed my second collection, *Luna de enfrente* (Moon Across the Way). It was published in 1925 and is a kind of riot of sham local color. Among its tomfooleries were the spelling of my first name in the nineteenth-century Chilean fashion as "Jorje" (it was a halfhearted attempt at phonetic spelling); the spelling of the Spanish for "and" as "*i*" instead of "*y*" (our greatest writer, Sarmiento, had done the same, trying to be as un-Spanish as he could); and the omission of the final "d" in words like "*autoridá*" and "*ciudá*." In later editions, I dropped the worst poems, pruned the eccentricities, and successively — through several reprintings — revised and toned down the verses. The third collection of the time, *Cuaderno San Martín* (the title has nothing to do with the national hero; it was merely the brand name of the out-of-fashion copybook into which I wrote the poems), includes some quite legitimate pieces, such as "La noche que en el Sur lo velaron," whose title has been strikingly translated by Robert Fitzgerald as "Deathwatch on the Southside," and "Muertes de Buenos Aires" (Deaths of Buenos Aires), about the two chief graveyards of the Argentine capital. One poem in the book (no favorite of mine) has somehow become a minor Argentine classic: "The Mythical Founding of Buenos Aires." This book, too, has been improved, or purified, by cuts and revisions down through the years.

In 1929, that third book of essays won the Second Municipal Prize of three thousand pesos, which in those days was a lordly sum of money. I was, for one thing, to acquire with it a secondhand set of the Eleventh Edition of the *Encyclopaedia Britannica*. For another, I was insured a year's leisure and decided I would write a longish book on a wholly Argentine subject. My mother wanted me to write about any of three really worthwhile poets — Ascasubi, Almafuerte, or Lugones. I now wish I had. Instead, I chose to write about a nearly invisible popular poet, Evaristo Carriego. My mother and father pointed out that his poems were not good. "But he was a friend and neighbor of ours," I said. "Well, if you think that qualifies him as the subject for a book, go ahead," they said. Carriego was the man who discovered the literary possibilities of the run-down and ragged outskirts of the city — the Palermo of my boyhood. His career followed the same evolution as the tango — rollicking, daring, courageous at first, then turning sentimental. In 1912, at the age of twenty-nine, he died of tuberculosis, leaving behind a single volume of his work. I remember that a copy of it, inscribed to my father, was one of several Argentine books we had taken to Geneva and that I read and reread there. Around 1909, Carriego had dedicated a poem to my mother. Actually, he had written it in her album. In it, he spoke of me: "And may your son . . . go forth, led by the trusting wing of inspiration, to carry out the vintage of a new annunication, which from lofty grapes will yield the wine of Song." But when I began writing my book the same thing happened to me that happened to Carlyle as he wrote his *Frederick the Great*. The more I wrote, the less I cared about my hero. I had started out to do a straight biography, but on the way I became more and more interested in old-time Buenos Aires. Readers, of course, were not slow in finding out that the book hardly lived up to its title, *Evaristo Carriego*, and so it fell flat. When the second edition appeared twenty-five years later, in 1955, as the fourth volume of my "complete" works, I enlarged the book with several new chapters, one a "History of the Tango." As a consequence of these additions, I feel *Evaristo Carriego* has been rounded out for the better.

Prisma (Prism), founded in 1921 and lasting two numbers, was the earliest of the magazines I edited. Our small ultraist group was eager to have a magazine of its own, but a real magazine was beyond our means. I had noticed billboard ads, and the thought came to me that we might similarly print a "mural magazine" and paste it up ourselves on the walls of buildings in different parts of town. Each issue was a large single sheet and contained a manifesto and some six or eight short, laconic poems, printed with plenty of white space around them, and a woodcut by my sister. We sallied forth at night—González Lanuza, Piñero, my cousin, and I—armed with pastepots and brushes provided by my mother, and, walking miles on end, slapped them up along Santa Fe, Callao, Entre Ríos, and Mexico Streets. Most of our handiwork was torn down by baffled readers almost at once, but luckily for us Alfredo Bianchi, of *Nosotros*, saw one of them and invited us to publish an ultraist anthology among the pages of his solid magazine. After *Prisma*, we went in for a six-page magazine, which was really just a single sheet printed on both sides and folded twice. This was the first *Proa* (Prow), and three numbers of it were published. Two years later, in 1924, came the second *Proa*. One afternoon, Brandán Caraffa, a young poet from Córdoba, came to see me at the Garden Hotel, where we were living upon return from our second European trip. He told me that Ricardo Güiraldes and Pablo Rojas Paz had decided to found a magazine that would represent the new literary generation, and that everyone had said that if that were its goal I could not possibly be left out. Naturally, I was flattered. That night, I went around to the Phoenix Hotel, where Güiraldes was staying. He greeted me with these words: "Brandán told me that the night before last all of you got together to found a magazine of young writers, and everyone said I couldn't be left out." At that moment, Rojas Paz came in and told us excitedly, "I'm quite flattered." I broke in and said, "The night before last, the three of us got together and decided that in a magazine of new writers you couldn't be left out." Thanks to this innocent stratagem, *Proa* was born. Each one of us put in fifty pesos, which paid for an edition of three to five hundred copies with no misprints and on fine paper. But a year and a half and fifteen issues later, for lack of subscriptions and ads, we had to give it up.

These years were quite happy ones because they stood for many friendships. They were those of Norah Lange, Macedonio, Piñero, and my father. Behind our work was a sincerity; we felt we were renewing both prose and poetry. Of course, like all young men, I tried to be as unhappy as I could—a kind of Hamlet and Raskolnikov rolled into one. What we achieved was quite bad, but our comradeships endured.

In 1924, I found my way into two different literary sets. One, whose memory I still enjoy, was that of Ricardo Güiraldes, who was yet to write *Don Segundo Sombra*. Güiraldes was very generous to me. I would give him a quite clumsy poem and he would read between the lines and divine what I had been trying to say but what my literary incapacity had prevented me from saying. He would then speak of the poem to other people, who were baffled not to find these things in the text. The other set, which I rather regret, was that of the magazine *Martín Fierro*. I disliked what *Martín Fierro* stood for, which was the French idea that literature is being continually renewed—that Adam is reborn every morning, and also for the idea that, since Paris had literary cliques that wallowed in publicity and bickering, we should be up to date and do the same. One result of this was that a sham literary feud was cooked up in Buenos Aires—that between Florida and Boedo. Florida represented downtown and Boedo the proletariat. I'd have preferred to be in the Boedo group, since I was writing about the old Northside and slums, sadness, and sunsets. But I was informed by one of the two conspirators—they were Ernesto Palacio, of Florida, and Roberto Mariani, of Boedo—that I was already one of the Florida warriors and that it was too late for me to change. The whole thing was just a put-up job. Some writers belonged to both groups— Roberto Arlt and Nicolás Olivari, for example. This sham is now taken into serious consideration by "credulous universities." But it was partly publicity, partly a boyish prank.

Linked to this time are the names of Silvina and Victoria Ocampo, of the poet Carlos Mastronardi, of Eduardo Mallea, and, not least, of Alejandro Xul-Solar. In a rough-and-ready way, it may be said that Xul, who was a mystic, a poet, and a painter, is our William Blake. I remember asking him on one particularly sultry afternoon about what he had done that stifling day. His answer was "Nothing whatever, except for founding twelve religions after lunch." Xul was also a philologist and the inventor of two languages. One was a philosophical language after the manner of John Wilkins and the other a reformation of Spanish with many English, German, and Greek words thrown in. He came of Baltic and Italian stock. "Xul" was his version of "Schulz" and "Solar" of "Solari." At this time, I also met Alfonso Reyes. He was the Mexican ambassador to Argentina, and used to invite me to dinner every Sunday at the embassy. I think of

Reyes as the finest Spanish prose stylist of this century, and in my writing I learned a great deal about simplicity and directness from him.

Summing up this span of my life, I find myself completely out of sympathy with the priggish and rather dogmatic young man I then was. Those friends, however, are still very living and very close to me. In fact, they form a precious part of me. Friendship is, I think, the one redeeming Argentine passion.

MATURITY

In the course of a lifetime devoted chiefly to books, I have read but few novels, and, in most cases, only a sense of duty has enabled me to find my way to their last page. At the same time, I have always been a reader and rereader of short stories. Stevenson, Kipling, James, Conrad, Poe, Chesterton, the tales of Lane's Arabian Nights, and certain stories by Hawthorne have been habits of mine since I can remember. The feeling that great novels like *Don Quixote* and *Huckleberry Finn* are virtually shapeless served to reinforce my taste for the short-story form, whose indispensable elements are economy and a clearly stated beginning, middle, and end. As a writer, however, I thought for years that the short story was beyond my powers, and it was only after a long and roundabout series of timid experiments in narration that I sat down to write real stories.

It took me some six years, from 1927 to 1933, to go from that all too self-conscious sketch "Hombres pelearon" to my first outright short story, "Hombre de la esquina rosada" (Streetcorner Man). A friend of mine, don Nicolás Paredes, a former political boss and former gambler of the Northside, had died, and I wanted to record something of his voice, his anecdotes, and his particular way of telling them. I slaved over my every page, sounding out each sentence and striving to phrase it in his exact tones. We were living out in Adrogué at the time and, because I knew my mother would heartily disapprove of the subject matter, I composed in secret over a period of several months. Originally titled "Hombres de las orillas" (Men from the Edge of Town), the story appeared in the Saturday supplement, which I was editing, of a yellow-press daily called *Crítica*. But out of shyness, and perhaps a feeling that the story was a bit beneath me, I signed it with a pen name—the name of one of my great-great grandfathers, Francisco Bustos. Although the story became popular to the point of embarrassment (today I only find it stagy and mannered and the characters bogus), I never regarded it as a starting point. It simply stands there as a kind of freak.

The real beginning of my career as a story writer starts with the series of sketches entitled *Historia universal de la infamia* (A Universal History of Infamy), which I contributed to the columns of *Crítica* in 1933 and 1934. The irony of this is that "Streetcorner Man" really was a story but that these sketches and several of the fictional pieces which followed them, and which very slowly led me to legitimate stories, were in the nature of hoaxes and pseudo-essays. In my *Universal History*, I did not want to repeat what Marcel Schwob had done in his *Imaginary Lives*. He had invented biographies of real men about whom little or nothing is recorded. I, instead, read up on the lives of known persons and then deliberately varied and distorted them according to my own whims. For example, after reading Herbert Asbury's *The Gangs of New York*, I set down my free version of Monk Eastman, the Jewish gunman, in flagrant contradiction of my chosen authority. I did the same for Billy the Kid, for John Murrel (whom I rechristened Lazarus Morell), for the Veiled Prophet of Khorassan, for the Tichborne Claimant, and for several others. I never thought of book publication. The pieces were meant for popular consumption in *Crítica* and were pointedly picturesque. I suppose now the secret value of those sketches—apart from the sheer pleasure the writing gave me—lay in the fact that they were narrative exercises. Since the general plots or circumstances were all given me, I had only to embroider sets of vivid variations.

My next story, "The Approach to al-Mu'tasim," written in 1935, is both a hoax *and* a pseudo-essay. It purports to be a review of a book published originally in Bombay three years earlier. I endowed its fake second edition with a real publisher, Victor Gollancz, and a preface by a real writer, Dorothy L. Sayers. But the author and the book are entirely my own invention. I gave the plot and details of some chapters—borrowing from Kipling and working in the twelfth-century Persian mystic Farid ud-Din Attar—and then carefully pointed out its shortcomings. The story appeared the next year in a volume of my essays, *Historia de la eternidad* (A History of Eternity), buried at the back of the book together with an article on the "Art of Insult." Those who read "The Approach to al-Mu'tasim" took it at face value, and one of my friends even ordered a copy from London. It was not until 1942 that I openly published it as a short story in my first story collection, *El jardín de senderos que se bifurcan* (The Garden of Branching Paths). Perhaps I have been unfair to this story; it now seems to me to foreshadow and even to set the pattern for those tales that were somehow awaiting me, and upon which my reputation as a storyteller was to be based.

Along about 1937, I took my first regular full-time job. I had previously worked at small editing tasks. There was the *Crítica* supplement, which was a heavily and even gaudily illustrated entertainment sheet. There was *El Hogar*, a popular society weekly, to which, twice a month, I contributed a couple of literary pages on foreign books and authors. I had also written newsreel texts and had been editor of a pseudo-scientific magazine called *Urbe*, which was really a promotional organ of a privately owned Buenos Aires subway system. These had all been small-paying jobs, and I was long past the age when I should have begun contributing to our household upkeep. Now, through friends, I was given a very minor position as First Assistant in the Miguel Cané branch of the Municipal Library, out in a drab and dreary part of town to the southwest. While there were Second and Third Assistants below me, there were also a Director and First, Second, and Third Officials above me. I was paid two hundred and ten pesos a month and later went up to two hundred and forty. These were sums roughly equivalent to seventy or eighty American dollars.

At the library, we did very little work. There were some fifty of us doing what fifteen could easily have done. My particular job, shared with fifteen or twenty colleagues, was classifying and cataloging the library's holdings, which until that time were uncatalogued. The collection, however, was so small that we knew where to find the books without the system, so the system, though laboriously carried out, was never needed or used. The first day, I worked honestly. On the next, some of my fellows took me aside to say that I couldn't do this sort of thing because it showed them up. "Besides," they argued, "as this cataloging has been planned to give us some semblance of work, you'll put us out of our jobs." I told them I had classified four hundred titles instead of their one hundred. "Well, if you keep that up," they said, "the boss will be angry and won't know what to do with us." For the sake of realism, I was told that from then on I should do eighty-three books one day, ninety another, and one hundred and four the third.

I stuck out the library for about nine years. They were nine years of solid unhappiness. At work, the other men were interested in nothing but horse racing, soccer matches, and smutty stories. Once, a woman, one of the readers, was raped on her way to the ladies' room. Everybody said such things were bound to happen, since the men's and ladies' rooms were adjoining. One day, two rather posh and well-meaning friends — society ladies — came to see me at work. They phoned me a day or two later to say, "You may think it amusing to work in a place like that, but promise us you will find at least a nine-hundred-peso job before the month is out." I gave them my word that I would. Ironically, at the time I was a fairly well-known writer — except at the library. I remember a fellow employee's once noting in an encyclopedia the name of a certain Jorge Luis Borges — a fact that set him wondering at the coincidence of our identical names and birth dates. Now and then during these years, we municipal workers were rewarded with gifts of a two-pound package of maté to take home. Sometimes in the evening, as I walked the ten blocks to the tramline, my eyes would be filled with tears. These small gifts from above always underlined my menial and dismal existence.

A couple of hours each day, riding back and forth on the tram, I made my way through *The Divine Comedy*, helped as far as "Purgatory" by John Aitken Carlyle's prose translation and then ascending the rest of the way on my own. I would do all my library work in the first hour and then steal away to the basement and pass the other five hours in reading or writing. I remember in this way rereading the six volumes of Gibbon's *Decline and Fall* and the many volumes of Vicente Fidel López' *History of the Argentine Republic*. I read Léon Bloy, Claudel, Groussac, and Bernard Shaw. On holidays, I translated Faulkner and Virginia Woolf. At some point, I was moved up to the dizzying height of Third Official. One morning, my mother rang me up and I asked for leave to go home, arriving just in time to see my father die. He had undergone a long agony and was very impatient for his death.

It was on Christmas Eve of 1938 — the same year my father died — that I had a severe accident. I was running up a stairway and suddenly felt something brush my scalp. I had grazed a freshly painted open casement window. In spite of first-aid treatment, the wound became poisoned, and for a period of a week or so I lay sleepless every night and had hallucinations and high fever. One evening, I lost the power of speech and had to be rushed to the hospital for an immediate operation. Septicemia had set in, and for a month I hovered, all unknowingly, between life and death. (Much later, I was to write about this in my story "The South.") When I began to recover, I feared for my mental integrity. I remember that my mother wanted to read to me from a book I had just ordered, C. S. Lewis' *Out of the Silent Planet*, but for two or three nights I kept putting her off. At last, she prevailed, and after hearing a page or two I fell to crying. My mother asked me why the tears. "I'm crying because I understand," I said. A bit later, I wondered whether I could ever write again. I had previously written quite a few poems and dozens of short reviews. I thought that if I tried to write a review now and failed, I'd be all through intellectually but that if I tried something I had never really done before and failed at that it wouldn't be so bad and might even prepare me for the final revelation. I decided I would try to write a story. The result was "Pierre Menard, Author of *Don Quixote*."

"Pierre Menard," like its forerunner "The Approach to al-Mu'tasim," was still a halfway house between the essay and the true tale. But the achievement spurred me on. I next tried something more ambitious — "Tlön, Uqbar, Orbis Tertius," about the discovery of a new world that finally replaces our present world. Both were published in Victoria Ocampo's magazine *Sur*. I kept up my writing at the library. Though my colleagues thought of me as a traitor for not sharing their boisterous fun, I went on with work of my own in the basement, or, when the weather was warm, up on the flat roof. My Kafkian story "The Library of Babel" was meant as a nightmare version or magnification of that municipal library, and certain details in the text have no particular meaning. The numbers of books and shelves that I recorded in the story were literally what I had at my elbow. Clever critics have worried over those ciphers, and generously endowed them with mystic significance. "The Lottery in Babylon," "Death and the Compass," and "The Circular Ruins" were also written, in whole or part, while I played truant. These tales and others were to become *The Garden of Branching Paths*, a book expanded and retitled *Ficciones* in 1944. *Ficciones* and *El Aleph* (1949 and 1952), my second story collection, are, I suppose, my two major books.

In 1946, a president whose name I do not want to remember came into power. One day soon after, I was honored with the news that I had been "promoted" out of the library to the inspectorship of poultry and rabbits in the public markets. I went to the City Hall to find out what it was all about. "Look here," I said. "It's rather strange that among so many others at the library, I should be singled out as worthy of this new position." "Well," the clerk answered, "you were on the side of the Allies — what do you expect?" His statement was unanswerable; the next day, I sent in my resignation. My friends rallied round me at once and offered me a public dinner. I prepared a speech for the occasion but, knowing I was too shy to read it myself, I asked my friend Pedro Henríquez Ureña to read it for me.

I was now out of a job. Several months before, an old English lady had read my tea leaves and had foretold that I was soon to travel, to lecture, and to make vast sums of money thereby. When I told my mother about it, we both laughed, for public speaking was far beyond me. At this juncture, a friend came to the rescue, and I was made a teacher of English literature at the Asociación Argentina de Cultura Inglesa. I was also asked at the same time to lecture on classic American literature at the Colegio Libre de Estudios Superiores. Since this pair of offers was made three months before classes opened, I accepted, feeling quite safe. As the time grew near, however, I grew sicker and sicker. My series of lectures was to be on Hawthorne, Poe, Thoreau, Emerson, Melville, Whitman, Twain, Henry James, and Veblen. I wrote the first one down. But I had no time to write out the second one. Besides, thinking of the first lecture as Doomsday, I felt that only eternity could come after. The first one went off well enough — miraculously. Two nights before the second lecture, I took my mother for a long walk around Adrogué and had her time me as I rehearsed my talk. She said she thought it was overlong. "In that case," I said, "I'm safe." My fear had been of running dry. So, at forty-seven, I found a new and exciting life opening up for me. I traveled up and down Argentina and Uruguay, lecturing on Swedenborg, Blake, the Persian and Chinese mystics, Buddhism, gauchesco poetry, Martin Buber, the Kabbalah, the Arabian Nights, T. E. Lawrence, medieval Germanic poetry, the Icelandic sagas, Heine, Dante, expressionism, and Cervantes. I went from town to town, staying overnight in hotels I'd never see again. Sometimes my mother or a friend accompanied me. Not only did I end up making far more money than at the library but I enjoyed the work and felt that it justified me.

One of the chief events of these years — and of my life — was the beginning of my friendship with Adolfo Bioy-Casares. We met in 1930 or

1931, when he was about seventeen and I was just past thirty. It is always taken for granted in these cases that the older man is the master and the younger his disciple. This may have been true at the outset, but several years later, when we began to work together, Bioy was really and secretly the master. He and I attempted many different literary ventures. We compiled anthologies of Argentine poetry, tales of the fantastic, and detective stories; we wrote articles and forewords; we annotated Sir Thomas Browne and Gracián; we translated short stories by writers like Beerbohm, Kipling, Wells, and Lord Dunsany; we founded a magazine, *Destiempo*, which lasted three issues; we wrote film scripts, which were invariably rejected. Opposing my taste for the pathetic, the sententious, and the baroque, Bioy made me feel that quietness and restraint are more desirable. If I may be allowed a sweeping statement, Bioy led me gradually toward classicism.

It was at some point in the early forties that we began writing in collaboration — a feat that up to that time I had thought impossible. I had invented what we thought was a quite good plot for a detective story. One rainy morning, he told me we ought to give it a try. I reluctantly agreed, and a little later that same morning the thing happened. A third man, Honorio Bustos Domecq, emerged and took over. In the long run, he ruled us with a rod of iron and to our amusement, and later to our dismay, he became utterly unlike ourselves, with his own whims, his own puns, and his own very elaborate style of writing. Domecq was the name of a great-grandfather of Bioy's and Bustos of a great-grandfather of mine from Córdoba. Bustos Domecq's first book was *Six Problems for don Isidro Parodi* (1942), and during the writing of that volume he never got out of hand. Max Carrados had attempted a blind detective; Bioy and I went one step further and confined our detective to a jail cell. The book was at the same time a satire on the Argentine. For many years, the dual identity of Bustos Domecq was never revealed. When finally it was, people thought that, as Bustos was a joke, his writing could hardly be taken seriously.

Our next collaboration was another detective novel, *A Model for Death*. This one was so personal and so full of private jokes that we published it only in an edition that was not for sale. The author of this book we named B. Suárez Lynch. The "B." stood, I think, for Bioy and Borges, "Suárez" for another great-grandfather of mine, and Lynch for another great-grandfather of Bioy's. Bustos Domecq reappeared in 1946 in another private edition, this time of two stories, entitled *Two Memorable Fantasies*. After a long eclipse, Bustos took up his pen again, and in 1967 brought out his *Chronicles*. These are articles written on imaginary, extravagantly modern artists — architects, sculptors, painters, chefs, poets, novelists, couturiers — by a devotedly modern critic. But both the author and his subjects are fools, and it is hard to tell who is taking in whom. The book is inscribed, "To those three forgotten greats — Picasso, Joyce, Le Corbusier." The style is itself a parody. Bustos writes a literary journalese,

abounding in neologisms, a Latinate vocabulary, clichés, mixed metaphors, non sequiturs, and bombast.

I have often been asked how collaboration is possible. I think it
requires a joint abandoning of the ego, of vanity, and maybe of common
politeness. The collaborators should forget themselves and think only in
terms of the work. In fact, when somebody wants to know whether such-
and-such a joke or epithet came from my side of the table or Bioy's, I
honestly cannot tell him. I have tried to collaborate with other friends —
some of them very close ones — but their inability to be blunt on the one
hand or thick-skinned on the other has made the scheme impossible. As to
the *Chronicles of Bustos Domecq*, I think they are better than anything I
have published under my own name and nearly as good as anything Bioy
has written on his own.

In 1950, I was elected President of the Sociedad Argentina de
Escritores (Argentine Society of Writers). The Argentine Republic, then as
now, is a soft country, and the S.A.D.E. was one of the few strongholds
against the dictatorship. This was so evident that many distinguished men
of letters did not dare set foot inside its doors until after the revolution.
One curious trait of the dictatorship was that even its professed upholders
made it clear that they did not really take the government seriously but
were acting out of self-interest. This was understood and forgiven, since
most of my countrymen have an intellectual, if not a moral, conscience.
Nearly all the smutty jokes made up about Perón and his wife were the
invention of Peronistas themselves, trying to save face. The S.A.D.E. was
eventually closed. I remember the last lecture I was allowed to give there.
The audience, quite a small one, included a very puzzled policeman who
did his clumsy best to set down a few of my remarks on Persian Sufism.
During this drab and hopeless period, my mother — then in her seventies —
was under house arrest. My sister and one of my nephews spent a month in
jail. I myself had a detective on my heels, whom I first took on long,
aimless walks and at last made friends with. He admitted that he too hated
Perón, but said that he was obeying orders. Ernesto Palacio once offered to
introduce me to the Unspeakable, but I did not want to meet him. How
could I be introduced to a man whose hand I would not shake?

The long-hoped-for revolution came in September, 1955. After a
sleepless, anxious night, nearly the whole population came out into the
streets, cheering the revolution and shouting the name of Córdoba, where
most of the fighting had taken place. We were so carried away that for
some time we were quite unaware of the rain that was soaking us to the
bone. We were so happy that not a single word was even uttered against
the fallen dictator. Perón went into hiding, and was later allowed to leave
the country. No one knows how much money he got away with.

Two very dear friends of mine, Esther Zemborain de Torres and
Victoria Ocampo, dreamed up the possibility of my being appointed
Director of the National Library. I thought the scheme a wild one, and

hoped at most to be given the directorship of some small-town library, preferably to the south of the city. Within the space of a day, a petition was signed by the magazine *Sur* (read Victoria Ocampo), by the reopened S.A.D.E. (read Carlos Alberto Erro), by the Sociedad Argentina de Cultura Inglesa (read Carlos del Campillo), and by the Colegio Libre de Estudios Superiores (read Luis Reissig). This was placed on the desk of the Minister of Education, and eventually I was appointed to the directorship by General Eduardo Lonardi, who was Acting President. A few days earlier, my mother and I had walked to the Library one night to take a look at the building, but, feeling superstitious, I refused to go in. "Not until I get the job," I said. That same week, I was called to come to the Library to take over. My family was present, and I made a speech to the employees, telling them I was actually the Director—the incredible Director. At the same time, José Edmundo Clemente, who a few years before had managed to persuade Emecé to bring out an edition of my works, became the Assistant Director. Of course, I felt very important, but we got no pay for the next three months. I don't think my predecessor, who was a Peronista, was ever officially fired. He just never came around to the Library again. They named me to the job but did not take the trouble to unseat him.

Another pleasure came to me the very next year, when I was named to the professorship of English and American Literature at the University of Buenos Aires. Other candidates had sent in painstaking lists of their translations, papers, lectures, and other achievements. I limited myself to the following statement: "Quite unwittingly, I have been qualifying myself for this position throughout my life." My plain approach gained the day. I was hired, and spent ten or twelve happy years at the University.

My blindness had been coming on gradually since childhood. It was a slow, summer twilight. There was nothing particularly pathetic or dramatic about it. Beginning in 1927, I underwent eight eye operations, but since the late 1950's, when I wrote my "Poem of the Gifts," for reading and writing purposes I have been blind. Blindness ran in my family; a description of the operation performed on the eyes of my great-grandfather, Edward Young Haslam, appeared in the pages of the London medical journal, the *Lancet*. Blindness also seems to run among the Directors of the National Library. Two of my eminent forerunners, José Mármol and Paul Groussac, suffered the same fate. In my poem, I speak of God's splendid irony in granting me at one time 800,000 books and darkness.

One salient consequence of my blindness was my gradual abandonment of free verse in favor of classical metrics. In fact, blindness made me take up the writing of poetry again. Since rough drafts were denied me, I had to fall back on memory. It is obviously easier to remember verse than prose, and to remember regular verse forms rather than free ones. Regular verse is, so to speak, portable. One can walk down the street or be riding the subway while composing and polishing a sonnet, for rhyme and meter have mnemonic virtues. In these years, I wrote dozens of sonnets and longer poems consisting of eleven-syllable quatrains. I thought I had taken Lugones as my master, but when the verses were written my friends told me that, regrettably, they were quite unlike him. In my later poetry, a narrative thread is always to be found. As a matter of fact, I even think of plots for poems. Perhaps the main difference between Lugones and me is that he held French literature as his model and lived intellectually in a French world, whereas I look to English literature. In this new poetic activity, I never thought of building a sequence of poems, as I always formerly did, but was chiefly interested in each piece for its own sake. In this way, I wrote poems on such different subjects as Emerson, and wine, Snorri Sturluson and the hourglass, my grandfather's death and the beheading of Charles I. I also went in for summing up my literary heroes: Poe, Swedenborg, Whitman, Heine, Camões, Jonathan Edwards, and Cervantes. Due tribute, of course, was also paid to mirrors, the Minotaur, and knives.

I had always been attracted to the metaphor, and this leaning led me to the study of the simple Saxon kennings and overelaborate Norse ones. As far back as 1932, I had even written an essay about them. The quaint notion of using, as far as it could be done, metaphors instead of straightforward nouns, and of these metaphors' being at once traditional and arbitrary, puzzled and appealed to me. I was later to surmise that the purpose of these figures lay not only in the pleasure given by the pomp and circumstance of compounding words but also in the demands of alliteration. Taken by themselves, the kennings are not especially witty, and calling a ship "a sea-stallion" and the open sea "the whale's-road" is no great feat. The Norse skalds went a step further, calling the sea "the sea-stallion's road," so that what originally was an image became a laborious equation. In turn, my investigation of kennings led me to the study of Old English and Old Norse. Another factor that impelled me in this direction was my ancestry. It may be no more than a romantic superstition of mine, but the fact that the Haslams lived in Northumbria and Mercia — or, as they are today called, Northumberland and the Midlands — links me with a Saxon and perhaps a Danish past. (My fondness for such a northern past has been resented by some of my more nationalistic countrymen, who dub me an Englishman, but I hardly need point out that many things English are utterly alien to me: tea, the Royal Family, "manly" sports, the worship of every line written by the uncaring Shakespeare.)

At the end of one of my University courses, several of my students came to see me at the Library. We had just polished off all English literature from Beowulf to Bernard Shaw in the span of four months, and I thought we might now do something in earnest. I proposed that we begin at the beginning, and they agreed. I knew that at home, on a certain top shelf, I had copies of Sweet's *Anglo-Saxon Reader* and the *Anglo-Saxon*

Chronicle. When the students came the next Saturday morning, we began reading these two books. We skipped grammar as much as we could and pronounced the words like German. All at once, we fell in love with a sentence in which Rome (Romeburh) was mentioned. We got drunk on these words and rushed down Peru Street shouting them at the top of our voices. And so we had set out on a long adventure. I had always thought of English literature as the richest in the world; the discovery now of a secret chamber at the very threshold of that literature came to me as an additional gift. Personally, I knew that the adventure would be an endless one, and that I could go on studying Old English for the rest of my days. The pleasure of studying, not the vanity of mastering, has been my chief aim, and I have not been disappointed these past twelve years. As for my recent interest in Old Norse, this is only a logical step, since the two languages are closely linked and since of all medieval Germanic literature Old Norse is the crown. My excursions into Old English have been wholly personal and, therefore, have made their way into a number of my poems. A fellow-academician once took me aside and said in alarm, "What do you mean by publishing a poem entitled 'Embarking on the Study of Anglo-Saxon Grammar'?" I tried to make him understand that Anglo-Saxon was as intimate an experience to me as looking at a sunset or falling in love.

Around 1954, I began writing short prose pieces — sketches and parables. One day, my friend Carlos Frías, of Emecé, told me he needed a new book for the series of my so-called complete works. I said I had none to give him, but Frías persisted, saying, "Every writer has a book if he only looks for it." Going through my drawers at home one idle Sunday, I began ferreting out uncollected poems and prose pieces, some of the latter going back to my days on *Crítica*. These odds and ends, sorted out and ordered and published in 1960, became *El hacedor* (The Maker). Remarkably, this book, which I accumulated rather than wrote, seems to me my most personal work and, to my taste, maybe my best. The explanation is only too easy: the pages of *El hacedor* contain no padding. Each piece was written for its own sake and out of an inner necessity. By the time it was undertaken, I had come to realize that fine writing is a mistake, and a mistake born out of vanity. Good writing, I firmly believe, should be done in an unobtrusive way.

On the closing page of that book, I told of a man who sets out to make a picture of the universe. After many years, he has covered a blank wall with images of ships, towers, horses, weapons, and men, only to find out at the moment of his death that he has drawn a likeness of his own face. This may be the case of all books; it is certainly the case of this particular book.

CROWDED YEARS

Fame, like my blindness, had been coming gradually to me. I had never expected it, I had never sought it. Néstor Ibarra and Roger Caillois, who in the early 1950's daringly translated me into French, were my first benefactors. I suspect that their pioneer work paved the way for my sharing with Samuel Beckett the Formentor Prize in 1961, for until I appeared in French I was practically invisible — not only abroad but at home in Buenos Aires. As a consequence of that prize, my books mushroomed overnight throughout the western world.

This same year, under the auspices of Edward Larocque Tinker, I was invited as Visiting Professor to the University of Texas. It was my first physical encounter with America. In a sense, because of my reading, I had always been there, and yet how strange it seemed when in Austin I heard ditch diggers who worked on campus speaking in English, a language I had until then always thought of as being denied that class of people. America, in fact, had taken on such mythic proportions in my mind that I was sincerely amazed to find there such commonplace things as weeds, mud, puddles, dirt roads, flies, and stray dogs. Though at times we fell into homesickness, I know now that my mother — who accompanied me — and I grew to love Texas. She, who always loathed football, even rejoiced over *our* victory when the Longhorns defeated the neighboring Bears. At the University, when I finished one class I was giving in Argentine literature, I would sit in on another as a student of Saxon verse under Dr. Rudolph Willard. My days were full. I found American students, unlike the run of students in the Argentine, far more interested in their subjects than in their grades. I tried to interest people in Ascasubi and Lugones, but they stubbornly questioned and interviewed me about my own output. I spent as much time as I could with Ramón Martínez López, who, as a philologist, shared my passion for etymologies and taught me many things. During those six months in the States, we traveled widely, and I lectured at universities from coast to coast. I saw New Mexico, San Francisco, New York, New England, Washington. I found America the friendliest, most forgiving, and most generous nation I had ever visited. We South Americans tend to think in terms of convenience, whereas people in the United States approach things ethically. This — amateur Protestant that I am — I admired above all. It even helped me overlook skyscrapers, paper bags, television, plastics, and the unholy jungle of gadgets.

My second American trip came in 1967, when I held the Charles Eliot Norton Chair of Poetry at Harvard, and lectured to well-wishing audiences on "This Craft of Verse." I spent seven months in Cambridge, also teaching a course on Argentine writers and traveling all over New England, where most things American, including the West, seem to have been invented. I made numerous literary pilgrimages — to Hawthorne's haunts in Salem, to Emerson's in Concord, to Melville's in New Bedford, to Emily Dickinson's in Amherst, and to Longfellow's around the corner from where I lived. Friends seemed to multiply in Cambridge: Jorge Guillén, John Murchison, Juan Marichal, Raimundo Lida, Héctor Ingrao, and a Persian physicist who had worked out a theory of spherical time that I do not quite understand but hope someday to plagiarize — Farid Hushfar. I also met writers like Robert Fitzgerald, John Updike, and the late Dudley Fitts. I availed myself of chances to see new parts of the continent: Iowa, where I found my native pampa awaiting me; Chicago, recalling Carl Sandburg; Missouri; Maryland; Virginia. At the end of my stay, I was greatly honored to have my poems read at the Y.M.H.A. Poetry Center in New York, with several of my translators reading and a number of poets in the audience. I owe a third trip to the United States, in November of 1969, to my two benefactors at the University of Oklahoma, Lowell Dunham and Ivar Ivask, who invited me to give talks there and called together a group of scholars to comment on, and enrich, my work. Ivask made me a gift of a fish-shaped Finnish dagger — rather alien to the tradition of the old Palermo of my boyhood.

Looking back on this past decade, I seem to have been quite a wanderer. In 1963, thanks to Neil MacKay of the British Council in Buenos Aires, I was able to visit England and Scotland. There, too, again in my mother's company, I made my pilgrimages: to London, so teeming with literary memories; to Lichfield and Dr. Johnson; to Manchester and De Quincey; to Rye and Henry James; to the Lake Country; to Edinburgh. I visited my grandmother's birthplace in Hanley, one of the Five Towns — Arnold Bennett country. Scotland and Yorkshire I think of as among the loveliest places on earth. Somewhere in the Scottish hills and glens I recaptured a strange sense of loneliness and bleakness that I had known before; it took me some time to trace this feeling back to the far-flung wastes of Patagonia. A few years later, this time in the company of María Esther Vázquez, I made another European trip. In England, we stayed with the late Herbert Read in his fine rambling house out on the moors. He took us to Yorkminster, where he showed us some ancient Danish swords in the Viking Yorkshire room of the museum. I later wrote a sonnet to one of the swords, and just before his death Sir Herbert corrected and bettered my original title, suggesting, instead of "To a Sword in York," "To a Sword in Yorkminster." We later went to Stockholm, invited by my Swedish publisher, Bonnier, and by the Argentine ambassador. Stockholm and Copenhagen I count among the most unforgettable cities I have seen, like San Francisco, New York, Edinburgh, Santiago de Compostela, and Geneva.

Early in 1969, invited by the Israeli government, I spent ten very exciting days in Tel Aviv and Jerusalem. I brought home with me the conviction of having been in the oldest and the youngest of nations, of having come from a very living, vigilant land back to a half-asleep nook of the world. Since my Genevan days, I had always been interested in Jewish culture, thinking of it as an integral element of our so-called Western civilization, and during the Israeli-Arab war of a few years back I found myself taking immediate sides. While the outcome was still uncertain, I wrote a poem on the battle. A week after, I wrote another on the victory. Israel was, of course, still an armed camp at the time of my visit. There, along the shores of Galilee, I kept recalling these lines from Shakespeare: "Over whose acres walk'd those blessed feet, / Which, fourteen hundred years ago, were nail'd, / For our advantage, on the bitter cross."

Now, despite my years, I still think of the many stones I have left unturned, and of others I would like to turn again. I hope yet to see Mormon Utah, to which I was introduced as a boy by Mark Twain's *Roughing It* and by the first book of the Sherlock Holmes saga, *A Study in Scarlet*. Another daydream of mine is a pilgrimage to Iceland, and another still to return again to Texas and to Scotland.

At seventy-one, I am still hard at work and brimming with plans. Last year I wrote a new book of poems, *Elogio de la sombra* (In Praise of Darkness). It was my first entirely new volume since 1960, and these were also my first poems since 1929 written with a book in mind. My main concern in this work, running through several of its pieces, is of an ethical nature, irrespective of any religious or antireligious bias. "Darkness" in the title stands for both blindness and death. To finish *Elogio*, I worked every morning, dictating at the National Library. By the time I ended, I had set up a comfortable routine—so comfortable that I kept it up and began writing tales. These, my first stories since 1953, I published this year. The collection is called *El informe de Brodie* (Doctor Brodie's Report). It is a set of modest experiments in straightforward storytelling, and is the book I have often spoken about in the past five years. Recently, I completed the script of a film to be called *Los otros* (The Others). Its plot is my own; the writing was done together with Adolfo Bioy-Casares and the young Argentine director Hugo Santiago. My afternoons now are usually given over to a long-range and cherished project: for nearly the past three years, I have been lucky to have my own translator at my side, and together we are bringing out some ten or twelve volumes of my work in English, a language I am unworthy to handle, a language I often wish had been my birthright.

I intend now to begin a new book, a series of personal—not scholarly—essays on Dante, Ariosto, and medieval northern subjects. I want also to set down a book of informal, outspoken opinions, whims, reflections, and private heresies. After that, who knows? I still have a number of stories, heard or invented, that I want to tell. At present, I am finishing a long tale called "The Congress." Despite its Kafkian title, I hope it will turn out more in the line of Chesterton. The setting is Argentine and Uruguayan. For twenty years, I have been boring my friends with the raw plot. Finally, I came to see that no further elaboration was needed. I have another project that has been pending for an even longer period of time—that of revising and perhaps rewriting my father's novel *The Caudillo*, as he asked me to years ago. We had gone as far as discussing many of the problems; I like to think of the undertaking as a continued dialogue and a very real collaboration.

People have been unaccountably good to me. I have no enemies, and if certain persons have masqueraded as such, they've been far too good-natured to have ever pained me. Anytime I read something written against me, I not only share the sentiment but feel I could do the job far better myself. Perhaps I should advise would-be enemies to send me their grievances beforehand, with full assurance that they will receive my every aid and support. I have even secretly longed to write, under a pen name, a merciless tirade against myself. Ah, the unvarnished truths I harbor!

At my age, one should be aware of one's limits, and this knowledge may make for happiness. When I was young, I thought of literature as a game of skillful and surprising variations; now that I have found my own voice, I feel that tinkering and tampering neither greatly improve nor greatly spoil my drafts. This, of course, is a sin against one of the main tendencies of letters in this century — the vanity of overwriting — which led a man like Joyce into publishing expensive fragments, showily entitled "Work in Progress." I suppose my best work is over. This gives me a certain quiet satisfaction and ease. And yet I do not feel I have written myself out. In a way, youthfulness seems closer to me today than when I was a young man. I no longer regard happiness as unattainable; once, long ago, I did. Now I know that it may occur at any moment but that it should never be sought after. As to failure or fame, they are quite irrelevant and I never bother about them. What I'm out for now is peace, the enjoyment of thinking and of friendship, and, though it may be too ambitious, a sense of loving and of being loved.

A Modern Master   Paul de Man*

> Empty eyeballs knew
> That knowledge increases unreality, that Mirror on mirror mirrored is
> all the show.
> —W. B. Yeats

Although he has been writing poems, stories, and critical essays of the highest quality since 1923, the Argentinian writer Jorge Luis Borges is still much better known in Latin America than in the U.S. For the translator of John Peale Bishop, Hart Crane, E. E. Cummings, William Faulkner, Edgar Lee Masters, Robert Penn Warren, and Wallace Stevens, this

*From the New York Review of Books, 19 November 1964. Reprinted by permission of University of Minnesota Press.

neglect is somewhat unfair. There are signs, however, that he is being discovered in this country with some of the same enthusiasm that greeted him in France, where he received major critical attention, and has been very well translated. Several volumes of translations in English have recently appeared, including a fine edition of his most recent book *El hacedor (Dreamtigers)*[1] and a new edition of *Labryinths*, which first appeared in 1962. American and English critics have called him one of the greatest writers alive today, but have not as yet (so far as I know) made substantial contributions to the interpretation of his work. There are good reasons for this delay. Borges is a complex writer, particularly difficult to place. Commentators cast around in vain for suitable points of comparison and his own avowed literary admirations add to the confusion. Like Kafka and contemporary French existential writers, he is often seen as a moralist, in rebellion against the times. But such an approach is misleading.

It is true that, especially in his earlier works, Borges writes about villains: The collection *History of Infamy (Historia universal de la infamia*, 1935) contains an engaging gallery of scoundrels. But Borges does not consider infamy primarily as a moral theme; the stories in no way suggest an indictment of society or of human nature or of destiny. Nor do they suggest the lighthearted view of Gide's Nietzschean hero Lafcadio. Instead, infamy functions here as an aesthetic, formal principle. The fictions literally could not have taken shape but for the presence of villainy at their very heart. Many different worlds are conjured up—cotton plantations along the Mississippi, pirate-infested South seas, the Wild West, the slums of New York, Japanese courts, the Arabian desert, etc.— all of which would be shapeless without the ordering presence of a villain at the center.

A good illustration can be taken from the imaginary essays on literary subjects that Borges was writing at the same time as the *History of Infamy*. Borrowing the stylistic conventions of scholarly critical writing, the essays read like a combination of Empson, Paulhan, and *PMLA*, except that they are a great deal more succinct and devious. In an essay on the translations of *The Thousand and One Nights*, Borges quotes an impressive list of examples showing how translator after translator mercilessly cut, expanded, distorted, and falsified the original in order to make it conform to his own and his audience's artistic and moral standards. The list, which amounts in fact to a full catalogue of human sins, culminates in the sterling character of Enna Littmann, whose 1923–1928 edition is scrupulously exact: "Incapable, like George Washington, of telling a lie, his work reveals nothing but German candor." This translation is vastly inferior, in Borges's eyes, to all others. It lacks the wealth of literary associations that allows the other, villainous translators to give their language depth, suggestiveness, ambiguity—in a word, style. The artist has to wear the mask of the villain or order to create a style.

So far, so good. All of us know that the poet is of the devil's party and that sin makes for better stories than virtue. It takes some effort to prefer *La nouvelle Héloise* to *Les liaisons dangereuses* or, for that matter, to prefer the second part of the *Nouvelle Héloise* to the first. Borges's theme of infamy could be just another form of *fin-de-siècle* aestheticism, a late gasp of romantic agony. Or, perhaps worse, he might be writing out of moral despair as an escape from the trappings of style. But such assumptions go against the grain of a writer whose commitment to style remains unshakable; whatever Borges's existential anxieties may be, they have little in common with Sartre's robustly prosaic view of literature, with the earnestness of Camus's moralism, or with the weighty profundity of German existential thought. Rather, they are the consistent expansion of a purely poetic consciousness to its furthest limits.

The stories that make up the bulk of Borges's literary work are not moral fables or parables like Kafka's, to which they are often misleadingly compared, even less attempts at psychological analysis. The least inadequate literary analogy would be with the eighteenth-century *conte philosophique:* their world is the representation, not of an actual experience, but of an intellectual proposition. One does not expect the same kind of psychological insight or the same immediacy of personal experience from *Candide* as from *Madame Bovary*, and Borges should be read with expectations closer to those one brings to Voltaire's tale than to a nineteenth-century novel. He differs, however, from his eighteenth-century antecedents in that the subject of the stories is the creation of style itself; in this Borges is very definitely post-romantic and even post-symbolist. His main characters are prototypes for the writer, and his worlds are prototypes for a highly stylized kind of poetry or fiction. For all their variety of tone and setting, the different stories all have a similar point of departure, a similar structure, a similar climax, and a similar outcome; the inner cogency that links these four moments together constitutes Borges's distinctive style, as well as his comment upon this style. His stories are about the style in which they are written.

At their center, as I have said, always stands an act of infamy. The first story in *Labyrinths*, "Tlön, Uqbar, Orbis Tertius," describes the totally imaginary world of a fictitious planet; this world is first glimpsed in an encyclopedia which is itself a delinquent reprint of the *Britannica*. In "The Shape of the Sword," an ignominious Irishman who, as it turns out, betrayed the man who saved his life, passes himself off for his own victim in order to tell his story in a more interesting way. In "The Garden of the Forking Paths" the hero is a Chinese who, during World War I, spies on the British mostly for the satisfaction of refined labyrinthine dissimulation. All these crimes are misdeeds like plagiarism, impersonation, espionage, in which someone pretends to be what he is not, substitutes a misleading appearance for his actual being. One of the best of his early stories describes the exploits of the religious imposter Hakim, who hides his face behind a mask of gold. Here the symbolic function of the villainous acts stands out very clearly: Hakim was at first a dyer, that is, someone who presents in bright and beautiful colors what was originally drab and gray. In this, he resembles the artist who confers irresistably attractive qualities upon something that does not necessarily possess them.

The creation of beauty thus begins as an act of duplicity. The writer engenders another self that is his mirror-like reversal. In this anti-self, the virtues and the vices of the original are curiously distorted and reversed. Borges describes the process poignantly in a later text called "Borges and I" (it appears in *Labyrinths* and also, in a somewhat better translation, in *Dreamtigers*). Although he is aware of the other Borges's "perverse habit of falsifying and exaggerating," he yields more and more to this poetic mask "who shares [his] preferences, but in a vain way that converts them into the attributes of an actor." This act, by which a man loses himself in the image he has created, is to Borges inseparable from poetic greatness. Cervantes achieved it when he invented and became Don Quixote; Valéry achieved it when he conceived and became Monsieur Teste. The duplicity of the artist, the grandeur as well as the misery of his calling, is a recurrent theme closely linked with the theme of infamy. Perhaps its fullest treatment appears in the story "Pierre Ménard, Author of the Quixote" in *Labyrinths*. The work and life of an imaginary writer is described by a devoted biographer. As the story unfolds, some of the details begin to have a familiar ring: even the phony, mercantile, snobbish Mediterranean atmosphere seems to recall to us an actual person, and when we are told that Ménard published an early sonnet in a magazine called *La conque*, a reader of Valéry will identify the model without fail. (Several of Valéry's early poems in fact appeared in *La conque*, which was edited by Pierre Louys, though at a somewhat earlier date than the one given by Borges for Ménard's first publication.) When, a litter later, we find out that Ménard is the author of an invective against Paul Valéry, as well as the perpetrator of the shocking stylistic crime of transposing *"Le cimetière marin"* into alexandrines (Valéry has always insisted that the very essence of this famous poem resides in the decasyllabic meter), we can no longer doubt that we are dealing with Valéry's anti-self, in other words, Monsieur Teste. Things get a lot more complicated a few paragraphs later, when Ménard embarks on the curious project of re-inventing Don Quixote word for word, and by the time Borges treats us to a "close reading" of two identical passages from Don Quixote, one written by Cervantes, the other by Pierre Ménard (who is also Monsieur Teste, who is also Valéry) such a complex set of ironies, parodies, reflections, and issues are at play that no brief commentary can begin to do them justice.

Poetic invention begins in duplicity, but it does not stop there. For the writer's particular duplicity (the dyer's image in "Hakim") stems from the fact that he presents the invented form as if it possessed the attributes of reality, thus allowing it to be mimetically reproduced, in its turn, in another mirror-image that takes the preceding pseudo-reality for *its* starting-point. He is prompted "by the blasphemous intention of attributing the divine category of *being* to some mere [entities]". Consequently, the duplication grows into a proliferation of successive mirror-images. In "Tlön, Uqbar Orbis Tertius," for example, the plagiarized encyclopedia is itself falsified by someone who adds an entry on the imaginary region Uqbar, presenting it as if it were part of an imaginary country as *his* starting point, another falsifier (who, by the way, is a Southern segregationist millionaire) conjures up, with the assistance of a team of shady experts, a complete encyclopedia of a fictional planet called Tlön—a pseudo-reality equal in size to our own real world. This edition will be followed in turn by a revised and even more detailed edition written not in English but in one of the languages of Tlön and entitled *Orbis Tertius*.

All the stories have a similar mirror-like structure, although the devices vary with diabolical ingenuity. Sometimes, there is only one mirror-effect, as when at the end of "The Shape of the Sword" Vincent Moon reveals his true identity as the villain, not the hero, of his own story. But in most of Borges's stories, there are several layers of reflection. In "Theme of the Traitor and the Hero" from *Labyrinths* we have: (1) an actual historic event—a revolutionary leader betrays his confederates and has to be executed; (2) a fictional story about such an occurrence (though in reversed form)—Shakespeare's *Julius Caesar*; (3) an actual historic event which copies the fiction: the execution is carried out according to Shakespeare's plot, to make sure that it will be a good show; (4) the puzzled historian reflecting on the odd alternation of identical fictional and historical events, and deriving a false theory of historical archetypes from them; (5) the smarter historian Borges (or, rather, his duplicitous anti-self) reflecting on the credulous historian and reconstructing the true course of events. In other stories from *Labyrinths*, "The Immortal," "The Zahir," or "Death and the Compass," the complication is pushed so far that it is virtually impossible to describe.

This mirror-like proliferation constitutes, for Borges, an indication of poetic success. The works of literature he most admires contain this element; he is fascinated by such mirror-effects in literature as the Elizabethan play within the play, the character Don Quixote reading *Don Quixote*, Scheherazade beginning one night to retell *verbatim* the story of *The Thousand and One Nights*. For each mirrored image is stylistically superior to the preceding one, as the dyed cloth is more beautiful than the plain, the distorted translation richer than the original, Ménard's Quixote aesthetically more complex than Cervantes's. By carrying this process to its limits, the poet can achieve ultimate success—an ordered picture of reality that contains the totality of all things, subtly transformed and enriched by the imaginative process that engendered them. The imaginary world of Tlön is only one example of this poetic achievement; it recurs throughout Borges's work and constitutes, in fact, the central, climactic image around which each of the stories is organized. It can be the philosophically coherent set of laws that makes up the mental universe of Tlön, or it can be the fantastic world of a man blessed (as well as doomed) with the frightening gift of total recall, a man "who knows by heart the forms of the southern clouds at dawn on the 30th of April 1882" as well as "the stormy mane of a pony, the changing fire and its innumerable ashes" ("Funes the Memorious," in *Labyrinths*). It can be vastly expanded, like the infinitely complex labyrinth that is also an endless book in "The Garden of the Forking Paths," or highly compressed, like a certain spot in a certain house from which one can observe the entire universe ("The Aleph"), or a single coin which, however insignificant by itself, contains "universal history and the infinite concatenation of cause and effect" ("The Zahir"). All these points or domains of total vision symbolize the entirely successful and deceiving outcome of the poets irrepressible urge for order.

The success of these poetic worlds is expressed by their all-inclusive and ordered wholeness. Their deceitful nature is harder to define, but essential to an understanding of Borges. Mirror images are indeed duplications of reality, but they change the temporal nature of this reality in an insidious fashion, even — one might say especially — when the imitation is altogether successful (as in Ménard's Quixote). In actual experience, time appears to us as continuous but infinite; this continuity may seem reassuring, since it gives us some feeling of identity, but it is also terrifying, since it drags us irrevocably towards an unknowable future. Our "real" universe is like space: stable but chaotic. If, by an act of the mind comparable to Borges's will to style, we order this chaos, we may well succeed in achieving an order of sorts, but we dissolve the binding, spatial substance that held our chaotic universe together. Instead of an infinite mass of substance, we have a finite number of isolated events incapable of establishing relations among one another. The inhabitants of Borges's totally poetic world of Uqbar "do not conceive that the spatial persists in time. The perception of a cloud of smoke on the horizon and then of the burning field and then of the half-extinguished cigarette that produced the blaze is considered an example of association of ideas." This style in Borges becomes the ordering but dissolving act that transforms the unity of experience into the enumeration of its discontinuous parts. Hence his rejection of *style lié* and his preference for what grammarians call parataxis, the mere placing of events side by side, without conjunctions; hence also his definition of his own style as baroque, "the style that deliberately exhausts (or tries to exhaust) all its possibilities."[2] The style is a mirror, but unlike the mirror of the realists that never lets us forget for a moment it creates what it mimics.

Probably because Borges is such a brilliant writer, his mirror-world is also profoundly, though always ironically, sinister. The shades of terror vary from the criminal gusto of the *History of Infamy* to the darker and shabbier world of the later *Ficciones*, and in *Dreamtigers* the violence is even starker and more somber, closer, I suppose, to the atmosphere of Borges's native Argentina. In the 1935 story, Hakim the impostor proclaimed: "The earth we live on is a mistake, a parody devoid of authority. Mirrors and paternity are abominable things, for they multiply this earth." This statement keeps recurring throughout the later work, but it becomes much more comprehensible there. Without ceasing to be the main metaphor for style, the mirror acquires deadly powers—a motif that runs throughout Western literature but of which Borges's version is particularly rich and complex. In his early work, the mirror of art represented the intention to keep the flow of time from losing itself forever in the shapeless void of infinity. Like the speculations of philosophers, style is an attempt at immortality. But this attempt is bound to fail. To quote one of Borges's favorite books, Sir Thomas Browne's *Hydrothapia, Urne-Buriall* (1658): "There is no antidote against the *Opium* of time, which temporarily considereth all things. . . ." This is not, as has been said, because Borges's God plays the same trick on the poet that the poet plays on reality; God does not turn out to be the arch-villain set to deceive man into an illusion of eternity. The poetic impulse in all its perverse duplicity, belongs to man alone, marks him as essentially human. But God appears on the scene as the power of reality itself, in the form of a death that demonstrates the failure of poetry. This is the deeper reason for the violence that pervades all Borges's stories. God is on the side of chaotic reality and style is powerless to conquer him. His appearance is like the hideous face of Hakim when he loses the shining mask he has been wearing and reveals a face worn away by leprosy. The proliferation of mirrors is all the more terrifying because each new image brings us a step closer to this face.

As Borges grows older and his eye-sight gets steadily weaker, this final confrontation throws its darkening shadow over his entire work, without however extinguishing the lucidity of his language. For although the last reflection may be the face of God himself, with his appearance the life of poetry comes to an end. The situation is very similar to that of Kierkegaard's aesthetic man, with the difference that Borges refuses to give up his poetic predicament for a leap into faith. This confers a somber glory on the pages of *Dreamtigers*, so different from the shining brilliance of the stories in *Labyrinths*. To understand the full complexity of this later mood, one must have followed Borges's enterprise from the start and see it as the unfolding of a poetic destiny. This would not only require the translation into English of Borges's earlier work, but also serious critical studies worthy of this great writer.

Notes

1. Other translations, aside from stories in anthologies or reviews, are to be found in *Ficciones*, edited by Anthony Kerrigan (New York: Grove Press, 1960). Bibliographical indications on the work of Borges, including mention of some critical studies, can be found in

the New Directions volume *Labyrinths*. A much more extensive bibliography has just appeared in Paris, in the latest issue of *L'herne*, which is entirely devoted to Borges (Paris: *Lettres modernes*).

2. Prologue to the 1954 edition of *Universal History of Infamy*.

The Author as Librarian   John Updike*

The belated North American acknowledgment of the genius of Jorge Luis Borges proceeds apace. The University of Texas Press last year published two volumes by this Argentine fantasist, critic, poet, and librarian. These translations, together with Grove Press's *Ficciones*, bring to three the number of complete books by Borges available in English. There is also New Directions' *Labyrinths*, a selection. And now the New York University Press has published a book *about* him.

Four years ago, when Borges shared with Samuel Beckett the Prix International des Éditeurs, he was known here to few but Hispanic specialists. A handful of poems and short stories had appeared in scattered anthologies and magazines. I myself had read only "The Garden of the Forking Paths," originally published in *Ellery Queen's Mystery Magazine* and subsequently a favorite of detective-story anthologies. Though vivid and intellectual beyond the requirements of its genre, the story can be read without awareness that its creator is a giant of world literature. I was prompted to read Borges seriously by a remark made—internationally enough—in Rumania, where, after a blanket disparagement of contemporary French and German fiction, Borges was praised by a young critic in a tone he had previously reserved for Kafka. An analogy with Kafka is inevitable, but I wonder if Borges' abrupt projection, by the university and avant-garde presses, into the bookstores will prove as momentous as Kafka's publication, by the commercial firm of Knopf, in the thirties. It is not a question of Borges' excellence. His driest paragraph is somehow compelling. His fables are written from a height of intelligence less rare in philosophy and physics than in fiction. Furthermore, he is, at least for anyone whose taste runs to puzzles or pure speculation, delightfully entertaining. The question is, I think, whether or not Borges' lifework, arriving in a lump now (he was born in 1899 and since his youth has been an active and honored figure in Argentine literature), can serve, in its gravely considered oddity, as any kind of clue to the way out of the dead-end narcissim and downright trashiness of present American fiction.

Borges' narrative innovations spring from a clear sense of technical

*From the *New Yorker*, 30 October 1965. Reprinted in *Picked-Up Pieces* (New York; Knopf, 1976). Reprinted by permission of Alfred A. Knopf, Inc.

crisis. For all his modesty and reasonableness of tone, he proposes some sort of essential revision in literature itself. The concision of his style and the comprehensiveness of his career (in addition to writing poems, essays, and stories, he has collaborated on detective novels, translated from many tongues, edited, taught, and even executed film scripts) produce a strangely terminal impression: he seems to be the man for whom literature has no future. I am haunted by knowing that this insatiable reader is now virtually blind.

A constant bookishness gives Borges' varied production an unusual consistency. His stories have the close texture of argument; his critical articles have the suspense and tension of fiction. The criticism collected in *Other Inquisitions, 1937–1952* almost all takes the form of detection, of uncovering what was secret. He looks for, and locates, the hidden pivots of history: the moment (in Iceland in 1225) when a chronicler first pays tribute to an enemy, the very line (in Chaucer in 1382) when allegory yields to naturalism. His interest gravitates toward the obscure, the forgotten: John Wilkins, the 17th-century inventor *ab nihilo* of an analytical language; J. W. Dunne, the 20th-century proponent of a grotesque theory of time; Layamon, the 13th-century poet isolated between the death of Saxon culture and the birth of the English language. Where an arcane quality does not already exist, Borges injects it. His appreciation of the classic Spanish satirist and stylist Francisco de Quevedo begins, "Like the history of the world, the history of literature abounds in enigmas. I found, and continue to find, none so disconcerting as the strange partial glory that has been accorded to Quevedo." His essay on Layamon concludes, " '*No one knows who he is,*' said Léon Bloy. Of that intimate ignorance no symbol is better than this forgotten man, who abhorred his Saxon heritage with Saxon vigor, and who was the last Saxon poet and never knew it."

Implacably, Borges reduces everything to a condition of mystery. His gnomic style and encyclopedic supply of allusions generate a kind of inverse illumination, a Gothic atmosphere in which the most lucid and famous authors loom somewhat menacingly. His essay on Bernard Shaw begins, "At the end of the thirteenth century Raymond Lully (Ramón Lull) attempted to solve all the mysteries by means of a frame with unequal, revolving, concentric disks, subdivided into sectors with Latin words." It ends on an equally ominous and surprising note: "[Existentialists] may play at desperation and anguish, but at bottom they flatter the vanity; in that sense, they are immoral. Shaw's work, on the other hand, leaves an aftertaste of liberation. The taste of the doctrines of Zeno's Porch and the taste of the sagas."

Borges' harsh conjunctions and plausible paradoxes are not confined to literary matters. In "A Comment on August 23, 1944." Borges meditates on the ambivalent reaction of his Fascist friends to the Allied occupation of Paris and ends with this daring paragraph:

I do not know whether the facts I have related require elucidation. I believe I can interpret them like this: for Europeans and Americans, one order—and only one—is possible: it used to be called Rome and now it is called Western Culture. To be a Nazi (to play the game of energetic barbarism, to play at being a Viking, a Tartar, a sixteenth-century conquistador, a Gaucho, a redskin) is, after all, a mental and moral impossibility. Nazism suffers from unreality, like Erigena's hells. It is uninhabitable; men can only die for it, lie for it, kill and wound for it. No one, in the intimate depths of his being, can wish it to triumph. I shall hazard this conjecture: *Hitler wants to be defeated.* Hitler is collaborating blindly with the inevitable armies that will annihilate him, as the metal vultures and the dragon (which must not have been unaware that they were monsters) collaborated, mysteriously, with Hercules.

The tracing of hidden resemblances, of philosophical genealogies, is Borges' favorite mental exercise. Out of his vast reading he distills a few related images, whose parallelism, tersely presented, has the force of a fresh thought. "Perhaps universal history is the history of a few metaphors. I should like to sketch one chapter of that history," he writes in "Pascal's Sphere," and goes on to compile, in less than four pages, twenty-odd instances of the image of a sphere "whose center is everywhere and whose circumference nowhere." These references are arranged like a plot, beginning with Xenophanes, who joyously substituted for the anthropomorphic gods of Greece a divine and eternal Sphere, and ending with Pascal, who, in describing nature as "an infinite sphere" had first written and then rejected the word *"effroyable"*—"a frightful sphere." Many of Borges' genealogies trace a degeneration: he detects a similar "magnification to nothingness" in the evolutions of theology and of Shakespeare's reputation; he watches an Indian legend succumb, through its successive versions, to the bloating of unreality. He follows in the works of Léon Bloy the increasingly desperate interpretations of a single phrase in St. Paul—*"per speculum in aenigmate"* ("through a glass darkly"). Borges himself recurrently considers Zeno's second paradox—the never-completed race between Achilles and the tortoise, the formal argument of *regressus in infinitum*—and comes to a conclusion that is, to use his favorite adjective, monstrous: "One concept corrupts and confuses the others. . . . I am speaking of the infinite. . . . We (the undivided divinity that operates within us) have dreamed the world. We have dreamed it strong, mysterious, visible, ubiquitous in space and secure in time; but we have allowed tenuous, eternal interstices of injustice in its structure so we may know that it is false."

Borges is not an antiseptic pathologist of the irrational; he is himself susceptible to infection. His connoisseurship has in it a touch of madness. In his "Kafka and His Precursors," he discovers, in certain parables and anecdotes by Zeno, Han Yü, Kierkegaard, Browning, Bloy, and Lord Dunsany, a prefiguration of Kafka's tone. He concludes that each writer creates his own precursors: "His work modifies our conception of the past, as it will modify the future." This is sensible enough, and, indeed, has been pointed out by T. S. Eliot, whom Borges cites in a footnote. But Borges goes on: "In this correlation the identity or plurality of men matters not at all." This sentence, I believe, expresses not a thought but a *sensation* that Borges has; he describes it — a mixture of deathlike detachment and ecstatic timelessness — in his most ambitious essay, "New Refutation of Time." It is this sensation that encourages his peculiar view of human thought as the product of a single mind, and of human history as a vast magic book that can be read cabalistically. His highest praise, bestowed upon the fantastic narratives of the early H. G. Wells, is to claim that "they will be incorporated, like the fables of Theseus of Ahasuerus, into the general memory of the species and even transcend the fame of their creator or the extinction of the language in which they were written."

As a literary critic, Borges demonstrates much sensitivity and sense. The American reader of these essays will be gratified by the general amount of space devoted to writers of the English language. Borges, from within the Spanish literary tradition of "dictionaries and rhetoric," is attracted by the oneiric and hallucinatory quality he finds in North American, German, and English writing. He values Hawthorne and Whitman for the intense unreality, and bestows special fondness upon the English writers he read in his boyhood. The *fin-de-siècle* and Edwardian giants, whose reputations are generally etiolated, excite Borges afresh each time he rereads thems: "Reading and rereading Wilde through the years, I notice something that his panegyrists do not seem to have even suspected: the provable and elementary fact that Wilde is almost always right. . . . he was a man of the eighteenth century who sometimes condescended to play the game of symbolism. Like Gibbon, like Johnson, like Voltaire, he was an ingenious man who was also right."

Borges' tributes to Shaw and Wells have been quoted above. In connection with Wells and Henry James, it is a salutary shock to find the terms of the usual invidious comparison reversed: "the sad and labyrinthine Henry James . . . a much more complex writer than Wells, although he was less gifted with those pleasant virtues that are usually called classical." But of this generation none is dearer to Borges than Chesterton, in whom he finds, beneath the surface of dogmatic optimism, a disposition like Kafka's: "Chesterton restrained himself from being Edgar Allan Poe or Franz Kafka, but something in the makeup of his personality leaned toward the nightmarish, something secret, and blind, and central . . . the powerful work of Chesterton, the prototype of physical and moral sanity, is always on the verge of becoming a nightmare . . . he tends inevitably to revert to atrocious observations." Much in Borges' fiction that suggests

Kafka in fact derives from Chesterton. As critic and artist both, Borges mediates between the post-modern present and the colorful, prolific, and neglected pre-moderns.

Of the moderns themselves, of Yeats, Eliot, and Rilke, of Proust and Joyce, he has, at least in *Other Inquisitions*, little to say. Pound and Eliot, he asserts in passing, practice "the deliberate manipulation of anachronisms to produce an appearance of eternity" (which seems, if true at all, rather incidentally so), and he admires Valéry less for his work than for his personality, "the symbol of a man who is infinitely sensitive to every fact." The essays abound in insights delivered parenthetically—"God must not theologize"; "to fall in love is to create a religion that has a fallible god"— but their texts as a whole do not open outward into enlightenment. Whereas, say, Eliot's relatively tentative considerations offer to renew a continuing tradition of literary criticism, Borges' tight arrangements seem a bizarre specialization of the tradition. His essays have a quality I can only call *sealed*. They are structured like mazes and, like mirrors, they reflect back and forth on one another. There is frequent repetition of the adjectives and phrases that denote Borges' favorite notions of mystery, of secrecy, of "intimate ignorance." From his immense reading he has distilled a fervent narrowness. The same parables, the same quotations recur; one lengthy passage from Chesterton is reproduced three times.

Here and there appear sentences ("One literature differs from another, either before or after it, not so much because of the text as for the manner in which it is read") that elsewhere have been developed into "fictions"; in "Pierre Menard, Author of Don Quixote," a modern writer as his masterwork reconstructs passages from *Don Quixote* that, though verbally identical, are read very differently. This story, in fact, was, according to an interview given in Buenos Aires in 1960, the first Borges ever wrote. Long a respected poet and critic, he turned to fiction with a grim diffidence. In his words:

> I know that the least perishable part of my literary production is the narrative, yet for many years I did not dare to write stories. I thought that the paradise of the tale was forbidden to me. One day, I suffered an accident. I was in a sanitarium where I was operated upon. . . . a time I cannot recall without horror, a period of fever, insomnia, and extreme insecurity. . . . If after the operation and the extremely long convalescence I tried to write a poem or an essay and failed, I would know that I had lost . . . intellectual integrity. Thus, I decided upon another approach. I said to myself: "I am going to write a story and if I cannot do so it does not matter because I have not written one before. In any case, it will be a first attempt." Then I began to write a story . . . which turned out rather well; this was followed by others . . . and I discovered that I had not lost my intellectual integrity and that I could now write stories. I have written many since.

Turning from Borges' criticism to his fiction, one senses the liberation he must have felt upon entering "the paradise of the tale." For there is something disturbing as well as fascinating, something distorted and strained about his literary essays. His ideas border on delusions; the dark hints — of a cult of books, of a cabalistic unity hidden in history — that he so studiously develops are special to the corrupt light of libraries and might vanish outdoors. It is uncertain how seriously he intends his textual diagrams, which seem ciphers for concealed emotions. Borges crowds into the margins of others' books passion enough to fill blank pages; his essays all tend to open inward, disclosing an obsessed imagination and a proud, Stoic, almost cruelly masculine personality.

Dreamtigers, a collection of paragraphs, sketches, poems, and apocryphal quotations titled in Spanish *El Hacedor (The Maker)*, succeeds in time the creative period of narrative fiction his essays foreshadow. It is frankly the miscellany of an aging man, fondly dedicated to a dead enemy — the Modernist poet Leopoldo Lugones, like Borges the director of a national library:

> Leaving behind the babble of the plaza, I entered the Library. I feel, almost physically, the gravitation of the books, the enveloping serenity of order, time magically desiccated and preserved. . . . These reflections bring me to the door of your office. I go in; we exchange a few words, conventional and cordial, and I give you this book. . . . My vanity and nostalgia have set up an impossible scene. Perhaps so (I tell myself), but tomorrow I too will have died, and our times will intermingle and chronology will be lost in a sphere of symbols. And then in some way it will be right to claim that I have brought you this book, and that you have accepted it.

The epilogue repeats this prediction of his own death:

> Few things have happened to me, and I have read a great many. Or rather, few things have happened to me more worth remembering than Schopenhauer's thought or the music of England's words.
>
> A man sets himself the task of portraying the world. Through the years he peoples a space with images of provinces, kingdoms, mountains, bays, ships, islands, fishes, rooms, instruments, stars, horses, and people. Shortly before his death, he discovers that that patient labyrinth of lines traces the image of his face.

The book is in two parts. The first, translated by Mildred Boyer, consists of those short prose sketches, musical and firm, that Borges, unable to see to write, composes in his head. The first of these describes Homer: "Gradually now the beautiful universe was slipping away from him. A stubborn mist erased the outline of his hand, the night was no longer peopled by stars, the earth beneath his feet was unsure." In a critical essay, Borges had traced the evolution of God and Shakespeare, as reputations, from something to nothing; now this nothingness is discovered in Shakespeare himself, intimately: "There was no one in him; behind his face (which even in the poor paintings of the period is unlike any other) and his words, which were copious, imaginative, and emotional, there was nothing but a little chill, a dream not dreamed by anyone." Dante is imagined dying in Ravenna, "as unjustified and as alone as any other man." God in a dream declares to him the secret purpose of his life and his work, which is like that of the leopard who endured a caged existence so that Dante might see him and place him in the first canto of the *Inferno*. "You suffer captivity, but you will have given a word to the poem," God told the leopard, "But when he awoke, there was only a dark resignation in him; a valiant ignorance. . . ." And the illustrious Italian Giambattista Marino—"proclaimed as the new Homer and the new Dante"—dying, perceives that "the tall, proud volumes casting a golden shadow in a corner were not—as his vanity had dreamed—a mirror of the world, but rather one thing more added to the world." It is as if, in his blindness and age, the oneness of all men that Borges had so often entertained as a theory and premonition has become a fact; he *is* Homer, Shakespeare, Dante, and tastes fully the bitter emptiness of creative splendor. The usurpation of a writer's private identity by his literary one has not been more sadly, or wittily, expressed than in "Borges and I": "It's the other one, it's Borges, that things happen to. I stroll about Buenos Aires and stop, perhaps mechanically now, to look at the arch of an entrance or an iron gate. News of Borges reaches me through the mail and I see his name on an academic ballot or in a biographical dictionary. I like hourglasses, maps, eighteenth-century typography, the taste of coffee, and Stevenson's prose. The other one shares these preferences with me, but in a vain way that converts them into the attributes of an actor."

Borges tempts one to quote him at too great length. These brief paragraphs composed in his head have an infrangible aptness. His ability to crystallize vague ideas and vaguer emotions into specific images has grown. The image of Layamon, the last Saxon poet, returns in the form of an anonymous old man, dying, unaware that he is the last man to have witnessed the worship of Woden. He lies in a stable: "Outside are the plowed fields and a deep ditch clogged with dead leaves and an occasional wolf track in the black earth at the edge of the forest." This stark sentence, with its unexpectedly vivid ditch, has in it the whole of a primitive England, and pierces us with a confused sense of elapsed time. These sketches see a diminishing of those adjectives—"mysterious," "secret," "atrocious"—with which the younger Borges insisted on his sense of strangeness. Instead, there is a delicate manipulation of the concrete—lists and catalogues in which one or two of the series seem anomalous (". . . islands, fishes, rooms, instruments, stars, horses . . .") and the application now and then of a surprising color adjective (the volumes' "golden shadow" above, "red Adam in Paradise," and, apropos of Homer, "black vessels searching the sea for a beloved isle"). Immensity is reified in terms of color: "Every hundred paces a tower cleft the air; to the eye their color was identical, yet the first of all was yellow, and the last, scarlet, so delicate were the gradations and so long the series." In this image the concept of the infinite—the concept that "corrupts and confuses the others"—is tamed into something lyrical and even pretty. One feels in *Dreamtigers* a calm, an intimation of truce, a tranquil fragility. Like so many last or near-last works—like *The Tempest, The Millionairess,* or "Investigations of a Dog"—*Dreamtigers* preserves the author's life-long concerns, but drained of urgency; horror has yielded to a resigned humorousness. These sketches can be read for their grace and wit but scarcely for narrative excitement; the most exciting of them, "Ragnarök," embodies Borges' most terrible vision, of an imbecilic God or body of gods. But it occurs within a dream, and ends easily: "We drew our heavy revolvers—all at once there were revolvers in the dream—and joyously put the Gods to death."

The second half of this slim volume consists of poems, late and early. Poetry was where Borges' ramifying literary career originally took root. The translations, by Harold Morland, into roughly four-beat and intermittently rhymed lines, seem sturdy and clear, and occasional stanzas must approximate very closely the felicity of the original:

> In their grave corner, the players
> Deploy the slow pieces. And the chessboard
> Detains them until dawn in its severe
> Compass in which two colors hate each other.

As a poet, Borges has some of the qualities—a meditative circularity, a heavy-lidded elegance—of Wallace Stevens:

> With slow love she looked at the scattered
> Colors of afternoon. It pleased her
> to lose herself in intricate melody
> or in the curious life of verses.

And

> We shall seek a third tiger. This
> Will be like those others a shape
> Of my dreaming, a system of words
> A man makes and not the vertebrate tiger
> That, beyond the mythologies,
> Is treading the earth.

But in English the poems are chiefly interesting for their content; they are more autobiographical and emotionally direct than Borges' prose. The first one, "Poem About Gifts," movingly portrays himself in his blindness:

> Slow in my darkness, I explore
> The hollow gloom with my hesitant stick,

> I, that used to figure Paradise
> In such a library's guise.

Thoughts anonymously cached in the maze of his fictions are enunciated
in his own voice. In a fabricated encyclopedia article he describes the
"philosophers of Uqbar" as believing that "Copulation and mirrors are
abominable. . . . For one of those gnostics, the visible universe was an
illusion or, more precisely, a sophism. Mirrors and fatherhood are abominable because they multiply it and extend it." In a poem, "Mirrors," the
belief turns out to be Borges' own:

> I see them as infinite, elemental.
> Executors of an ancient pact,
> To multiply the world like the act
> Of begetting. Sleepless. Bringing doom.

The profound sense of timelessness that in the prose activates so much
textual apparatus becomes in verse an elementary nostalgia:

> Rain is something happening in the past. . . .
> And the drenched afternoon brings back the sound
> How longed for, of my father's voice, not dead.

And his long poem about his childhood home at Adrogué culminates:

> The ancient amazement of the elegy
> Loads me down when I think of that house
> And I do not understand how time goes by,
> I, who am time and blood and agony.

Together, the prose and poetry of *Dreamtigers* afford some glimpses
into Borges' major obscurities—his religious concerns and his affective life.
Physical love, when it appears at all in his work, figures as something
remote, like an ancient religion. "[Shakespeare] thought that in the
exercise of an elemental human rite he might well find what he sought,
and he let himself be initiated by Anne Hathaway one long June afternoon." And Homer remembers when "a woman, the first the gods set aside
for him, had waited for him in the shadow of a hypogeum, and he had
searched for her through corridors that were like stone nets, along slopes
that sank into the shadow." Though *Dreamtigers* contains two fine poems
addressed to women—Susana Soca and Elvira de Alvear—they are eulo-
gies couched in a tone of heroic affection not different from the affection
with which he writes elsewhere of male friends like Alfonso Reyes and
Macedonio Fernández. This is at the opposite pole from homosexuality;
femaleness, far from being identified with, is felt as a local estrangement
that blends with man's cosmic estrangement. There are two prose sketches
that, by another writer, might have shown some erotic warmth, some
surrender to femininity. In one, he writes of Julia, a "sombre girl" with "an
unbending body," in whom he sensed "an intensity that was altogether

foreign to the erotic." In their walks together, he must have talked about mirrors, for now (in 1931) he has learned that she is insane and has draped her mirrors because she imagines that his reflection has replaced her own. In the other, he writes of Delia Elena San Marco, from whom he parted one day beside "a river of vehicles and people." They did not meet again, and in a year she was dead. From the casualness of their unwitting farewell, he concludes, tentatively, that we are immortal. "For if souls do not die, it is right that we should not make much of saying goodbye."

It would be wrong to think that Borges dogmatically writes as an atheist. God is invoked by him, not always in an ironical or pantheistic way.

> God has created nighttime, which he arms
> With dreams, and mirrors, to make clear
> To man he is a reflection and a mere
> Vanity.

He hopes seriously for immortality. Death is "the mirror / In which I shall see no-one or I shall see another." One of the many riddles that interest him is Christ's aspect, and he is moved by the possibility that "the profile of a Jew in the subway is perhaps the profile of Christ; perhaps the hands that give us our change at a ticket window duplicate the ones some soldiers nailed one day to the cross." But we feel that he *entertains* these possibilities, almost blasphemously; they are isolated, for him, from the corpus of ethics and argument which is historical Christianity. He dismisses the orthodox afterlife: "We distrust his intelligence, as we would distrust the intelligence of a God who maintained heavens and hells." He ransacks Christian apologetics for oddities of forced reasoning. He writes, "Those who automatically reject the supernatural (I try, always, to belong to this group). . . ." While Christianity is not dead in Borges, it *sleeps* in him, and its dreams are fitful. His ethical allegiance is to pre-Christian heroism, to Stoicism, to "the doctrines of Zeno's Porch and . . . the sagas," to the harsh gaucho ethos celebrated in the Argentine folk poem of Martín Fierro. Borges is a pre-Christian whom the memory of Christianity suffuses with premonitions and dread. He is European in everything except the detachment with which he view's European civilization, as something intrinsically strange—a heap of relics, a universe of books without a central clue. This detachment must be, in part, geographical; by many devious routes he returns to the home in space and time that he finds:

>   in the tumbledown
> Decadence of the widespread suburbs,
> And in the thistledown that the pampas wind
> Blows into the entrance hall . . .
> And in a flag sort of blue and white
> Over a barracks, and in unappetizing stories

> Of street-corner knifings, and in the sameness
> Of afternoons that are wiped out and leave us . . .

Perhaps Latin America, which has already given us the absolute skepticism of Machado de Assis, is destined to reënact the intellectual patterns of ancient Greece. Borges' voracious and vaguely idle learning, his ecumenic and problematical and unconsoling theology, his willingness to reconsider the most primitive philosophical questions, his tolerance of superstition in both himself and others, his gingerly and regretful acknowledgment of women and his disinterest in the psychological and social worlds that women dominate, his almost Oriental modesty, his final solitude, his serene pride — this constellation of Stoic attributes, mirrored in the southern hemisphere, appears inverted and frightful.

Borges the Labyrinth Maker, by Ana María Barrenechea, has for its jacket design a labyrinth from which there is no exit. I do not know whether this is intentional or a mistake in drawing. The book is a methodical and efficient arrangement of quotations from Borges in abstract categories — The Infinite, Chaos and the Cosmos, Pantheism and Personality, Time and Eternity, Idealism and Other Forms of Unreality. In a foreword, Borges says that the book "has unearthed many secret links and affinities in my own literary output of which I had been quite unaware. I thank her for those revelations of an unconscious process." Professor Barrenechea's collations, however — including many sentences and paragraphs of Borges not elsewhere translated — seem to me an admirable explication of his conscious philosophical concerns as they shape, adjective by adjective, his fiction. What is truly unconscious — the sense of life that drives him from unequivocal philosophical and critical assertion to the essential ambiguity of fiction — she scarcely touches. The labyrinth of his thought-forms is drawn without an indication of how his concrete and vigorous art has emerged. She admits this: "Only one aspect of the writer's work — the expression of irreality — has been treated; but Borges' creativity is characterized by the richness and complexity of his art."

The great achievement of his art is his short stories. To round off this review of accessory volumes, I will describe two of my favorites.

"The Waiting" is from his second major collection, *El Aleph*, and is found, translated by James E. Irby, in *Labyrinths*. It is a rarity in Borges' *oeuvre* — a story in which nothing incredible occurs. A gangster fleeing from the vengeance of another gangster seeks anonymity in a northwest part of Buenos Aires. After some weeks of solitary existence, he is discovered and killed. These events are assigned a detailed and mundane setting. The very number of the boarding house where he lives is given (4004: a Borgian formula for immensity), and the neighborhood is flatly described: "The man noted with approval the spotted plane trees, the square plot of earth at the foot of each, the respectable houses with their little balconies, the pharmacy alongside, the dull lozenges of the paint and hardware store. A long windowless hospital wall backed the sidewalk on the other side of the street; the sun reverberated, farther down, from some greenhouses." Yet much information is withheld. "The man" mistakenly gives a cabdriver a Uruguayan coin, which "had been in his pocket since that night in the hotel at Melo." What had happened that night in Melo and the nature of his offense against his enemy are not disclosed. And when the landlady — herself unnamed, and specified as having "a distracted or tired air" — asks the man his name he gives the name, Villari, of the man hunting him! He does this, Borges explains, "not as a secret challenge, not to mitigate the humiliation which actually he did not feel, but because that name troubled him, because it was impossible for him to think of any other. Certainly he was not seduced by the literary error of thinking that assumption of the enemy's name might be an astute maneuver."

Villari — Villari the hunted — is consistently prosaic, even stupid. He ventures out to the movies and, though he sees stories of the underworld that contain images of his old life, takes no notice of them, "because the idea of a coincidence between art and reality was alien to him." Reading of another underworld in Dante, "he did not judge the punishments of hell to be unbelievable or excessive." He has a toothache and is compelled to have the tooth pulled. "In this ordeal he was neither more cowardly nor more tranquil than other people." His very will to live is couched negatively: "It only wanted to endure, not to come to an end." The next sentence, grounding the abhorrence of death upon the simplest and mildest, recalls Unamuno. "The taste of the maté, the taste of black tobacco, the growing line of shadows gradually covering the patio — these were sufficient incentives."

Unobtrusively, the reader comes to love Villari, to respect his dull humility and to share his animal fear. Each brush with the outer world is a touch of terror. The toothache — "an intimate discharge of pain in the back of his mouth" — has the force of a "horrible miracle." Returning from the movies, he feels pushed, and, turning "with anger, with indignation, with secret relief," he spits out "a coarse insult." The passerby and the reader are alike startled by this glimpse into the savage criminal that Villari has been. Each night, at dawn, he dreams of Villari — Villari the hunter — and his accomplices overtaking him, and of shooting them with the revolver he keeps in the drawer of the bedside table. At last — whether betrayed by the trip to the dentist, the visits to the movie house, or the assumption of the other's name we did not know — he is awakened one July dawn by his pursuers:

> Tall in the shadows of the room, curiously simplified by those shadows (in the fearful dreams they had always been clearer), vigilant, motionless and patient, their eyes lowered as if weighed down by the heaviness of their weapons, Alejandro Villari and a stranger had

overtaken him at last. With a gesture, he asked them to wait and turned his face to the wall, as if to resume his sleep. Did he do it to arouse the pity of those who killed him, or because it is less difficult to endure a frightful happening than to imagine it and endlessly await it, or — and this is perhaps most likely — so that the murderers would be a dream, as they had already been so many times, in the same place, at the same hour?

So the inner action of the narrative has been to turn the utterly unimaginative hero into a magician. In retrospect, this conversion has been scrupulously foreshadowed. The story, indeed, is a beautiful cinematic succession of shadows; the most beautiful are those above, which simplify the assassins — "(in the fearful dreams they had always been clearer)." The parenthesis of course makes a philosophic point: it opposes the ambiguity of reality to the relative clarity and simplicity of what our minds conceive. It functions as well in the realistic level of the story, bodying forth all at once the climate, the moment of dawn, the atmosphere of the room, the sleeper's state of vision, the menace and matter-of-factness of the men, "the eyes lowered as if weighted down by the heaviness of their weapons." Working from the artificial reality of films and gangster novels, and imposing his hyper-subtle sensations of unreality on the underworld of his plot, Borges has created an episode of criminal brutality in some ways more convincing that those in Hemingway. One remembers that in "The Killers" Ole Andreson also turns his face to the wall. It is barely possible that Borges had in mind a kind of gloss of Hemingway's classic. If that is so, with superior compassion and keener attention to peripheral phenomena he has enriched the theme. In his essay on Hawthorne, Borges speaks of the Argentine literary aptitude for realism; his own florid fantasy is grafted onto that native stock.

"The Library of Babel," which appears in *Ficciones*, is wholly fantastic, yet refers to the librarian's experience of books. Anyone who has been in the stacks of a great library will recognize the emotional aura, the wearying impression of an inexhaustible and mechanically ordered chaos, that suffuses Borges' mythical universe, "composed of an indefinite, perhaps an infinite, number of hexagonal galleries, with enormous ventilation shafts in the middle, encircled by very low railings." Each hexagon contains twenty shelves, each shelf thirty-two books, each book four hundred and ten pages, each page forty lines, each line eighty letters. The arrangement of these letters is almost uniformly chaotic and formless. The nameless narrator of "The Library of Babel" sets forward, pedantically, the history of philosophical speculation by the human beings who inhabit this inflexible and inscrutable cosmos, which is equipped, apparently for their convenience, with spiral stairs, mirrors, toilets, and lamps ("The light they emit is insufficient, incessant").

This monstrous and comic model of the universe contains a full range of philosophical schools — idealism, mysticism, nihilism:

The idealists argue that the hexagonal halls are a necessary form of absolute space, or, at least, of our intuition of space. They contend that a triangular or pentagonal hall is inconceivable.

The mystics claim that to them ecstasy reveals a round chamber containing a great book with a continuous back circling the walls of the room. . . . That cyclical book is God.

I know of a wild region whose librarians repudiate the vain superstitious custom of seeking any sense in books and compare it to looking for meaning in dreams or in the chaotic lines of one's hands. . . . They speak (I know) of "the febrile Library, whose hazardous volumes run the constant risk of being changed into others and in which everything is affirmed, denied, and confused as by a divinity in delirium."

Though the Library appears to be eternal, the men within it are not, and they have a history punctuated by certain discoveries and certain deductions now considered axiomatic. Five hundred years ago, in an upper hexagon, two pages of homogeneous lines were discovered that within a century were identified as "a Samoyed-Lithuanian dialect of Guaraní, with classical Arabic inflections" and translated. The contents of these two pages — "notions of combinational analysis" — led to the deduction that the Library is total; that is, its shelves contain all possible combinations of the orthographic symbols: "Everything is there: the minute history of the future, the autobiographies of the archangels, the faithful catalogue of the Library, thousands and thousands of false catalogues, a demonstration of the fallacy of these catalogues, a demonstration of the fallacy of the true catalogue, the Gnostic gospel of Basilides, the commentary on this gospel, the commentary on the commentary on this gospel, the veridical account of your death, a version of each book in all languages, the interpolations of every book in all books."

Men greeted this revelation with joy; "the universe suddenly expanded to the limitless dimensions of hope." They surged onto the stairs, searching for Vindications — books that would vindicate and explain his life to each man. Sects sprang up. One used dice and metal letters in an attempt to "mimic the divine disorder" and compose by chance the canonical volumes. Another, the Purifiers, destroyed millions of books, hurling them down the air shafts. They believed in "the Crimson Hexagon: books of a smaller than ordinary format, omnipotent, illustrated, magical." A third sect worshipped the Man of the Book — a hypothetical librarian who, in some remote hexagon, must have perused a book, "which is the cipher and perfect compendium of *all the rest*." This librarian is a god. "Many pilgrimages have sought Him out."

The analogies with Christianity are pursued inventively and without the tedium of satire. The narrator himself confides, "To me, it does not seem unlikely that on some shelf of the universe there lies a total book. I pray the unknown gods that some man — even if only one man, and though it have been thousands of years ago! — may have examined and read it." But in his own person he has only the "elegant hope" that the Library, if traversed far enough, would repeat itself in the same disorder, which then would constitute an order. At hand, in the illegible chaos, are only tiny rays of momentary sense, conglomerations of letters spelling *O Time your pyramids, Combed Clap of Thunder,* or *The Plaster Cramp.*

This kind of comedy and desperation, these themes of vindication and unattainability, suggest Kafka. But *The Castle* is a more human work, more personal and neurotic; the fantastic realities of Kafka's fiction are projections of the narrator-hero's anxieties, and have no communion, no interlocking structure, without him. The Library of Babel instead has an adamant solidity. Built of mathematics and science, it will certainly survive the weary voice describing it, and outlast all its librarians, already decimated, we learn in a footnote, by "suicide and pulmonary diseases." We move, with Borges, beyond psychology, beyond the human, and confront, in his work, the world atomized and vacant. Perhaps not since Lucretius has a poet so definitely felt men as incidents in space.

What are we to make of him? The economy of his prose, the tact of his imagery, the courage of his thought are there to be admired and emulated. In resounding the note of the marvellous last struck in English by Wells and Chesterton, in permitting infinity to enter and distort his imagination, he has lifted fiction away from the flat earth where most of our novels and short stories still take place. Yet discouragingly large areas of truth seem excluded from his vision. Though the population of the Library somehow replenishes itself, and "fecal necessities" are provided for, neither food nor fornication is mentioned — and in truth they are not generally seen in libraries. I feel in Borges a curious implication: the unrealities of physical science and the senseless repetitions of history have made the world outside the library an uninhabitable vacuum. Litera-ture — that European empire augmented with translations from remote kingdoms — is now the only world capable of housing and sustaining new literature. Is this too curious? Did not Eliot recommend forty years ago, in reviewing *Ulysses,* that new novels be retellings of old myths? Is not the greatest of modern novels, *Remembrance of Things Past,* about its own inspiration? Have not many books already been written from within Homer and the Bible? Did not Cervantes write from within Ariosto and Shakespeare from within Holinshed? Borges, by predilection and by program, carries these inklings toward a logical extreme: the view of books as, in sum, an alternate creation, vast, accessible, highly colored, rich in arcana, possibly sacred. Just as physical man, in his cities, has manufac-tured an environment whose scope and challenge and hostility eclipse that of the natural world, so literate man has heaped up a counterfeit universe capable of supporting life. Certainly the traditional novel as a transparent imitation of human circumstances has "a distracted or tired air." Ironic and blasphemous as Borges' hidden message may seem, the texture and method of his creations, though strictly inimitable, answer to a deep need in contemporary fiction — the need to confess the fact of artifice.

Borges and the Fictive Narrative   Pierre Macherey*

> Here something returns upon itself, something coils around itself, and yet does not enclose itself, but frees itself in its very coils. (Heidegger, *The Essence of Reasons*)

Borges is essentially preoccupied by problems of narrative: but he poses these problems idiosyncratically, fictively (one of his collections is entitled, significantly, *Fictions*). He offers a fictive theory of narrative, and thereby runs the risk of being taken too seriously, or taken too far.

The obsessional idea which shapes the book (*Fictions*) is that of necessity and duplication realised to the fullest in the Library (see the story "The Library of Babel"); here each book is in its exact place as an element in a sequence. The book (the narrative, in fact) only exists in its recognisable form because it is implicitly related to the totality of all possible books. It exists, it has its allotted place in the universe of books, because it is an element in a totality. Around this theme Borges weaves all the paradoxes of the infinite. The book exists only by its possible multiplication: externally, in relation to other books, but also internally, as it is itself structured like a library. The substance of the book is its self-identity; but identity is only ever a limit-form of variation. One of the principles of the library, which lends it an almost Leibnizian character, is that no two books are identical. This may be transposed and used to define the book as a "unity": there are not two identical books in the same book. Each book remains deeply different from itself because it implies an indefinite repertoire of "bifurcations." This subtle meditation on the "same" and the "other" is the object of the story about Pierre Ménard, who "writes" two chapters of *Don Quixote*. "The text of Cervantes and that of Ménard are verbally identical": but the analogy is purely formal; it contains a radical diversity. The stratagem of a new reading, of deliberate anachronism, which consists of reading, for example, the *Imitatio Christi* as though it were the work of Louis-Ferdinand Céline or James Joyce, is not just for the sake of the incidental surprises thus procured; it relates inevitably to a process of *writing*. The meaning of Ménard's apologue is now obvious:

*First published in *Temps Modernes* (Paris), 21 (1966). Reprinted in *A Theory of Literary Production* (Routledge & Kegan Paul, 1978). Reprinted here by permission of Routledge & Kegan Paul.

reading is in the end only a reflection of the wager of writing (and not vice versa); the hesitations of reading reproduce, perhaps by distortion, *the modifications inscribed in the narrative itself.* The book is always incomplete because it harbours the promise of an inexhaustible variety. "No book is published without some discrepancy between each copy" (*The Lottery in Babylon*): the slightest material defect evokes the inevitable inadequacy of the narrative to itself; the narrative speaks to us only in so far as time permits itself to be determined by the operations of chance.

The narrative thus exists on the basis of its internal division, which makes it appear in itself as a dissymmetrical relation and as a term in such a relation. Every narrative, even in the moment of utterance, is the revelation of a self-contradictory *reprise.* The investigation of the work of Herbert Quain introduces us to that exemplary problem-novel *The God of the Labyrinth*: "There is an incomprehensible assassination in the opening pages, a slow discussion in the middle, a solution at the end. Once the mystery has been solved there is a long retrospective paragraph which contains this sentence: 'All the world thought that the meeting between the two chessplayers was fortuitous'. This sentence implies that the solution is incorrect. The anxious reader looks back to the relevant chapters and discovers a different solution, the correct one. The reader of this unusual book is shrewder than the detective."

From a certain moment the narrative begins to turn inside out: any story worthy of the name contains, even if in a concealed form, this retrogression which opens up unsuspected avenues of interpretation. In this Borges belongs with Kafka, who makes the anxieties of interpretation the centre of his work.

The allegory of the labyrinth barely assists our understanding of this theory of narrative; too simple, yielding too readily to the perils of reverie. The labyrinth, rather than the enigma, the unfolding of the narrative, this is the inverted image which the story reflects from its end, in which is crystallised the idea of an inexhaustible division: the labyrinth of the narrative is traversed backwards, with a derisory exit in sight, an exit which leads to nothing, neither a centre nor a content, since one might just as well retreat as advance. The narrative derives its purpose from this dislocation which links it to its double — ever more ineluctable as we realise that it corresponds less with its initial conditions. On this theme, one might quote the detective story "Death and the Compass," which might well have been written by Herbert Quain: the progress of Lonnrot, the detective, towards a solution announces a meta-problem; the solving of the mystery was in fact one of the terms of the mystery itself; to resolve the problem, to avoid the trap, would have been to have failed, etc. The narrative contains several versions of itself which are all so many predictable failures. Here is a certain affinity with the art of Poe: the narrative is inscribed on its reverse side, begun from the end, but this time in the form of a *radical* art; the story is begun at the end in such a way that we no longer know which is the end and which is the beginning, the story having wound around itself to produce the illusory coherence of an infinite perspective.

But Borges' writing has a value other than that of the riddle. If he seems to make the reader think (and the best specimen of this genre is the story "The Circular Ruins," in which the man who dreams a man is himself dreamt), it is because he deprives the reader of anything to think about: hence his predilection for the paradoxes of illusion which do not strictly contain any ideas at all (the label on the bottle which shows a label on a bottle which shows . . .). Borges at his simplest, but probably the Borges who tricks us, makes great use of these dots. His best stories are not the ones that open out so easily, but those which are entirely sealed off.

"Readers will witness the execution and all the preliminaries of a crime, the intention of which is known to them, but which they will not understand, it seems to me, until the very last paragraph." When Borges, in a prologue, thus summarises "The Garden of Forking Paths" we are obliged to believe his promise. The story is shut in, encompassed, between the problem (no need to pose it) and the solution. And the last paragraph, truthfully announced in the prologue, does in fact give us the key to the mystery. But this is accomplished at the cost of a formidable confusion which is established retrospectively in all that precedes the conclusion. The solution seems just as derisory: only at the cost of a trick, apparently, can it carry the burden of a story. The author is cheating by making a mystery out of insignificance. But the solution is on display; it just runs along the edges of the story's meaning: it is a new fork which closes off the plot at the same moment as it gives notice of its inexhaustible content. A possible exit is blocked, and the narrative is concluded: but where are the other doors? Or is the ending defective? And the story escapes, flies out of the false window, in a vague interruption. The problem seems perfectly clear: either the story has a meaning and the false ending is therefore an allegory, or the story may not have a meaning and the false ending is then an allegory of absurdity. This is how Borges is usually interpreted: he is made to conclude by having attributed to him the appearances of an intelligent scepticism. It is not established that the scepticism is in fact intelligent, or that the deep meanings of his stories lie in their apparent subtlety.

Accordingly, the problem would seem to be wrongly stated. The story certainly has a meaning, but not the one that we think. The meaning does not follow from the possible choice between several interpretations. The meaning is not an interpretation; meaning is not to be sought in a reading, but in the writing: the footnotes, incessant and indiscreet, indicate the great difficulty that the story has in developing at all, as though it were initially arrested. Hence the relatively simple editorial technique of copious allusion. Rather than writing it, Borges *indicates* his story: not only the one that he could write, but those that others could have written.

This can be seen in the analysis of *Bouvard et Pécuchet*, which is printed in the Borges special number of *L'Herne*, a fair specimen of the style of Ménard. Instead of tracing the line of the story he indicates its possibility, generally postponed or deferred. This is why his critical essays are fictional even when they are about actual works; and this is also why his stories are told largely for the sake of the explicit self-criticism which they embody. This is the culmination and the fulfilment of Valéry's hollow project: to watch what one does when one is writing or thinking. Borges has found the authentic method of achieving this. How to write the most simple story, when it implies an infinite possibility of variations, when its chosen form will always lack those other forms which might have clothed it? Borges' art is to answer this question with a story; by choosing from amongst these forms precisely that which best preserves the question, by its instability, its obvious artificiality and its contradictions. There is a great distance between these efficacious fictions and the complacently annotated delayings of the sinister academic poetician: the distance which separates the lips from the cup.

Before we return to the forking paths, we can take another example, more transparent (not that it is to be condemned for that, if in spite of appearances there really is something in what Borges has written), "The Shape of the Sword." Using a technique from the detective novel, as made famous by Agatha Christie in *The Murder of Roger Ackroyd*, the story is told in the third person by the protagonist (I tell that he; he tells that I: the "I" is not the same; only the "he" is the common term which makes the narrative possible.) A man tells the story of a betrayal but does not discover until the end that he is the betrayer. This revelation is effected by the deciphering of a sign; the narrator has a scar on his face, and when the same scar appears in the story the identity is revealed. All explanation is thus superfluous: the presence of this eloquent token (the story is its discourse) serves the purpose. But the token itself has to be used in a discourse, otherwise its significance would remain hidden. It is sufficient for the token to reappear at a privileged moment of the story in order to assume its full meaning. This is rather like Racine's *Phèdre*, when the queen announces at the opening of the play that she is going to die, that her robes are stifling her . . . and then actually dies at the end of Act 5. Nothing seems to have happened: fifteen hundred lines have been needed to charge this decisive gesture with its meaning, to give it its truth in language, its literary truth. Evidently the function of the discourse of the narrative is to deliver *the truth*. But this is done at the cost of a very long detour, a cost which must be met. The discourse shapes a truth only by bringing itself into question, only by adopting the appearance of pure artifice. It only progresses inevitably towards its end by elaborating its own futility (since everything was given in advance); its episodes are freely improvised only in order to deceive the reader (since everything will be given at the end). The discourse winds around its object, enveloping it, so as to combine two narratives in its single movement: a right side and a reverse side. The foreseen is unforeseen because the unforeseen is foreseen. This is the privileged point of view that Borges chooses: the one that precipitates the dissymmetry between a subject (the plot) and the writing which is our access to it. In so far as the story begins to make sense, the narrative diverges, calling attention to all the other possible ways of telling it as well as all the other meanings that it could have.

In fact the story of the *Garden*, which could have been part of a spy story, veers towards a controlled surprise. In the narrative something happens which the initial plot would have done without. The protagonist, a spy, has to solve a problem which is posed in a very confused way. He goes to the house of a certain Albert, and does what had to be done there; when he has done this we are told what it was, and the mystery is solved in the last paragraph, just as promised. The completed story conveys a certain fact, which is nevertheless not very interesting. In order to signal the bombardment of a town called Albert, the spy commits a crime against a man called Albert whose name he has found in a telephone directory. This resolves the mystery, but what of it? This insignificant meaning has migrated to produce another meaning, and even another story which in contrast is more important. In Albert's house, apart from the name of Albert, which will be used as a cipher, there is something else: the labyrinth itself. The spy, whose job is to hunt out other people's secrets, has gone inadvertently to the place of the secret: just when he was not looking for the secret but for the means of communicating one. Albert keeps in his house the most elaborate labyrinth that could be devised by a perversely subtle mind: a book. Not a book in which one is bewildered, but a book which is itself bewildered on every page, "The Garden of the Forking Paths." Albert has deciphered this fundamental secret: he has not found the translation (except for a linear translation, one which deciphers without decoding, refrains from interpretation: the motive of the secret is that it is the geometrical place of all interpretations); he has recognised it. He knows that the book is an ultimate labyrinth — to enter it is to be lost; he also knows that this labyrinth is a book in which anything can be read since this is the way it is written (or rather *is not written*, since, as we shall see, such a writing is impossible).

In fact, the labyrinthine novel of the scholarly Ts'ui Pen resolves all the problems of the narrative (though naturally it does so on condition of not existing: in a real narrative, one can only pose a few problems): "In all fictions, whenever several solutions present themselves, men choose one and eliminate all the others; in the fiction of the almost inextricable Ts'ui Pen they are all chosen simultaneously" (J. L. Borges, *Labyrinths*, ed. Donald A. Yates, and J. E. Irby, Penguin Modern Classics, 1970). The perfect book is the one which succeeds in eliminating all its doubles, all the simple pathways which pretend to cross it; or rather it has succeeded in absorbing them: for a given event all the interpretations coexist. Let a character knock on a door, and if the narrative is freely improvised we can expect anything and everything. The door may open or may not open, or any other solution (if there are any); the artifice of the labyrinth is founded on an axiom: these solutions form an enumerable whole, finite or infinite. A narrative will ordinarily privilege one of these solutions, which will then seem inevitable, or at least true: the narrative takes sides, moves in a determinate direction. The myth of the labyrinth corresponds to the idea of a completely objective narrative, one which takes all sides at once and develops them to their conclusions: but this ending is impossible, and the narrative only ever gives the *image* of a labyrinth, because, condemned to choose a definite term, it is compelled to conceal all the forkings, and to drown them in the line of a discourse. The labyrinth of the Garden is the analogue of the Library of Babel, but the real book has only the labyrinth of its own incompleteness in which to lose itself. Just as Borges had promised in the prologue, the last paragraph gives us the solution: it gives us, as it were, the key to the labyrinth, by pointing out that the only real traces of the labyrinth will be found in the form of the narrative, precarious and finite, but precisely achieved. Each story discloses the idea of the labyrinth, but it gives us the only *readable* reflection. Borges has been able to conclude his demonstration without falling into the expository gesture of the traditional mystery writers (given that a rhetoric of the mysterious had been elaborated in the eighteenth century): in a story concerned with Melmoth there is someone who tells us a story about Melmoth in which there is . . . and no story could ever finish because of this system of Chinese boxes. The real labyrinth is that there is no longer a labyrinth: to write is to lose the labyrinth.

The real narrative is then determined by the absence of all the other possible narratives from amongst which it could have been chosen: this absence hollows out the form of the book by putting it into endless conflict with itself. Then instead of the ultimately convivial allegory of the Library in which one can be lost, instead of the Garden big enough to wander in, we have now the critical allegory of the lost book which survives only in its traces and insufficiencies, the Encyclopaedia of Tlön: "Let it suffice for me to recall that the apparent contradictions of the Eleventh Volume are the fundamental basis for the proof that the other volumes exist, so lucid and exact is the order observed in it" (Ibid.). The incomplete or missing book is present in its fragments. It is not therefore absurd to imagine that, instead of a total book which would regroup all the combinations, it would be possible to write one of such insufficiency that the importance of what had been lost would shine forth from it: "a vast polemic concerning the composition of a novel in the first person, whose narrator would omit or disfigure the facts and indulge in various contradictions which would permit a few readers — very few readers — to perceive an atrocious or banal reality" (Ibid.). The stratagems of Borges all ultimately lead towards the possibility of such a narrative. The enterprise can be deemed both a success and a failure in so far as Borges manages to show us by means of the insufficiencies of a narrative that we have lost nothing.

The Literature of Exhaustion   John Barth*

I want to discuss three things more or less together: first, some old questions raised by the new intermedia arts; second, some aspects of the Argentine writer Jorge Luis Borges, whom I greatly admire; third, some professional concerns of my own, related to these other matters and having to do with what I'm calling "the literature of exhausted possibility" — or, more chicly, "the literature of exhaustion."

By "exhaustion" I don't mean anything so tired as the subject of physical, moral, or intellectual decadence, only the used-upness of certain forms or exhaustion of certain possibilities — by no means necessarily a cause for despair. That a great many Western artists for a great many years have quarreled with received definitions of artistic media, genres, and forms goes without saying: pop art, dramatic and musical "happenings," the whole range of "intermedia" or "mixed-means" art, bear recentest witness to the tradition of rebelling against Tradition. A catalogue I received some time ago in the mail, for example, advertises such items as Robert Filliou's *Ample Food for Stupid Thought*, a box full of postcards on which are inscribed "apparently meaningless questions," to be mailed to whomever the purchaser judges them suited for; Ray Johnson's *Paper Snake*, a collection of whimsical writings, "often pointed," once mailed to various friends (what the catalogue describes as The New York Correspondence School of Literature); and Daniel Spoerri's *Anecdoted Typography of Chance*, "on the surface" a description of all the objects that happen to be on the author's parlor table — "in fact, however . . . a cosmology of Spoerri's existence."

"On the surface," at least, the document listing these items is a catalogue of The Something Else Press, a swinging outfit. "In fact, however," it may be one of their offerings, for all I know: The New York Direct-Mail Advertising School of Literature. In any case, their wares are lively to read about, and make for interesting conversation in fiction-writing classes, for example, where we discuss Somebody-or-other's un-bound, unpaginated, randomly assembled novel-in-a-box and the desirability of printing *Finnegans Wake* on a very long roller-towel. It's easier and sociabler to talk technique than it is to make art, and the area of "happenings" and their kin is mainly a way of discussing aesthetics,

*First published in the *Atlantic* (August 1967). Reprinted in *The Friday Book* (New York: Putnam Publishing Group, 1985). Reprinted here by permission of Putnam.

really; illustrating "dramatically" more or less valid and interesting points about the nature of art and the definition of its terms and genres.

One conspicuous thing, for example, about the "intermedia" arts is their tendency (noted even by *Life* magazine) to eliminate not only the traditional audience — "those who apprehend the artist's art" (in "happenings" the audience is often the "cast," as in "environments," and some of the new music isn't intended to be performed at all) — but also the most traditional notion of the artist: the Aristotelian conscious agent who achieves with technique and cunning the artistic effect; in other words, one endowed with uncommon talent, who has moreover developed and disciplined that endowment into virtuosity. It's an aristocratic notion on the face of it, which the democratic West seems eager to have done with; not only the "omniscient" author of older fiction, but the very idea of the controlling artist, has been condemned as politically reactionary, even fascist.

Now, personally, being of the temper that chooses to "rebel along traditional lines," I'm inclined to prefer the kind of art that not many people can *do*: the kind that requires expertise and artistry as well as bright aesthetic ideas and / or inspiration. I enjoy the pop art in the famous Albright-Knox collection, a few blocks from my house in Buffalo, like a lively conversation for the most part, but was on the whole more impressed by the jugglers and acrobats at Baltimore's old Hippodrome, where I used to go every time they changed shows: genuine *virtuosi* doing things that anyone can dream up and discuss but almost no one can do.

I suppose, the distinction is between things worth remarking — preferably over beer, if one's of my generation — and things worth doing. "Somebody ought to make a novel with scenes that pop up, like the old children's books," one says, with the implication that one isn't going to bother doing it oneself.

However, art and its forms and techniques live in history and certainly do change. I sympathize with a remark attributed to Saul Bellow, that to be technically up to date is the least important attribute of a writer, though I would have to add that this least important attribute may be nevertheless essential. In any case, to be technically *out* of date is likely to be a genuine defect: Beethoven's Sixth Symphony or the Chartres Cathedral if executed today would be merely embarrassing. A good many current novelists write turn-of-the-century-type novels, only in more or less mid-twentieth-century language and about contemporary people and topics; this makes them considerably less interesting (to me) than excellent writers who are also technically contemporary: Joyce and Kafka, for instance, in their time, and in ours, Samuel Beckett, and Jorge Luis Borges. The intermedia arts, I'd say, tend to be intermediary too, between the traditional realms of aesthetics on the one hand and artistic creation on the other; I think the wise artist and civilian will regard them with quite the kind and degree of seriousness with which he regards good shoptalk: he'll listen carefully, if noncommittally, and keep an eye on his intermedia colleagues, if only the corner of his eye. They may very possibly suggest something usable in the making or understanding of genuine works of contemporary art.

The man I want to discuss a little here, Jorge Luis Borges, illustrates well the difference between a technically old-fashioned artist, a technically up-to-date civilian, and a technically up-to-date artist. In the first category I'd locate all those novelists who for better or worse write not as if the twentieth century didn't exist, but as if the great writers of the last sixty years or so hadn't existed (*nota bene* that our century's more than two-thirds done; it's dismaying to see so many of our writers following Dostoevsky or Tolstoy or Flaubert or Balzac, when the real technical question seems to me to be how to succeed not even Joyce and Kafka, but those who've *succeeded* Joyce and Kafka and are now in the evenings of their own careers). In the second category are such folk as an artist-neighbor of mine in Buffalo who fashions dead Winnies-the-Pooh in sometimes monumental scale out of oilcloth stuffed with sand and impaled on stakes or hung by the neck. In the third belong the few people whose artistic thinking is as hip as any French new-novelist's, but who manage nonetheless to speak eloquently and memorably to our still-human hearts and conditions, as the great artists have always done. Of these, two of the finest living specimens that I know of are Beckett and Borges, just about the only contemporaries of my reading acquaintance mentionable with the "old masters" of twentieth-century fiction. In the unexciting history of literary awards, the 1961 International Publishers' Prize, shared by Beckett and Borges, is a happy exception indeed.

One of the modern things about these two is that in an age of ultimacies and "final solutions" — at least *felt* ultimacies, in everything from weaponry to theology, the celebrated dehumanization of society, and the history of the novel — their work in separate ways reflects and deals with ultimacy, both technically and thematically, as, for example, *Finnegans Wake* does in its different manner. One notices, by the way, for whatever its symptomatic worth, that Joyce was virtually blind at the end, Borges is literally so, and Beckett has become virtually mute, musewise, having progressed from marvelously constructed English sentences through terser and terser French ones to the unsyntatical, unpunctuated prose of *Comment C'est* and "ultimately" to wordless mimes. One might extrapolate a theoretical course for Beckett: language, after all, consists of silence as well as sound, and the mime is still communication — "that nineteenth-century idea," a Yale student once snarled at me — but by the language of action. But the language of action consists of rest as well as movement, and so in the context of Beckett's progress immobile, silent figures still aren't altogether ultimate. How about an empty, silent stage, then, or blank pages[1] — a "happening" where nothing happens, like Cage's *4' 33"* performed in an empty hall? But dramatic communication consists of the absence as well as the presence of the actors; "we have our exits and our entrances"; and so even that would be imperfectly ultimate in Beckett's case. Nothing at all, then, I suppose: but Nothingness is necessarily and inextricably the background against which Being et cetera; for Beckett, at this point in his career, to cease to create altogether would be fairly meaningful: his crowning work, his "last word." What a convenient corner to paint yourself into! "And now I shall finish," the valet Arsene says in *Watt*, "and you will hear my voice no more." Only the silence *Molloy* speaks of, "of which the universe is made."

After which, I add on behalf of the rest of us, it might be conceivable to rediscover validly the artifices of language and literature—such far-out notions as grammar, punctuation . . . even characterization! Even *plot!*—if one goes about it the right way, aware of what one's predecessors have been up to.

Now J. L. Borges is perfectly aware of all these things. Back in the great decades of literary experimentalism he was associated with *Prisma*, a "muralist" magazine that published its pages on walls and billboards; his later *Labyrinths* and *Ficciones* not only anticipate the farthest-out ideas of The Something-Else Press crowd—not a difficult thing to do—but being marvelous works of art as well, illustrate in a simple way the difference between the *fact* of aesthetic ultimacies and their artistic *use*. What it comes to is that an artist doesn't merely exemplify an ultimacy; he employs it.

Consider Borges' story "Pierre Menard, Author of the *Quixote*": the hero, an utterly sophisticated turn-of-the-century French Symbolist, by an astounding effort of imagination, produces—not *copies* or *imitates*, mind, but *composes*—several chapters of Cervantes' novel.

> It is a revelation [Borges' narrator tells us] to compare Menard's *Don Quixote* with Cervantes'. The latter, for example, wrote (part one, chapter nine):
>
>> . . . truth, whose mother is history, rival of time, depository of deeds, witness of the past, exemplar and adviser to the present, the future's counselor.
>
> Written in the seventeenth century, written by the "lay genius" Cervantes, this enumeration is a mere rhetorical praise of history. Menard, on the other hand, writes:
>
>> . . . truth, whose mother is history, rival of time, depository of deeds, witness of the past, exemplar and adviser to the present, the future's counselor.
>
> History, the *mother* of truth: the idea is astounding. Menard, a contemporary of William James, does not define history as an inquiry into reality but as its origin. . . .

Et cetera. Now, this is an interesting idea, of considerable intellectual validity. I mentioned earlier that if Beethoven's Sixth were composed today, it would be an embarrassment; but clearly it wouldn't be, necessarily, if done with ironic intent by a composer quite aware of where we've been and where we are. It would have then potentially, for better or worse, the kind of significance of Warhol's Campbell's Soup ads, the difference being that in the former case a work of art is being reproduced instead of a work of non-art, and the ironic comment would therefore be more directly on the genre and history of the art than on the state of the culture. In fact, of course, to make the valid intellectual point one needn't even recompose the Sixth Symphony, any more than Menard really needed to re-create the *Quixote*. It would've been sufficient for Menard to have *attributed* the novel to himself in order to have a new work of art, from the intellectual point of view. Indeed, in several stories Borges plays with this very idea, and I can readily imagine Beckett's next novel, for example, as *Tom Jones*, just as Nabokov's last was that multivolume annotated translation of Pushkin. I myself have always aspired to write Burton's version of *The 1001 Nights*, complete with appendices and the like, in twelve volumes, and for intellectual purposes I needn't even write it. What evenings we might spend (over beer) discussing Saarinen's Parthenon, D. H. Lawrence's *Wuthering Heights*, or the Johnson Administration by Robert Rauschenberg!

The idea, I say, is intellectually serious, as are Borges' other characteristic ideas, most of a metaphysical rather than an aesthetic nature. But the important thing to observe is that Borges *doesn't* attribute the *Quixote* to himself, much less recompose it like Pierre Menard; instead, he writes a remarkable and original work of literature, the implicit theme of which is the difficulty, perhaps the unnecessity, of writing original works of literature. His artistic victory, if you like, is that he confronts an intellectual dead end and employs it against itself to accomplish new human work. If this corresponds to what mystics do—"every moment leaping into the infinite," Kierkegaard says, "and every moment falling surely back into the finite"—it's only one more aspect of that old analogy. In homelier terms, it's a matter of every moment throwing out the bath water without for a moment losing the baby.

Another way of describing Borges' accomplishment is in a pair of his own favorite terms, *algebra and fire*. In his most often anthologized story, "Tlön, Uqbar, Orbis Tertius," he imagines an entirely hypothetical world, the invention of a secret society of scholars who elaborate its every aspect in a surreptitious encyclopedia. This *First Encyclopaedia of Tlön* (what fictionist would not wish to have dreamed up the *Britannica*?) describes a coherent alternative to this world complete in every respect from its algebra to its fire, Borges tells us, and of such imaginative power that, once conceived, it begins to obtrude itself into and eventually to supplant our prior reality. My point is that neither the algebra nor the fire, metaphorically speaking, could achieve this result without the other. Borges' algebra is what I'm considering here—algebra is easier to talk about than fire—but any intellectual giant could equal it. The imaginary authors of the *First Encyclopaedia of Tlön* itself are not artists, though their work is in a manner of speaking fictional and would find a ready publisher in New York nowadays. The author of the story "Tlön, Uqbar, Orbis Tertius," who merely *alludes* to the fascinating *Encyclopaedia, is* an artist; what makes him one of the first rank, like Kafka, is the combination of that intellectually profound vision with great human insight, poetic power, and consummate mastery of his means, a definition which would have gone without saying, I suppose, in any century but ours.

Not long ago, incidentally, in a footnote to a scholarly edition of Sir Thomas Browne (*The Urn Burial*, I believe it was), I came upon a perfect Borges datum, reminiscent of Tlön's self-realization: the actual case of a book called *The Three Impostors*, alluded to in Browne's *Religio Medici* among other places. *The Three Impostors* is a non-existent blasphemous treatise against Moses, Christ, and Mohammed, which in the seventeenth century was widely held to exist, or to have once existed. Commentators attributed it variously to Boccaccio, Pietro Aretino, Giordano Bruno, and Tommaso Campanella, and though no one, Browne included, had ever seen a copy of it, it was frequently cited, refuted, railed against, and generally discussed as if everyone had read it—until, sure enough, in the *eighteenth* century a spurious work appeared with a forged date of 1598 and the title *De Tribus Impostoribus*. It's a wonder that Borges doesn't mention this work, as he seems to have read absolutely everything, including all the books that don't exist, and Browne is a particular favorite of his. In fact, the narrator of "Tlön, Uqbar, Orbis Tertius" declares at the end: ". . . English and French and mere Spanish will disappear from the globe. The world will be Tlön. I pay no attention to all this and go on revising, in the still days at the Adrogué hotel, an uncertain Quevedian translation (which I do not intend to publish) of Browne's *Urn Burial*."[2]

This "contamination of reality by dream," as Borges calls it, is one of his pet themes, and commenting upon such contaminations is one of his favorite fictional devices. Like many of the best such devices, it turns the artist's mode or form into a metaphor for his concerns, as does the diary-ending of *Portrait of the Artist As a Young Man* or the cyclical construction of *Finnegans Wake*. In Borges' case, the story "Tlön," etc., for example, is a real piece of imagined reality in our world, analogous to those Tlönian artifacts called *hrönir*, which imagine themselves into existence. In short, it's a paradigm of or metaphor for itself; not just the *form* of the story but the *fact* of the story is symbolic; "the medium is the message."

Moreover, like all of Borges' work, it illustrates in other of its aspects my subject: how an artist may paradoxically turn the felt ultimacies of our time into material and means for his work—*paradoxically* because by doing so he transcends what had appeared to be his refutation, in the same way that the mystic who transcends finitude is said to be enabled to live, spiritually and physically, in the finite world. Suppose you're a writer by vocation—a "print-oriented bastard," as the McLuhanites call us—and you feel, for example, that the novel, if not narrative literature generally, if not the printed word altogether, has by this hour of the world just about shot its bolt, as Leslie Fiedler and others maintain. (I'm inclined to agree, with reservations and hedges. Literary forms certainly have histories and historical contingencies, and it may well be that the novel's time as a major art form is up, as the "times" of classical tragedy, grand opera, or the sonnet sequence came to be. No necessary cause for alarm in this at all, except perhaps to certain novelists, and one way to handle such a feeling might be to write a novel about it. Whether historically the novel expires or persists seems immaterial to me; if enough writers and critics *feel* apocalyptical about it, their feeling becomes a considerable cultural fact, like the *feeling* that Western civilization, or the world, is going to end rather soon. If you took a bunch of people out into the desert and the world didn't end, you'd come home shamefaced, I imagine; but the persistence of an art form doesn't invalidate work created in the comparable apocalyptic ambience. That's one of the fringe benefits of being an artist instead of a prophet. There are others.) If you happened to be Vladimir Nabokov you might address that felt ultimacy by writing *Pale Fire*: a fine novel by a learned pedant, in the form of a pedantic commentary on a poem invented for the purpose. If you were Borges you might write *Labyrinths*: fictions by a learned librarian in the form of footnotes, as he describes them, to imaginary or hypothetical books.[3] And I'll add, since I believe Borges' idea is rather more interesting, that if you were the author of this paper, you'd have written something like *The Sot-Weed Factor* or *Giles Goat-Boy*: novels which imitate the form of the Novel, by an author who imitates the role of Author.

If this sort of thing sounds unpleasantly decadent, nevertheless it's about where the genre began, with *Quixote* imitating *Amadis of Gaul*, Cervantes pretending to be the Cid Hamete Benengeli (and Alonso Quijano pretending to be Don Quixote), or Fielding parodying Richardson. "History repeats itself as farce"—meaning, of course, in the form or mode of farce, not that history is farcical. The imitation (like the Dadaist echoes in the work of the "intermedia" types) is something new and *may be* quite serious and passionate despite its farcical aspect. This is the important difference between a proper novel and a deliberate imitation of a novel, or a novel imitative of other sorts of documents. The first attempts (has been historically inclined to attempt) to imitate actions more or less directly, and its conventional devices—cause and effect, linear anecdote,

characterization, authorial selection, arrangement, and interpretation—
can be and have long since been objected to as obsolete notions, or
metaphors for obsolete notions: Robbe-Grillet's essays *For a New Novel*
come to mind. There are replies to these objections, not to the point here,
but one can see that in any case they're obviated by imitations-of-novels,
which attempt to represent not life directly but a representation of life. In
fact, such works are no more removed from "life" than Richardson's or
Goethe's epistolary novels are: both imitate "real" documents, and the
subject of both, ultimately, is life, not the documents. A novel is as much a
piece of the real world as a letter, and the letters in *The Sorrows of Young
Werther* are, after all, fictitious.

One might imaginably compound this imitation, and though Borges
doesn't, he's fascinated with the idea: one of his frequenter literary
allusions is to the 602nd night of *The 1001 Nights*, when, owing to a
copyist's error, Scheherezade begins to tell the King the story of the 1001
nights, from the beginning. Happily, the King interrupts; if he didn't
there'd be no 603rd night ever, and while this would solve Scheherezade's
problem—which is every storyteller's problem: to publish or perish—it
would put the "outside" author in a bind. (I suspect that Borges dreamed
this whole thing up: the business he mentions isn't in any edition of *The
1001 Nights* I've been able to consult. Not *yet*, anyhow: after reading
"Tlön, Uqbar," etc., one is inclined to recheck every semester or so.)

Now Borges (whom someone once vexedly accused *me* of inventing) is
interested in the 602nd Night because it's an instance of the story-within-
the-story turned back upon itself, and his interest in such instances is
threefold: first, as he himself declares, they disturb us metaphysically:
when the characters in a work of fiction become readers or authors of the
fiction they're in, we're reminded of the fictitious aspect of our own
existence, one of Borges's cardinal themes, as it was of Shakespeare,
Calderón, Unamuno, and other folk. Second, the 602nd Night is a literary
illustration of the *regressus in infinitum*, as are almost all of Borges'
principal images and motifs. Third, Scheherezade's accidental gambit,
like Borges' other versions of the *regressus in infinitum*, is an image of the
exhaustion, or attempted exhaustion, of possibilities—in this case literary
possibilities—and so we return to our main subject.

What makes Borges' stance, if you like, more interesting to me than,
say, Nabokov's or Beckett's, is the premise with which he approaches
literature; in the words of one of his editors: "For [Borges] no one has
claim to originality in literature; all writers are more or less faithful
amanuenses of the spirit, translators and annotators of pre-existing archetypes." Thus his inclination to write brief comments on imaginary books:
for one to attempt to add overtly to the sum of "original" literature by even
so much as a conventional short story, not to mention a novel, would be
too presumptuous, too naïve; literature has been done long since. A
librarian's point of view! And it would itself be too presumptuous if it

weren't part of a lively, passionately relevant metaphysical vision, and slyly employed against itself precisely to make new and original literature. Borges defines the Baroque as "that style which deliberately exhausts (or tries to exhaust) its possibilities and borders upon its own caricature." While his own work is *not* Baroque, except intellectually (the Baroque was never so terse, laconic, economical), it suggests the view that intellectual and literary history has been Baroque, and has pretty well exhausted the possibilities of novelty. His *ficciones* are not only footnotes to imaginary texts, but postscripts to the real corpus of literature.

This premise gives resonance and relation to all his principal images. The facing mirrors that recur in his stories are a dual *regressus*. The doubles that his characters, like Nabokov's, run afoul of suggest dizzying multiples and remind one of Browne's remark that "every man is not only himself . . . men are lived over again." (It would please Borges, and illustrate Browne's point, to call Browne a precursor of Borges. "Every writer," Borges says in his essay on Kafka, "creates his own precursors.") Borges' favorite third-century heretical sect is the Histriones—I think and hope he invented them—who believe that repetition is impossible in history and therefore live viciously in order to purge the future of the vices they commit: in other words, to exhaust the possibilities of the world in order to bring its end nearer.

The writer he most often mentions, after Cervantes, is Shakespeare; in one piece he imagines the playwright on his deathbed asking God to permit him to be one and himself, having been everyone and no one; God replies from the whirlwind that He is no one either; He has dreamed the world like Shakespeare, and including Shakespeare. Homer's story in Book IV of the *Odyssey*, of Menelaus on the beach at Pharos, tackling Proteus, appeals profoundly to Borges: Proteus is he who "exhausts the guises of reality" while Menelaus—who, one recalls, disguised his own identity in order to ambush him—holds fast. Zeno's paradox of Achilles and the Tortoise embodies a *regressus in infinitum* which Borges carries through philosophical history, pointing out that Aristotle uses it to refute Plato's theory of forms, Hume to refute the possibility of cause and effect, Lewis Carroll to refute syllogistic deduction, William James to refute the notion of temporal passage, and Bradley to refute the general possibility of logical relations; Borges himself uses it, citing Schopenhauer, as evidence that the world is our dream, our idea, in which "tenuous and eternal crevices of unreason" can be found to remind us that our creation is false, or at least fictive.

The infinite library of one of his popular stories is an image particularly pertinent to the literature of exhaustion; the "Library of Babel" houses every possible combination of alphabetical characters and spaces, and thus every possible book and statement, including your and my refutations and vindications, the history of the actual future, the history of every possible future, and, though he doesn't mention it, the

encyclopedias not only of Tlön but of every imaginable other world—
since, as in Lucretius' universe, the number of elements, and so of
combinations, is finite (though very large), and the number of instances of
each element and combination of elements is infinite, like the library
itself.

That brings us to his favorite image of all, the labyrinth, and to my
point. *Labyrinths* is the name of his most substantial translated volume,
and the only full-length study of Borges in English, by Ana María
Barrenechea, is called *Borges the Labyrinth-Maker*. A labyrinth, after all,
is a place in which, ideally, all the possibilities of choice (of direction, in
this case) are embodied, and—barring special dispensation like Theseus'—
must be exhausted before one reaches the heart. Where, mind, the
Minotaur waits with two final possibilities: defeat and death, or victory
and freedom. Now, in fact, the legendary Theseus is non-Baroque; thanks
to Ariadne's thread he can take a shortcut through the labyrinth at
Knossos. But Menelaus on the beach at Pharos, for example, is genuinely
Baroque in the Borgesian spirit, and illustrates a positive artistic morality
in the literature of exhaustion. He is not there, after all, for kicks (any
more than Borges and Beckett are in the fiction racket for their health):
Menelaus is *lost*, in the larger labyrinth of the world, and has got to hold
fast while the Old Man of the Sea exhausts reality's frightening guises so
that he may extort direction from him when Proteus returns to his "true"
self. It's a heroic enterprise, with salvation as its object—one recalls that
the aim of the Histriones is to get history done with so that Jesus may come
again the sooner, and that Shakespeare's heroic metamorphoses culminate
not merely in a theophany but in an apotheosis.

Now, not just any old body is equipped for this labor, and Theseus in
the Cretan labyrinth becomes in the end the aptest image for Borges after
all. Distressing as the fact is to us liberal Democrats, the commonality,
alas, will *always* lose their way and their souls: it's the chosen remnant,
the virtuoso, the Thesean *hero*, who, confronted with Baroque reality,
Baroque history, the Baroque state of his art, need *not* rehearse its
possibilities to exhaustion, any more than Borges needs actually to *write*
the *Encyclopaedia of Tlön* or the books in the Library of Babel. He need
only be aware of their existence or possibility, acknowledge them, and
with the aid of *very special gifts*—as extraordinary as saint- or hero-hood
and not likely to be found in The New York Correspondence School of
Literature—go straight through the maze to the accomplishment of his
work.

Notes

1. An ultimacy already attained in the nineteenth century by that *avant-gardiste* of
East Aurora, New York, Elbert Hubbard, in his *Essay on Silence*.

2. Moreover, on rereading "Tlön," etc., I find now a remark I'd swear wasn't in it last

year: that the eccentric American millionaire who endows the *Encyclopaedia* does so on condition that "the work will make no pact with the imposter Jesus Christ."

3. Borges was born in Argentina in 1899, educated in Europe, and for some years worked as director of the National Library in Buenos Aires, except for a period when Juan Perón demoted him to the rank of provincial chicken inspector as a political humiliation. Currently he's the *Beowulf*-man at the University of Buenos Aires.

A Game with Shifting Mirrors   John Ashbery*

In the six years since he won the International Publishers Prize, Jorge Luis Borges has been belatedly recognized in this country as the greatest living Spanish-language writer. "A Personal Anthology," first published in Buenos Aires in 1961, is the fifth of his books to appear in English in as many years. It is the author's own choice of his favorite works, arranged without regard for chronology but according to "sympathies and differences."

Speaking of his choice in a prologue, Borges announces: "I should like to be judged by it, justified or reproved because of it, and not by certain exercises in excessive and apocryphal local color which keep cropping up in anthologies and which I can not recall without a blush." It would seem that he is referring to some of the very pieces on which his reputation rests, such as "The Garden of Forking Paths," "The Immortal," "The Bablyon Lottery," "Tlön, Uqbar, Orbis Tertius," "Pierre Menard, Author of Don Quixote" and "The Approach to Al-Mu'tasim." To describe these masterpieces as exercises in local color is either some elaborate Borgesian jest or else the sign of an urge toward auto-da-fé as obscure to us as Kafka's deathbed injunction to destroy his works.

Indeed, a reader coming to Borges's books for the first time would do better to begin with "Ficciones" or "Labyrinths," for not only does the present collection omit the works mentioned earlier, but it also overemphasizes the somewhat less satisfactory poetry and the brief, rather fragile parables which were collected in "Dreamtigers." Nevertheless, "A Personal Anthology" does include "The Aleph," a magnificent and celebrated story not hitherto available in English, as well as a number of other well-known pieces: "Death and the Compass," "Funes, the Memorious," "A New Refutation of Time."

Of course, there is no reason to believe that this book is intended for the "general reader," nor even to take Borges's own statement of its purpose too seriously, in view of the examples of literary duplicity that abound in his work. And then there is the curious fact that this book partially

*From the *New York Times Book Review*, 17 April 1967. Reprinted by permission of the author.

duplicates his other books available in English, which in turn partially duplicate each other, so that the very form of his English-language *oeuvre* is, in his own phrase, "a game with shifting mirrors." Could the author in fact have planned it this way? His Pierre Menard is a minor 20th-century French writer who succeeds so well in totally identifying himself with Cervantes that he is actually able to write a couple of chapters of "Don Quixote" exactly as Cervantes wrote them. Borges quotes two identical passages from the Cervantes and Menard versions, praising the latter as more remarkable given the circumstances and time of its creation. And he concludes: "Would not the attributing of 'The Imitation of Christ' to Louis-Ferdinand Céline or James Joyce be a sufficient renovation of its tenuous spiritual counsels?"

Perhaps a similar if contrary idea presided over the selection of "A Personal Anthology." Mightn't as strange and marvelous a writer as Jorge Luis Borges appear even more so when stripped of his finest creations, or rather with just enough of them put together with enough lesser pieces to persuade the reader that Borges is someone else: perhaps that "other" Borges in his parable "Borges and I" — not the one who "contrives his literature" but the one who likes "hourglasses, maps, eighteenth-century typography, the taste of coffee and Robert Louis Stevenson's prose"?

Borges's prologue also contains what I believe to be another red herring. He writes: "Croce held that art is expression; to this exigency, or to a deformation of this exigency, we owe the worst literature of our time. . . . Sometimes I, too, sought expression. I know now that my gods grant me no more than allusion or mention." This might in fact be true of some of the more schematic tales in this volume, such as "The End" or "The Captive" — bony allegories with some of the aridity of Unamumo's fiction, or, at worst, suggestive of O. Henry, Richard Harding Davis or Lord Dunsany. But elsewhere Borges is revealed as a master of "expression," which he defines as the ability to "reproduce a mental process with precision." Sometimes he even carries it to the point of expressionism in phrases like "from the dusty garden arose the useless cry of a bird"; but oftener it is fantastic accuracy — or accurate fantasy — that overpowers us, as in this description of the Emperor of China's vast palace: "It seemed impossible that the earth should be anything other than gardens, watercourses, architectural and other forms of splendor. Each hundred steps a tower cut the air; to the eye their color was identical, though the first one was yellow and the last scarlet, so delicate were the gradations and so long the series."

In fact, the danger with Borges is that the reader may overlook texture and content for the implacable outline that contains them. In her book "Borges, the Labyrinth Maker," Ana María Barrenechea calls him "an admirable writer pledged to destroy reality and convert Man into a shadow." But she immediately adds, "Nonetheless, a purely negative and false idea of Borges's work should not result . . . Borges's creativity is characterized by the richness and complexity of his art." Nor are the catalogues of minutiae and trivial events which he translates into desolate visions of eternity as discouraging as their infiniteness at first suggests.

True, Funes the Memorious can remember everything he has ever experienced, and the sum total of these memories is chaos. "He remembered the shapes of the clouds in the south at dawn on the 30th of April 1882, and he could compare them in his recollection with the marbled grain in the design of a leather-bound book which he had seen only once, and with the lines in the spray which an oar raised in the Río Negro on the eve of the battle of the Quebracho"; at the same time he is "almost incapable of general, platonic ideas. It was not only difficult for him to understand that the generic term *dog* embraced so many unlike specimens of differing sizes and different forms; he was disturbed by the fact that a dog at three-fourteen (seen in profile) should have the same name as the dog at three-fifteen (seen from the front)."

Similarly, the narrator in "The Aleph" has a sudden vision of everything in the universe: "I saw the delicate bone structure of a hand; I saw the survivors of a battle sending out post cards. . . . I saw the oblique shadow of some ferns on the floor of a hot-house; I saw tigers, emboli, bison, ground swells and armies; I saw all the ants in the world." It is a numbing message, like that intoned in E. M. Forster's Malabar Caves: "Everything exists, nothing has value"; but with the slight difference that everything has value—an equal value, but a value nevertheless. This is implied by the colossal scale and also the intricacy which have gone into the staging of the fraudulent tableau of eternity. And though it is true, as Borges wrote in "The Immortal," that we know nothing of the gods "except that they do not resemble man," someone evidently cares enough to clothe the dream with an air of truth. Borges is at times close to affirming this, as when he says in "The Wall and the Books," "Music, states of happiness, mythology, faces scored by time, certain twilights, certain places, all want to tell us something, or told us something we should not have missed, or are about to tell us something. This imminence of a revelation that does not take place is, perhaps, the esthetic fact."

One always ends up comparing Borges to Kafka, and it is true that each is obsessed by the same enigma: the fabulous complexity of the universe confronting man's ridiculously inadequate attempts at unraveling it. Occasionally both writers use the same symbols to project this enigma: bureaucracy, the Great Wall of China, Don Quixote and Sancho Panza. Each adds a reluctant codicil: Kafka's is the lighted window that is Joseph K.'s, last vision before his execution; Borges's is the "imminence of a revelation that does not take place." But Ana María Barrenechea warns us: "Kafka's anguish derives from being excluded from participation in an order in which he exists; Borges is indifferent because he does not believe in that order." And belief or its opposite determines a different kind of art in both cases: in Kafka's an "open form," self-propelling, open to modification, not unlike Charles Olson's "projective verse"; in Borges a closed one, self-contained, pre-determined, the work of a metaphysical Fabergé.

A similar opposition underlies much of the art of our time, and it determines opposite responses: we read Kafka from something like necessity; we read Borges for enjoyment, our own indifference taking pleasure in the frightful but robust spectacle of a disinherited cosmos. Each, like the northern and southern hemispheres of Borges's Tlön, is a different aspect of the same aggressive, enigmatic planet.

The Politics of Self-Parody   Richard Poirier*

From Chaucer's "Sir Thopas" through Max Beerbohm's "The Mote in the Middle Distance" on to Hemingway's *The Torrents of Spring* and Henry Reed's Eliotic "Chard Whitlow," parody constitutes criticism of the truest, often the best kind. For one thing, it demands the closest possible intimacy with the resources of a given style; for another, it treats writing as a performance, rather than as a codification of significances. Up to now, excepting a sport like Laurence Sterne, parody has been almost entirely other-directed—by one writer against another or at the literary modes of a particular period. Even self-parody has traditionally been other-directed, as in Coleridge's "On a Ruined Cottage in a Romantic Country" or Swinburne's "Nephelidia," a way of externalizing and disowning the mannerisms of earlier work.

As against these recognized forms of parody, I want to define a newly developed one: a literature of self-parody that makes fun of itself *as it goes along*. It proposes not the rewards so much as the limits of its own procedures; it shapes itself around its own dissolvents; it calls into question not any particular literary structure so much as the enterprise, the activity itself of creating any literary form, of empowering an idea with a style. The literature of self-parody continues, then, the critical function that parody has always assumed, but with a difference. While parody has traditionally been anxious to suggest that life or history or reality has made certain literary styles outmoded, the literature of self-parody, quite unsure of the relevance of such standards, makes fun of the effort even to verify them by the act of writing.

Thus the difference between older kinds of parody and this newer one is a measure of the difference between concepts of criticism. Very roughly, the distinction is between a (to me) discredited but still dominant criticism that trusts in *a priori* standards of life, reality, and history, and a criticism

*First published in *Partisan Review*, no. 3 (1968). Reprinted in *The Performing Self* (New York: Oxford University Press, 1971). Reprinted here by permission of the author.

that finds only provisional support in these terms. So far as I am concerned, the terms point to nothing authoritative. They refer instead to constructs as tentative as the fictions they are supposed to stabilize. But especially in America, and nearly without exception among Americanists, the great majority of critics still operate as if *articulated* forms of life or reality or history were uncontaminated by human contrivance and could thus be a measure for such obvious contrivances as literature and literary criticism.

In loyal opposition while fancying itself truly at odds, a much smaller group would claim that literature creates a reality of its own, and we must therefore avoid what Richard Gilman considers "a confusion of realms." Literature is itself an act of history, so this argument runs, and not a reflection of the history put together by historians; it can give us while we read a consciousness of life just as "real" as any accredited to daily living. But this admirable minority is still bound by the essential suppositions of the majority: it, too, depends on a radical differentiation between literary shapings of life, reality and history, and analogous shapings in presumably non-fictional sources like news-reporting (preferably on-the-spot), documents (especially hidden ones), sociological and anthropological researches (constituting to my mind the most interesting novels and stories now being written), and of course history (meaning history books, the best of which are usually written by people who share Martin Duberman's skepticism about the "limitations of being an historian.)"

Literature, in which I'd include literary criticism and, in another argument, nearly everything in print, is in a realistic and rationalistic trap. And it will escape only when more than a very few endorse a position which to many will seem obstinately inhuman, namely, that while all expressed forms of life, reality, and history have a status different from fiction as it exists in novels, poems, or plays, they are all fictions nonetheless and they can be measured on the same scale. To talk or to write is to fictionalize. More than that, to talk or to write about novels or poems or plays is only to re-fictionalize them. These propositions are scarcely new. They are generally accepted, however, only as part of some larger acknowledgments about language: that language is often felt to be inadequate to the pressure of something needing to get expressed, that to say anything is *not* to say something else at that moment.

What I want to urge is some less casual assurance within the area of these generally accepted limitations. Insofar as they are available for discussion life, reality, and history exist only as discourse, and no form of discourse, as Santayana insisted, can *be* what it expresses; no form of discourse can *be* life, reality, or history. Where is the Civil War and how do we know it? Where is the President and how does anyone know him? Is he a history book, an epic poem or a cartoon by David Levine? Who invents him, when and for what immediate purpose? Think of the inventions that crumbled, of the new ones that emerged at the end of

President Johnson's speech of renunciation. Earlier, in one of his 1967 press conferences, his mannerisms, though unfamiliar in their variations and in his frightening relaxations, were reported in the press to be those, at last, of the "real" Johnson, the Johnson his friends had always known and of whom the public had never had a glimpse — after nearly thirty-seven years of public exposure! And how about Richard Nixon, with what Chet Huntley, who observed him closely, calls his "overwhelming shallowness"? Where does Nixon's fictional self-creation end and the historical figure begin? Can such a distinction be made about a man who watches the movie *Patton* for the third or fourth time and then orders an invasion of Cambodia meant to destroy the Vietcong Pentagon, which he told us was there, but which has never been found?

No wonder anyone who cares about politics now finds the claims made for literature by most critics ridiculously presumptuous. Why should literature be considered the primary source of fictions, when fictions are produced at every press conference; why should novelists or dramatists be called "creative" when we have had Rusk and McNamara and Kissinger, the mothers of invention, "reporting" on the war in Vietnam?

Challenges to the fictional uniqueness of literature have come, oddly enough, from those most likely to suffer from the challenge — from the people, especially the novelists and dramatists, who create it. For some of these, the escape from the notion of a special status for literature has involved at least one kind of political stimulation: their occupational preferences for intricate fictional plots has been broadened by a Hegelian suspicion that the world itself is governed by self-generating political plots and conspiracies more intricate than any they could devise. Such is the logic of the "plotting" in Pynchon's *V.* and *The Crying of Lot 49*, as I've proposed in the previous chapter, of the invented "quests" of Wurlitzer's *Nog*, and of Mailer's *An American Dream*. Mailer's way of writing in that brilliant and almost wholly misunderstood book asks, in effect: what can I invent that the Kennedys haven't actually accomplished, what hyperboles are left to the imagination when reality is almost visibly exceeding any hyperboles? The damning reviews, notably by Philip Rahv and Elizabeth Hardwick, neither of whom can be called out of touch with what goes on in contemporary literature, testify to the persistence of neo-classical standards in most criticism of fiction, a persistence exposed by Leo Bersani's corrective essay on *An American Dream* and its reviewers.

Literature has only one responsibility — to be compelled and compelling about its own inventions. It can do this without paying strict attention to alternative inventions co-existing under the titles of history, life, reality, or politics. Indeed, there's plenty of evidence that writers who operate on the assumption that the public world they live in is also compulsively fictional are not denuded or depressed by the competition. Joyce and Nabokov derive their energies from it, and it sets in motion the creative powers of Jorge Borges, John Barth, and Iris Murdoch, among others.

Distinctions have to be made, however—nowhere in the works of the last three named, not even in the brilliant contrivances of Borges, is there a competitive response equal to the vitality of Joyce or Nabokov. Borges, Barth, and Miss Murdoch, however different from one another in many respects, share a debilitating assumption: that it is interesting, in and of itself, to make the formal properties of fiction into the subject matter of fiction. While it isn't wholly uninteresting to do so, those readers most capable of appreciating the idea are also apt to be the most impatient with any lengthy demonstrations, with the repetitive effort, page after page, to show that literature is, to take a phrase from *Finnegans Wake*, "the hoax that joke bilked."

The intellectual prowess of Borges, Barth, and Miss Murdoch is not in question. They are perhaps more intellectually attuned, and they are surely more philosophically adroit, than all but a few of the exclusively literary critics now writing in America or Europe. But admiration for their thinking about literature must very often contend with the experience of reading their novels. They all show an amused and theoretical impatience about the fact that literary conventions deteriorate with the passage of time. And yet in a curious way their desire to show the factitiousness of these conventions is accompanied by an illusion that their own works exist not in time but in space, like a painting.

A novel is not a painting, however, and the perpetrated notion of similarity has a great deal to do with some of the innocent lies we tell ourselves about what it is like to read a book. Reading is a very special activity, quite different if not more arduous than looking intensely at a painting. It is sequential but patterned activity, more like listening to music. But it is an altogether more sequestered act than listening to music, much less looking at paintings. It takes hours or days during which our interest must be propelled forward by something promised in the sounds and images we encounter. We sit in a favorite chair with a favorite light and some assurance of quiet, and we open, let us say, *Giles Goat-Boy*. Several days later we're probably no longer infatuated with repeated illustrations that literary and philosophical structures are really put-ons, that what we are doing is kind of silly.

As the previous chapter suggests, John Barth seems to me a writer of evident genius; I wrote a long and enthusiastic review of *Giles Goat-Boy* when it came out, and I'd take none of it back now. Even while writing the review, however, I was conscious of forgetting what it has been like at certain moments to read the book, what a confining, prolonged, and even exasperating experience it had sometimes been. Now and again I'd been bored and disengaged, and if I hadn't promised to review it I might not have finished it at all. To say this isn't really to disparage Barth or his achievement, surely not to anyone sufficiently honest about his own experience of "great" books. How many would ever have finished *Moby Dick*—read all of it, I mean—or *Ulysses*, not to mention *Paradise Lost* or other monsters of that kind, if it weren't for school assignments, the academic equivalent of being asked to write a review? And some of these, even-in university courses, are read only in part, especially *Paradise Lost; Finnegans Wake* is almost always merely sampled, and has been handsomely published in a shorter version, if you can believe the cynicism, by the novelist Anthony Burgess.

The university study of English and American literature, a quite recent phenomenon . . . tends to obscure many of the conventional questions about the true audience for literary works. Without the academic pressure which has forced some of the books I've mentioned and some of the most difficult modern poetry onto the shelves of near illiterates, what shape would the literature of this century have assumed? What would be considered the "important" books and what different myths would be accepted now about the "modern world"? One reads and writes within institutional pressures, within the exigencies of time and space, and therefore with something less than complete integrity. Partly because I felt that Barth wasn't at all receiving his proper due, the fairest thing, given the options and a limit of length for the review, was to report that in reading the book I'd been witness to certain acts of genius, both of invention and of philosophical playfulness, and to make altogether less of the fact that I was sometimes a rather bored witness. It is an exasperating fact, then, that it takes such a lot of time, a part of one's life, to discover in some of the most demanding of contemporary literature that its creators are as anxious to turn you off as to turn you on, that they want to show not the decisiveness but rather the triviality of literary structuring. Let's assume the triviality, but only because we then can insist all the more that fiction is something that has to be *made* worth the effort of reading it.

Life in literature is exhibited by the acts of performance that make it interesting, not by the acts of rendition that make it "real." "We must," as James puts it, "grant the artist his subject, his idea, his donnée: our criticism is applied only to what he makes of it." On performance, on the excitement of doing, on what literature creates by way of fun — that's where more of the emphasis should be. Lawrence was right — if it isn't fun don't do it. Equally right, but with different reasons, as I tried to show in *The Comic Sense of Henry James*, is the James who claims in the Preface to *The Golden Bowl*: "It all comes back to that, to my and your 'fun' — if we but allow the term its full extension; to the production of which no humblest question involved, even to that of the shade of a cadence or the position of a comma, is not richly pertinent."

If such standards do not inform academic criticism or reviews in journals where one hopes for something better, it is if possible even less evident among proponents of the "new." From the champions of "what's happening," one hears, amusingly enough, mostly irritable versions of William Dean Howells. The difference between them and Howells isn't in critical standards, but in decisions about the shapes of American reality.

Substitute the word "underground" for "smiling aspects" of American life, and Howells will seem out of touch only in his concept of reality, not in his literary criteria. And in any case, he expected that reality, as he conceived it, would become dated. He knew it would be changed by time, and he was naïve only in believing that time would change it for the better.

Maybe the best clue to what Howells was up to, and to his peculiarly modern tedium, is in his blandness about the workings of time. Knowing that its mere passage can dispel any dramatic accumulations, any gatherings of disaster, and that even the chance operations of daily living, like a good breakfast or a change in the weather, can ameliorate the anguish of romance or failure, he actually tried to make his novels duller than they potentially needed to have been. Time has indeed, up to now, given the lie to the imagination of apocalypse or endings, and in this conviction Howells is apt to seem especially, if eccentrically, a precursor of some contemporary fashions. This is hardly a reason to revive interest in most of his novels, however. He achieved what he called "the art of not arriving" — of not reaching for melodramatic and symbolic summaries — at disastrous cost to any continuing interest in most of his fashion. What he did was done out of literary convictions that are a child's version of novelistic practices like those of Iris Murdoch in *The Red and the Green:* if novels are to be like life, she tediously insists, then of course they should forswear any "false" shapings of material toward a prescribed and therefore unnecessarily fictitious finale.

Howells' parodies of literary summation, his refusal to exploit the dramatic heightening of the forces he brings into play (as in the little masterpiece *Indian Summer*, where past and present, youth and age, Italy and America are given a nearly Jamesian development), his opposition to whatever he recognized as belonging to literary romance — these restraints were all at the service of "reality" and "American life." Until the mid-eighties he couldn't see that what he called reality and American life were fictions manufactured out of his own placid and mostly uninterrupted personal success. He read his life as the history of his times. But again, was he much different, in his way of proceeding, from critics who now celebrate the fact, as did Zola in novels about the various industries and occupations, that a new book has finally "made available" some aspect of reality hitherto sequestered? The novel has been called many things, but is it at last only a procurer? Even Joyce had to wait for wide recognition until he could be properly misread, until, that is, it could be reported that he only put out the kind of thing academically trained readers had come to accept as "real." As a result, he does not even now get credit for his true and heroic achievement: as a writer who parodies, as I've suggested earlier, not only his meanings, but his methods, and does so while he enthusiastically moves into some new, wholly different kind of performance.

The risks inherent in self-parody can't be ignored, however, even in

Ulysses. It, too, is at times boring on purpose and for too long. Who can deny a tedious lack of economy in Joyce — or in Beckett or Borges, Burroughs or Barth — an overindulgence in mostly formal displays where little more is accomplished than a repetitive exposure of some blatantly obtuse formal arrangement? In *Ulysses* the so-called "Aeolus" and "Oxen of the Sun" episodes are instances, the former being an early version of Burroughs' "cut-ups." But the *longeurs* in Joyce are relieved by his complicity in momentary acts of faith: he participates in the productive illusions of Bloom and Molly and in the nostalgia of Stephen Dedalus for the possible saving grace of institutions whose impotence he is also exposing. So that while he seems more often than not to subscribe to the credo of Barth's hero in *The Floating Opera*—"Nothing is of intrinsic value"— Joyce is never as happy as Barth with the necessities of novelistically enacting it. It is an idea that can be rendered in fiction mostly by the deflations of any heroic (or Homeric) claim on the world.

In the literature of self-parody efforts to project a self of historical consequence are largely missing or the object of mockery. Plots seldom issue, as they do in earlier fiction, from the interplay and pressure of individual human actions, and can be said to exist, as in Pynchon and Heller, prior to the book. Plot, to recall some earlier remarks, becomes a self-generating, even possibly self-generated formula of myths and conspiracies whose source is as mysterious as the source of life itself, and within it characters try, often vainly, to find a role, or to find any possible human tie not implicated in the impersonality of plot. And the role of the novelist in the book is equally insecure — as if others had a prior claim to his material. Within the vastness of *V.* is there any locatable presence of Thomas Pynchon? The novelist in such instances is the distracted servant to servants, discovering that none of his material is original, none of it truly his, none of it derived from any state of "nature" or "life." Life, even before the novelist proposes to represent it, exists, it would seem, in the conditions and shapes imposed upon it by art, by the pastoral, allegorical, epic, narrative, political imaginations, all as much as by the myths and rituals that are the accompaniment of nationality and religion.

The literature of self-parody is bound by its allegiance, minute by minute, to the passage of time. Its practitioners are doing what Griffith thought of doing with his camera: of holding it on a scene so long that the scene would have to break up. Hold the camera, that is, on the noble rider until he climbs down, and after the hilarity of watching a line of men fall into an open manhole, keep your camera there until they have to crawl out, bloody, bruised and half-conscious. The passage of time distorts any shapes proposed by art, and this has by now become a major theme of literature no less than of painting and film.

Necessarily, the theme belongs to artists of a classic rather than a romantic inclination, to writers as culturally conditioned as Joyce or Eliot, as incredibly well-read as Borges, as learned as Barth, as encyclopedic as

Pynchon. They are all, to different degrees, burdened with the wastes of time, with cultural shards and rubbish. Joyce's great theme, finally, is that the mind, the conservative and responsible mind, can hold its contents only by acts of perverse and mechanical will. In *Ulysses* his own acts of historical and literary recollection are exposed to the modifications that are the inescapable result of their being inserted into the passage of time, here and now. It is as if Joyce wanted to show why it is no longer possible to be a poet in the sense proposed by Kierkegaard. It is no longer possible, that is, to be a happy genius of recollection, striving day and night "against the cunning of oblivion which would trick him," he says in *Fear and Trembling*, "out of his hero."

In assessing the grandeur of Joyce's achievement as against that of any writer since, one has to consider the scale of the objects which provoked his memory and its sufferings. The kind of object that excites memory need make no difference to the intensity of memory: in that respect the Catholic Church is no more imposing than a fishing trip to the Big Two-Hearted River. But the nature of the object can make a considerable difference to the texture of prose. Nostalgia for the Church can easily pass beyond personal deprivations to incorporate, by images and styles derived from it, the supposed agony of a culture facing the horrors of institutional collapse. The failure of endurance in institutions has a literary analogue in those works of literature which expose their own shapings to the dilapidating effects of duration. Nostalgia for lost or desiderated orders that in the past let a writer participate in a cultural or social complex—such nostalgia gives enormously richer pathos to the self-parody of Joyce or Nabokov or Borges than it does to Barth or Iris Murdoch. (Pynchon and sometimes Barthelme seem to me to succeed in making such orders out of the cults of young people of the sixties, a remarkable thing to have done. They are able to show, with pathos and wit, how a favorite bar, a prospect of Los Angeles, a current fashion can now have, for a time, the resonance of cultural tradition.)

The limited durability of any sense-making structures bedevils the careers of Joyce's characters, but it is felt with equal acuteness by Joyce himself, as he progresses through any given unit of his work. The drama of *Ulysses* is only incidentally that of Stephen, Bloom, and Molly; more poignantly it is the drama of Joyce himself making the book. The fact that its many and various techniques are made to appear forced, superimposed, and mechanical, that each in turn is dispensed with so that another might be tried—this fact in itself constitutes the drama of the novel. Joyce enacts by his performance in the book the problem which is felt with a sentimental enervation by Stephen: the problem of being unable to build, as it's phrased in *A Portrait* ". . . breakwaters of order and elegance against the sordid tide of life." It is a mistake, I think, to assume that the last section, Molly Bloom's soliloquy, is meant either to represent the disorganized flow of that life or that it constitutes some sort of Joycean affirmation.

Molly is merely saying "yes" to whatever has happened to her. Because of the increasingly tight organizational schemes of the immediately preceding sections, this last one does seem free, at least of punctuational barriers, to the flow of life independent of time. But like all other sections of the book, it takes form from a compulsive feeling about the ravages of time, a compulsive recollection.

Time in Molly's soliloquy has eroded not the great schemas of western civilization or even the lesser ones of the modern city. It has instead begun to lay waste the body of a very human woman in the early middle age of her life. Molly's self-consciousness about sex should be thought of no differently from Joyce's self-consciousness about the institutions that appeal to his imagination. In both cases, recollection has become the subject of nostalgic jokes, of longing chastened by a nervous confidence in the salvation afforded by some present or anticipated performance. There are analogues in Bloom thinking of Rudy and being pacified by his saving of Stephen at the end of the Circe episode, in Stephen thinking about the Church he has disowned and living with unacceptable substitutes for it — the blasphemies and medical logic of Buck, and myths of Pateresque art — and in Joyce making parodies now of one structural organization, now of another, and discovering in the process that he exults in and must parody his own fiction-making powers.

Creation follows on the discovery of waste. Fictions with the semblance and stimulus of reality, like God, become exposed by the pressure of time as no more than feeble fictions. They are strong enough only to promote nostalgia for the power they once exerted and excited, and to produce, in reaction against waste and loss, the desire to create new fictions, the excuse for new performances, new assertions of life. Joyce initiates a tradition of self-parody now conspiciously at work in literature. But he does far more than that. He simultaneously passes beyond it into something which writers of the present and future have still to emulate. He is not at all satisfied merely with demonstrating how any effort at the creation of shapes is an exercise in factitiousness. Instead, he is elated and spurred by this discovery; he responds not only by the contemplation of futility or with ironies about human invention and its waste, but with wonder at the human power to create and then to create again under the acknowledged aegis of death.

A roughly similar interaction between expiring and evolving fictions of reality is at the center of Nabokov's novelistic and autobiographical writings. Yet it is a mistake to say, as most commentators have, that he "believes" in aesthetic form: he would in the first place have had to construe a reality for which aesthetic form is the proposed substitute. And having dispensed with the idea that any articulated reality can escape the taint of fiction, why then turn to fictions for reality? Instead of doing so, Nabokov, like Joyce, parodies the very activities in which they both persist. By no accident, a hero of one is a would-be artist, while many of

Nabokov's heroes are writers, some of whom, like Humbert Humbert in *Lolita*, actually record for us an autobiography which they now recognize to have been a fiction. Reality, Nabokov once said, is "an infinite succession of levels, levels of perception, false bottoms and hence unquenchable, unattainable." Like Joyce, he directly parodies traditional forms such as melodrama, critical analysis in *Pale Fire*, the mystery story in *Laughter in the Dark*, the definitive biography in *The Real Life of Sebastian Knight* — and all of these parodies are intended to expose the deadness of characters who express themselves in obedience to some literary mode, who follow what Nabokov calls an "adopted method."

But Nabokov does not write parody merely to show that "an adopted method" is more remote from reality than is some method devised by him or by his characters. His other-directed parody merely clears the ground and establishes some of the criteria for a parody of the creativity being exercised in his own works. The parody in *The Real Life of Sebastian Knight* or *Lolita* or *Pale Fire* is directed at his authorial as much as at his characters' efforts to make others believe in the reality of schemes, plots, games, deceptions. While Nabokov's parody is of an extraordinarily compassionate kind, resisting all but the most delicate translation into interpretive language, nearly all of his interpreters continue to insist on irrelevant distinctions between art and life, fiction and reality. Humbert is not an example of a man victimized by mistaking art for reality or for living in a relationship that violates the limitations of time and physical nature. These things may be said, of course, and they are true, just as it is true that King Lear had a bad temper. It is possible to be right and vapid, and such a way of being right about Humbert thwarts precisely those responses of fascination, affection, bewilderment, and awe that Humbert and Nabokov call for.

To put it another way, we are faced in *Lolita* with a performed "thing," existing in spite of the realities and moralities anyone can propose against it. That's true for the book as much as for the career of Humbert. Performance creates more life and reality than do any of the fictions opposed to it either by readers, as against Nabokov, by other characters, like Quilty, as against Humbert, or by America, to whose fictions the book gives a guided transcontinental tour. When it comes to living there is nothing in Nabokov other than games and fictions to live by; when it comes to dying or to the passage of time, then all fictions are equally good and equally useless. Nabokov is quite capable of proposing, as Borges more assertively does, that he has dreamed even himself into existence and that, biggest joke of all, he comes into existence, for himself and for us, only by expressing himself in fiction.

Borges pushes this parody of creation to its furthest limits. Altogether obliterating any distinction between fiction and the analysis of it, he unabashedly makes into his subject what I've suggested is always implicit in the literature of self-parody: that it is necessarily a species of critical analysis. Instead of writing novels, he pretends that they already exist. He therefore offers only résumé and commentary. Sometimes confining himself to specific books, as in his essay on "The Approach to Al-Mu'tasim" (a novel ascribed to a Bombay lawyer named Mir Bahadur Ali), he can also invent whole canons by fictitious authors, as in "An Examination of the Work of Herbert Quain," which begins with some wonderfully accurate parody of Leavisite literary invective. And the parody of literary creation extends even to books that do exist, as in "Pierre Menard, Author of Don Quixote." Parody of creation cannot go further, except for blank pages, than the pretension that a work of creation does exist when it doesn't or the claim that a classic belongs to anyone who cares later to imagine that he wrote it. One of his most ambitious pieces, "Tlön, Uqbar, Orbis Tertius," is written in the manner of a geographic history, and not content with being a literary parody of that genre, manufactures for the occasion a wholly non-existent planet with "its architectures and quarrels, with the terror of its mythologies and the uproar of its languages, its emperors and seas, its minerals and birds and fish, its algebra and fire, its theological and metaphysical controversies." This invention of a new world is a little like Swift, closer to Kafka, and a preparation for Pynchon's Tristero system in *The Crying of Lot 49* and for the West Campus of Barth's *Giles Goat-Boy.*

Like these invented worlds and systems, the Tlön of Borges' story is apparently the work of a mysterious group of astronomers, biologists, engineers, metaphysicians, poets, chemists, mathematicians, moralists, painters and geometricians, all under the supervision of "an unknown genius." When a reporter from the Nashville, Tennessee *American* chances upon the forty-volume *First Encyclopedia of Tlön* in a Memphis library, where it was probably planted by an agent of the cabal.

> The international press infinitely proclaimed the "find." Manuals, anthologies, summaries, literal versions, authorized re-editions and pirated editions of the Greatest Work of Man flooded and still flood the earth. Almost immediately, reality yielded on more than one account. The truth is that it longed to yield. Ten years ago any symmetry with a semblance of order — dialectical materialism, anti-Semitism, Nazism — was sufficient to entrance the minds of men. How could one do other than submit to Tlön, to the minute and vast evidence of an orderly planet? It is useless to answer that reality is also orderly. Perhaps it is but in accordance with divine laws — I translate: inhuman laws — which we never quite grasp. Tlön is surely a labyrinth, but it is a labyrinth devised by men, a labyrinth destined to be deciphered by men.

The joke, if it might be called one, is that any inventiveness thorough enough, any inventiveness that can be made into a "strict, systematic plan" can take over the world. And why? Because the existent reality by which the world is governed is itself only an alternate invention. One point of the joke is that if invention is probably endless, forever displacing itself, if the most solid-seeming contrivance is merely contingent, then literature, Borges' own writing and especially this piece of writing, is one of the expendable forms of fiction-making. Its great and unique value is that it can elucidate its own expendability, as more pompous forms of fiction-making, especially in the political realm, cannot.

In fact, literature is only incidentally the object of Borges' parody, as we see even more plainly in the text which Michel Foucault says inspired his *Les Mots et les choses*. In this text Borges quotes "a certain Chinese encyclopedia" where it is written that " 'Animals are divided into a) belonging to the Emperor, b) embalmed, c) tamed, d) suckling pigs, e) sirens, f) fabulous, g) dogs at liberty, h) included in the present classification, i) which act like madmen, j) innumerable, k) drawn with a very fine camel's hair brush, l) et cetera, m) which have just broken jugs, n) which from afar look like flies.' "

What fascinates Foucault in this passage is that the exotic charm of another system of thought can so far expose the limitations of our own. But I think Borges is being more foxy than that: he won't allow *any* element of this or of any of his texts, not even the inferred standards behind his verbal parodies, to become stabilized or authoritative. Borges himself cannot be located in most of his writing and we're instead engaged by relatively anonymous narrators. These, while instrumental to Borges' parody, are also its object, much as is Joyce's nameless narrator within the complex of parodies in the Cyclops episode of *Ulysses*. Self-enclosed and remotely special in their interests, Borges' narrators are concerned with essentially cabalistic facts and systems of very questionable derivation. Everything in his texts is, in the literal sense of the word, eccentric: he is a writer with no center, playing off, one against the other, all those elements in his work which aspire to centrality. Thus, while the division of animals in "a certain Chinese encyclopedia" does indeed make currently accepted divisions seem tiresomely arbitrary, the effect of its utterly zany yet precise enumeration is momentarily to collapse our faith in taxonomy altogether, to free us from assumptions that govern the making of classifications, including those of an encyclopedia of no verifiable existence. Self-parody in Borges, as in Joyce and Nabokov, goes beyond the mere questioning of the validity of any given invention by proposing the unimpeded opportunity for making new ones.

Performance creates life in literature in the sense that it is itself the act and evidence of life. It is a way of being present, in every sense of that word. And yet, Borges is for my taste too little concerned with the glory of the human presence within the wastes of time, with human agencies of invention, and he is too exclusively amused by the careers of competing systems, the failed potencies of techniques and structures. We remember the point of his texts, especially since it is so often the same point, but he gives us few people to remember or care about. Our greatest invention so

far remains ourselves, what we call human beings, and enough inventing
of that phenomenon still goes on to make the destiny of persons altogether
more compelling in literature than the destiny of systems or of literary
modes. Nothing we have created, in politics or literature, is necessary —
that is what humanly matters, by way of liberation, in the writings of self-
parody.

Imaginary Borges and His Books   William H. Gass*

Among Paul Valéry's jottings, André Maurois observes the following:
"Idea for a frightening story: it is discovered that the only remedy for
cancer is living human flesh. Consequences."

One humid Sunday afternoon during the summer of 1969, in a slither
of magazines on a library table, I light like a weary fly upon this, reported
by Pierre Schneider: "One of Jean-Paul Riopelle's stories is about a village
librarian who was too poor to buy new books; to complete his library he
would, whenever he came across a favorable review in a learned journal,
write the book himself, on the basis of its title."

Both of these stories are by Borges; we recognize the author at once;
and their conjunction here is by Borges, too: a diverse collection of names
and sources, crossing like ignorant roads: Valéry, Maurois, Riopelle,
Schneider — who could have foreseen this meeting of names in *The New
York Review*?

Shaken out of sleep on a swift train at night we may unblind our
compartment window to discover a dim sign making some strange
allegation; and you, reader, may unfist this paper any moment and pick
up a book on raising herbs instead, a travel folder, letter from a lover,
novel by Colette; the eye, mind, memory which encounters them as vague
about the distance traversed as any passenger, and hardly startled anymore
by the abrupt change in climate or terrain you've undergone.[1] How calm
we are about it; we pass from a kiss to a verb and never tremble; and
having performed that bound, we frolic or we moon among our symbols,
those we've assigned to Henry Adams or those we say are by Heraclitus, as
if there were nothing to it. Like the hours we spent mastering speech, we
forget everything; nor do our logicians, our philosophers of language,
though they may coax us like cats do their fish, very often restore what we
once might have had — a sense of wonder at the mental country we
inhabit, lost till we wander lost into Borges, a man born as if between
syllables in Argentina where even he for many years believed he had been
raised in a suburb of Buenos Aires, a suburb of adventurous streets and

*First published in the *New York Review of Books*, 20 November 1969. Reprinted in
Fiction and the Figures of Life (New York: Knopf, 1970). Reprinted here by permission
of the author.

visible sunsets, when what was certain was that he was raised in a garden, behind a wrought-iron gate, and in a limitless library of English books.[2]

Just as Carriego, from the moment he recognized himself as a poet, became the author of verses which only later he was permitted to invent, Borges thought of himself as a writer before he ever composed a volume. A nearsighted child, he lived where he could see—in books and illustrations (Borges says "short-sighed," which will not do); he read English authors, read and read; in clumsy English wrote about the Golden Fleece and Hercules (and inevitably, the Labyrinth), publishing, by nine, a translation of *The Happy Prince* which a local teacher adopted as a text under the impression it was the father's doing, not the son's. In Switzerland, where his family settled for a time, he completed his secondary education, becoming more and more multitongued (acquiring German), yet seeing no better, reading on. He then traveled extensively to Spain, as if to meet other authors, further books, to enlarge the literary landscape he was already living in—deepening, one imagines daily, his acquaintance with the conceptual country he would eventually devote his life to. Back in Argentina, he issued his first book of poems. He was twenty. They sang of Buenos Aires and its streets, but the few lines [Ronald]Christ quotes gives the future away:

> Perhaps that unique hour
> increased the prestige of the street,
> giving it privileges of tenderness,
> making it as real as legend or verse.

Thus he was very soon to pass, as he says himself, from "the mythologies of the suburbs to the games with time and infinity" which finally made him infamous—made him that imaginary being, the Borges of his books.

Becoming Borges, Borges becomes a librarian, first a minor municipal one like our poor French village author, and then later, with the fall of Perón, after having been removed for political reasons from that lesser post, the director of the National Library itself.

Idea for a frightening story: the books written by the unknown provincial librarian ultimately replace their originals, which are declared to be frauds. Consequences.

Inside the library, inside the books, within their words: the world. Even if we feel it no longer, we can remember from our childhood the intenser reality which opened toward us when like a casket lid a cover rose and we were kings on clipper ships, cabin boys on camel back, Columbuses crossing swimming holes to sack the Alps and set free Lilliput, her golden hair climbing like a knight up the wall of some crimson battle tent . . . things, men, and moments more than merely lived but added to ourselves like the flesh of a fruit. In Borges' case, for instance, these included the lamp of Aladdin, the traitor invented by H. G. Wells who abandoned his friend to the moonmen, and a scene which I shall never forget either, Blind Pew tapping toward the horses which will run him down. Señor Borges confides to Burgin's tape that "I think of reading a book as no less an experience than traveling or falling in love. I think that reading Berkeley or Shaw or Emerson, those are quite as real experiences to me as seeing London. . . . Many people are apt to think of real life on the one side, that means toothache, headache, traveling and so on, and then on the other side, you have imaginary life and fancy and that means the arts. But I don't think that distinction holds water. I think that everything is a part of life."

Emerson? Many of Borges' other enthusiasms are equally dismaying, like the Russians' for Jack London, or the symbolist poets' for Poe; on the whole they tend to be directed toward obscure or marginal figures, to stand for somewhat cranky, wayward, even decadent choices: works at once immature or exotic, thin though mannered, clever rather than profound, neat instead of daring, too often the products of learning, fancy, and contrivance to make us comfortable; they exhibit a taste that is still in its teens, one becalmed in backwater, and a mind that is seriously intrigued by certain dubious or jejune forms, forms which have to be overcome, not simply exploited: fantastic tales and wild romances, science fiction, detective stories, and other similar modes which, with a terrible theological energy and zeal, impose upon implausible premises a rigorous gamelike reasoning; thus for this minutely careful essayist and poet it's not Aristotle, but Zeno, it's not Kant, but Schopenhauer; it's not even Hobbes, but Berkeley, not Mill or Bradley, but — may philosophy forgive him — Spencer; it's Dunne, Beckford, Blöy, the Cabbalists; it's Stevenson, Chesterton, Kipling, Wells and William Morris, Browne and De Quincey Borges turns and returns to, while admitting no such similar debt to James, Melville, Joyce, and so on, about whom, indeed, in these *Conversations*, he passes a few mildly unflattering remarks.[3]

Yet in the country of the word, Borges is well traveled, and has some of the habits of a seasoned, if not jaded, journeyer. What? see Mont Saint Michel again? that tourist trap? far better to sip a local wine in a small café, watch a vineyard comb its hillside. There are a thousand overlooked delights in every language, similarities and parallels to be remarked, and even the mightiest monuments have their neglected beauties, their unexplored crannies; then, too, it has been frequently observed that our childhood haunts, though possibly less spectacular, less perfect, than other, better advertised, places, can be the source of a fuller pleasure for us because our familiarity with them is deep and early and complete, because the place is ours; while for other regions we simply have a strange affinity — they do not threaten, like Dante or the Alps, to overwhelm us — and we somehow find our interests, our designs, reflected in them. Or is it we who function as the silvered glass? Idea for a frightening story.

Thus, reading Borges, we must think of literature as a landscape, present all at once like space, and we must remember that literary events,

unlike ordinary ones—drinking our coffee or shooting our chancellor—
repeat themselves, although with variations, in every mind the text fills.
Books don't plop into time like stones in a pond, rippling the surface for a
while with steadily diminishing waves. There is only one Paris, we
suppose, and one Flaubert, one *Madame Bovary*, but the novel has more
than a million occurrences, often in different languages, too. Flaubert
may have ridden a whore with his hat on, as has been reported, but such
high jinks soon spend their effects (so, comparatively, does the murder of
any Caesar, although its initial capital is greater), whereas one sentence,
divinely composed, goes on and on like the biblical proverbs, the couplet
of Pope, or the witticisms of Wilde.

We may indeed suspect that the real power of historical events lies in
their descriptions; only by virtue of their passage into language can they
continue to occur, and once recorded (even if no more than as gossip), they
become peculiarly atemporal, residing in that shelved-up present which
passes for time in a library, and subject to a special kind of choice, since I
can choose now to read about the war on the Peloponnesus or the invasion
of Normandy; change my climate more easily than my clothes; rearrange
the map; while on one day I may have traveled through Jonson to reach
Goldsmith, they are not villages, and can be easily switched, so that on the
next I may arrive directly from De Quincey, Goethe, or Thomas Aquinas.
New locations are constantly being created, like new islands rising from
the sea, yet when I land, I find them never so new as all that, and having
appeared, it is as if they had always been.[4]

It is a suggestion, I think, of Schopenhauer[5] (to whom Borges turns as
often as he does to Berkeley), that what we remember of our own past
depends very largely on what of it we've put our tongue to telling and
retelling. It's our words, roughly, we remember; oblivion claims the rest—
forgetfulness. Historians make more history than the men they write
about, and because we render our experience in universals, experience
becomes repetitious (for if events do not repeat, accounts do), and time
doubles back in confusion like a hound which has lost the scent.

Troy, many times, was buried in its own body, one city standing on
the shoulders of another, and students of linguistic geography have
observed a similar phenomenon. Not only are there many accounts, both
factual and fictional, of Napoleon's invasion of Russia (so that the event
becomes multiplied in the libraries), there are, of course, commentaries
and critiques of these, and then again examinations of those, which lead,
in turn, to reflections upon them, and so on, until it sometimes happens
that the originals are quite buried, overcome (idea for a frightening story),
and though there may be a definite logical distance between each level,
there is no other; they sit side by side on our shelves. We may read the
critics first, or exclusively; and is it not, in fact, true that our knowledge of
most books is at least second hand, as our knowledge of nearly everything
else is?

Borges knows of the treacheries of our histories (treachery is one of his principal subjects)[6] — they are filled with toothache — and in his little essay called "The Modesty of History" suggests that most of its really vital dates are secret — for instance, the introduction, by Aeschylus, of the second actor.[7] Still, this is but one more example of how, by practicing a resolute forgetfulness, we select, we construct, we compose our pasts, and hence make fictional characters of ourselves, as it seems we must to remain sane (Funes the Memorious remembers everything, while the Borges who receives a zahir in his drink change following a funeral one day finds the scarred coin literally unforgettable; both suffer).

It isn't always easy to distinguish *ficciones* from *inquisiciones*, even for Borges (of the famous Pierre Menard, he says: ". . . it's not wholly a story . . . it's a kind of essay . . ."), though the latter are perhaps more unfeignedly interrogations. It is his habit to infect these brief, playful, devious, solemn, *outré* notes, which, like his fictions, are often accounts of treacheries of one sort or other, with small treacheries of his own, treasons against language and its logic, betrayals of all those distinctions between fact and fancy, real life and dreaming, memory and imagination, myth and history, word and thing, fiction and essay, which we're so fond of, and find so necessary, even though keeping them straight is a perpetual difficulty.

If, as Wittgenstein thought, "philosophy is a battle against the bewitchment of our intelligence by means of language," then Borges' prose, at least, performs a precisely similar function, for there is scarcely a story which is not built upon a sophistry, a sophistry so fanatically embraced, so pedantically developed, so soberly defended, it becomes the principal truth in the world his parables create (puzzles, paradoxes, equivocations, and obscure and idle symmetries which appear as menacing laws); and we are compelled to wonder again whether we are awake or asleep, whether we are a dreamer or ourselves a dream, whether art imitates nature or nature mirrors art instead; once more we are required to consider whether things exist only while they are being perceived, whether change can occur, whether time is linear and straight or manifold and curved, whether history repeats, whether space is a place of simple locations, whether words aren't more real than their referents — whether letters and syllables aren't magical and full of cabbalistic contents — whether it is universals or particulars which fundamentally exist, whether destiny isn't in the driver's seat, what the determinate, orderly consequences of pure chance come to, whether we are the serious playthings of the gods or the amusing commercial enterprises of the devil.

It is not the subject of these compulsions, however, but the manner in which they are produced that matters, and makes Borges an ally of Wittgenstein. It is not hard to feel that Borges' creatures are mostly mad. This is, in many ways, a comforting conclusion. The causes, on the other hand, remain disturbing; they resemble far too literally those worlds theologians and metaphysicians have already made for us and in which we have so often found ourselves netted and wriggling. When Schopenhauer argues that the body in all its aspects is a manifestation of the will, he is composing poetry; he is giving us an idea for a frightening story, one which derives its plausibility from facts we are quite unpoetically aware of (teeth are for biting), but the suggestion that the will grew its body as a man might make some tool to do his bidding is a fiction which, if we responded to the cry for consequences implicit in it, would advertise its absurdity with the mad metaphysical fantasy which would grow from its trunk like a second head.

Thus the effect of Borges' work is suspicion and skepticism. Clarity, scholarship, and reason: they are all here, yet each is employed to enlarge upon a muddle without disturbing it, to canonize a confusion. Ideas become plots (how beautifully ambiguous, for Borges, that word is), whereupon those knotty tangles the philosopher has been so patiently picking at can be happily reseen as triumphs of esthetic design.[8] In the right sun suspicion can fall far enough to shadow every ideology; the political schemes of men can seem no more than myths through which they move like imaginary creatures, like fabulous animals in landscapes of pure wish; the metaphors upon which they ride toward utopia now are seldom seen (such is the price one pays for an ignorance of history) to be the same overfat or scrawny nags the old political romancers, puffing, rode at windmills in their time, and always futilely. "The illusions of patriotism are limitless." Hitler tries to turn the world into a book; he suffered from unreality, Borges claims, and collaborated in his own destruction. Under the right sun one may observe little that is novel. The world of words spins merrily around, the same painted horses rising and falling to the same tunes, and our guide delights in pointing out each reappearance. We have seen this before: in Persepolis, and also in Peking . . . in Pascal, in Plato, in Parmenides. The tone, throughout, is that of a skeptical conservative (this shows up very clearly, too, in his conversations with Burgin). Least government is best, and all are bad. They rest on myth. "Perhaps universal history is the history of a few metaphors." And we have had them all already, had them all.

As a young poet Borges pledged himself to Ultraism, a Spanish literary movement resembling Imagism in many ways, whose principles he carried back to Argentina in his luggage. It demanded condensation, the suppression of ornament, modifiers, all terms of transition; it opposed exhortation and vagueness — flourish; it praised impersonality, and regarded poetry as made of metaphors in close, suggestive combinations. It was primarily a poetry of *mention*, as Borges' prose is now, and Christ has no difficulty in showing how these early slogans, like the literary enthusiasms of his childhood, continue to affect the later work. Any metaphor which is taken with literal seriousness requires us to imagine a world in which it can be true; it contains or suggests a metaphorical principle that in turn gives form to a fable. And when the *whole* is an image, local images can be removed.

Borges makes much of the independence of the new worlds implied by his fiction; they are "contiguous realities"; the poet annexes new provinces to Being; but they remain mirror worlds for all that; it is our own world, *misthought*, reflected there. And soon we find in Wittgenstein, himself, this ancient idea for a frightening story: "Logic is not a body of doctrine, but a mirror-image of the world."

Mirrors are abominable. A photographer points her camera at Borges like a revolver. In his childhood he feared mirrors—mahogany—being repeated . . . and thus becoming increasingly imaginary? In the beautiful bestiary (*The Book of Imaginary Beings*) which has just been translated for us,[9] it is suggested that one day the imprisoned creatures in our looking glasses will cease to imitate us; fish will stir in the panes as though in clear water; and "we will hear from the depths of mirrors the clatter of weapons." How many times, already, have we been overcome by imaginary beings?

This bouquet which Borges has gathered in his travels for us consists largely of rather harmless animals from stories, myths, and legends, alphabetically arranged here in the texts which first reported them or in descriptions charmingly rebuilt by Borges. Most of these beasts are mechanically made—insufficiently imaginary to be real, insufficiently original to be wonderful or menacing. There are the jumbles, created by collage: centaurs, griffins, hydras, and so on; the mathematicals, fashioned by multiplication or division: one-eyed, half-mouthed monsters or those who are many-headed, sixteen-toed, and triple-tongued; there are those of inflated or deflated size: elves, dwarfs, brownies, leviathans, and fastitocalon; and finally those who have no special shape of their own—the proteans—and who counterfeit the forms of others. A few, more interesting, are made of metal, and one, my favorites, the A Bao A Qu, is almost wholly metaphysical, and very Borges.

There's no longer a world left for these creatures to inhabit—even our own world has expelled them—so that they seem like pieces from a game we've forgotten how to play. They are objects now of curiosity or amusement, and even the prospect of one's being alive and abroad, like the Loch Ness serpent or abominable snowman (neither of whom is registered here), does not deeply stir us. Borges' invented library of Babel is a far more compelling monster, with its mirrored hallways and hexagonal galleries, its closets where one may sleep standing up, its soaring and spiral stairways. Even those lady-faced vultures the harpies cannot frighten us, and hippogriffs are tame. It is that library we live in; it is that library we dream; our confusions alter not the parts of animals anymore, they lead on our understanding toward a culmination in illusion like a slut.

And which is Borges, which his double? which is the photograph? the face perverted by a mirror? image in the polish of a writing table? There is the Borges who compiles *A Personal Anthology*,[10] and says he wishes to be remembered by it, and there is the Borges who admits to Burgin that he did not put all of his best things in it; there is the Borges who plays with the notion that all our works are products of the same universal Will so that one author impersonally authors everything (thus the labors of that provincial librarian are not vain), and the Borges whose particular mark is both idiosyncratic and indelible. The political skeptic and the fierce opponent of Perón: are they one man? Can the author of *The Aleph* admire Chesterton? Wells? Croce? Kipling? And what about those stories which snap together at the end like a cheap lock? with a gun shot? Is this impish dilettante the same man who leaves us so often uneasily amazed? Perhaps he is, as Borges wrote so wonderfully of Valéry, "A man whose admirable texts do not exhaust, or even define, his all-embracing possibilities. A man who, in a century that adores the chaotic idols of blood, earth, and passion, always preferred the lucid pleasures of thought and the secret adventures of order." Yet can this be a figure that same age salutes? Consequences.

Notes

1. Unless the changes are forcibly called to our attention. See "The Leading Edge of the Trash Phenomenon."

2. Or so he asserts in the prologue to *Evaristo Carriego*, according to Ronald J. Christ (*The Narrow Act: Borges' Art of Allusion* [New York: New York University Press, 1969]), although errors are constantly creeping in — his, Christ's, mine — errors, modifications, corruptions, which, nevertheless, may take us nearer the truth. In his little note on Carriego, does he not warn us that Carriego is a creation of Carriego? and in the parable "Borges and I" does he not say, "I am quite aware of his perverse custom of falsifying and magnifying things"? does he not award all the mischievous translations of *A Thousand and One Nights* higher marks than the pure and exact one of Enna Littmann? and in his conversations with Richard Burgin (*Conversations with Jorge Luis Borges* [New York: Holt, Rinehart & Winston, 1969]) does he not represent memory as a stack of coins, each coin a recollection of the one below it, and in each repetition a tiny distortion? Still we can imagine, over time, the distortions correcting themselves, and returning to the truth through a circle like a stroller and his dog.

3. I am of course not suggesting that Borges regards Wells, say, as a better writer than Joyce, or that he pays no heed or tribute to major figures. Christ's treatment of this problem is fair and thorough. He tells us, incidentally, that in an introductory course on English literature, Borges' own interests led him to stress the importance of William Morris. Though Borges himself appears in most ways a modest man, such preferences are nevertheless personal and somewhat vain. Just as Borges becomes important by becoming Borges, Morris becomes important by becoming Borges, too. "An author may suffer from absurd prejudices," he tells us in his fine and suggestive lecture on Hawthorne, "but it will be impossible for his work to be absurd if it is genuine, if it responds to a genuine vision." As for Spencer, it might be worth noting that this philosopher tended to think of art as a form of *play*.

4. That all our messages are in the present tense, as I have tried to suggest, is fundamental to Barthelme's method of composition. See "The Leading Edge of the Trash Phenomenon."

5. Borges' good friend and collaborator, Bioy Casares, once attributed to a heresiarch

of Uqbar the remark that both mirrors and copulation were abominable because they increased the number of men. Borges momentarily wondered, then, whether this undocumented country and its anonymous heresiarch weren't a fiction devised by Bioy's modesty to justify a statement, and perhaps it's the same here. It should be perfectly clear, in any case, that Schopenhauer has read Borges and reflects him, just as Borges reflects both Bioy and Borges, since the remark about mirrors and copulation appears more than once.

6. He published his *Universal History of Infamy* in 1935, a work which is very carefully not a universal history of infamy. See Paul de Man, "A Modern Master," *New York Review*, No. 19, 1964.

7. Professor Celerent has complained bitterly that there is scarcely a history of Western Europe which troubles itself to mention Aristotle's invention of the syllogism — one of that continent's most formative events. "Suppose," he says, "that small matter had been put off, as it was in India, to the 16th century?"

8. Borges has made this point repeatedly himself (in the Epilogue to *Other Inquisitions*, for example); yet his commentators persist in trying to pin on him beliefs which, for Borges, are merely materials. They want him more imaginary than he already is. Perhaps this accounts for the statement, written we can imagine with a smile, which Borges includes in each of the little prefaces he has written to imprimatur the books about him: in Barrenechea, in Burgin (he "has helped me to know myself"), in Christ ("Some unsuspected things, many secret links and affinities, have been revealed to me by this book"), though he does not refrain, in the latter instance, from adding: ". . . I have no message. I am neither a thinker nor a moralist, but simply a man of letters who turns his own perplexities and that respected system of perplexities we call philosophy into the forms of literature."

9. *The Book of Imaginary Beings* by Jorge Luis Borges with Margarita Guerrero, trans. by Norman Thomas di Giovanni in collaboration with the author (New York: Dutton, 1969).

10. *Personal Anthology*, ed. Anthony Kerrigan (New York: Grove, 1967).

Tigers in the Mirror   George Steiner*

Inevitably, the current world fame of Jorge Luis Borges entails a sense of private loss. As when a view long treasured — the shadow-mass of Arthur's Seat in Edinburgh seen, uniquely, from the back of numbers sixty The Pleasance, or Fifty-first Street in Manhattan angled to a bronze and racing canyon through a trick of elevation and light in my dentist's window — a collector's item of and for the inner eye, becomes a panoptic spectacle for the tourist horde. For a long time, the splendor of Borges was clandestine, signaled to the happy few, bartered in undertones and mutual recognitions. How many knew of his first work, a summary of Greek myths, written in English in Buenos Aires, the author aged seven? Or of opus two, dated 1907 and distinctly premonitory, a translation into Spanish of Oscar Wilde's *The Happy Prince*? To affirm today that "Pierre Menard, Author of the Quixote" is one of the sheer wonders of human

*First published in the *New Yorker*, 20 June 1970. Reprinted in *Extraterritorial: Papers on Literature and the Language Revolution* (New York: Atheneum, 1976). © 1971 by George Steiner. Reprinted here with the permission of Atheneum Publishers, Inc.

contrivance, that the several facets of Borges' shy genius are almost wholly gathered in that spare fable, is a platitude. But how many own the *editio princeps* of *El jardin de senderos que bifurcan* (*Sur*, Buenos Aires, 1941) in which the tale first appeared? Only ten years ago, it was a mark of arcane erudition and wink to the initiate to realize that H. Bustos Domecq was the joint pseudonym of Borges and his close collaborator, Adolfo Bioy Casares, of that the Borges who, with Delia Ingenieros, published a learned monograph on ancient Germanic and Anglo-Saxon literatures (Mexico, 1951) was indeed the Master. Such information was close-guarded, parsimoniously dispensed, often nearly impossible to come by, as were Borges' poems, stories, essays themselves, scattered, out of print, pseudonymous. I recall an early connoisseur, in the cavernous rear of a bookstore in Lisbon, showing me — this, remember, was in the early 1950's — Borges' translation of Virginia Woolf's *Orlando*, his preface to a Buenos Aires edition of Kafka's *Metamorphosis*, his key essay on the artificial language devised by Bishop John Wilkins, published in *La Nación* on February 8, 1942, and, rarest of rare items, *Dimensions of My Hope*, a collection of short essays issued in 1926 but, by Borges' own wish, not reprinted since. These slim objects were displayed to me with an air of fastidious condescension. And rightly so. I had arrived late at the secret place.

The turning point came in 1961. Together with Beckett, Borges was awarded the Formentor Prize. A year later, *Labyrinths* and *Fictions* appeared in English. Honors rained. The Italian government made Borges *Commendatore*. At the suggestion of M. Malraux, President de Gaulle conferred on his illustrious fellow writer and master of myths the title of Commander of the *Ordre des Lettres et des Arts*. The sudden lion found himself lecturing in Madrid, Paris, Geneva, London, Oxford, Edinburgh, Harvard, Texas. "At a ripe old age," muses Borges, "I began to find that many people were interested in my work all over the world. It seems strange: many of my writings have been done into English, into Swedish, into French, into Italian, into German, into Portuguese, into some of the Slav languages, into Danish. And always this comes as a great surprise to me, because I remember I published a book — that must have been way back in 1932, I think — and at the end of the year I found out that no less than thirty-seven copies had been sold!" A leanness that had its compensations: "Those people are real, I mean every one of them has a face of his own, a family, he lives in his own particular street. Why, if you sell, say, two thousand copies, it is the same thing as if you had sold nothing at all, because two thousand is too vast, I mean for the imagination to grasp . . . perhaps seventeen would have been better or even seven." Cognoscenti will spot the symbolic role of each of these numbers, and of the kabbalistic diminishing series, in Borges' fables.

Today, the secret thirty-seven have become an industry. Critical commentaries on Borges, interviews with, memoirs about, special issues of quarterlies devoted to, editions of, pullulate. Already the 520-page exegetic, biographical, and bibliographical Borges compendium issued in Paris, by *L'Herne*, in 1964, is out of date. The air is gray with theses: on "Borges and Beowulf," on "The Influence of the Western on the Narrative Pace of the Later Borges," on "Borges' Enigmatic Concern with *West Side Story*" ("I have seen it many times"), on "The Real Origins of the Words *Tlön* and *Uqbar* in Borges' Stories," on "Borges and the Zohar." There have been Borges weekends at Austin, seminars at Harvard, a large-scale symposium at the University of Oklahoma — a festivity perhaps previewed in Kafka's *Amerika*. Borges himself was present, watching the learned sanctification of his other self, or, as he calls it, *Borges y yo*. A journal of Borgesian studies is being founded. Its first issue will deal with the function of the mirror and the labyrinth in Borges' art, and with the dreamtigers that wait behind the mirror or, rather, in its silent crystal maze.

With the academic circus have come the mimes. Borges' manner is being widely aped. There are magic turns which many writers, and even undergraduates gifted with a knowing ear, can simulate: the self-deprecatory deflection of Borges' tone, the occult fantastications of literary, historical reference which pepper his narrative, the alternance of direct, bone-spare statement with sinuous evasion. The key images and heraldic markers of the Borges world have passed into literary currency. "I've grown weary of labyrinths and mirrors and of tigers and of all that sort of thing. Especially when others are using them. . . . That's the advantage of imitators. They cure one of one's literary ills. Because one thinks: there are so many people doing that sort of thing now, there's no need for one to do it any more. Now let the others do it, and good riddance." But it is not pseudo-Borges that matters.

The enigma is this: that tactics of feeling so specialized, so intricately enmeshed with a sensibility that is private in the extreme, should have so wide, so natural, an echo. Like Lewis Carroll, Borges has made of his autistic dreams discreet but exacting summons which readers the world over are responding to with a sense of recognition. Our streets and gardens, the arrowing of a lizard across the warm light, our libraries and circular staircases are beginning to look precisely as Borges dreamed them, though the sources of his vision remain irreducibly singular, hermetic, at moments almost moon-mad.

The process whereby a fantastically private picture of the world leaps beyond the wall of mirrors behind which it was created, and reaches out to change the general landscape of awareness, is manifest but exceedingly difficult to talk about (how much of the vast critical literature on Kafka is baffled verbiage). That Borges' entrance on the larger scene of the imagination was preceded by a local genius of extreme rigor and linguistic *métier* is certain. But that will not get us very far. The fact is that even lame translations communicate much of his spell. The message, set in a kabbalistic code, written, as it were, in invisible ink, thrust, with the proud casualness of deep modesty, into the most fragile of bottles, has crossed the seven seas (there are, of course, many more in the Borges atlas, but they are always multiples of seven), to reach every kind of shore. Even to those who know nothing of his masters and early companions — Lugones, Macedonio Fernandez, Evaristo Carriego — or to whom the Palermo district of Buenos Aires and the tradition of gaucho ballads are little more than names, have found access to Borges' *Fictions*. There is a sense in which the Director of the Biblioteca Nacional of Argentina is now the most original of Anglo-American writers. This extraterritoriality may be a clue.

Borges is a universalist. In part, this is a question of upbringing, of the years from 1914 to 1921, which he spent in Switzerland, Italy, Spain. And it arises from Borges' prodigious talents as a linguist. He is at home in English, French, German, Italian, Portuguese, Anglo-Saxon, and Old Norse, as well as in a Spanish that is constantly shot through with Argentine elements. Like other writers whose sight has failed, Borges moves with a cat's assurance through the sound-world of many tongues. He tells memorably of "Beginning the Study of Anglo-Saxon Grammar":

> At fifty generations' end
> (And such abysses time affords us all)
> I returned to the further shore of a great river
> That the vikings' dragons did not reach,
> To the harsh and arduous words
> That, with a mouth now turned to dust,
> I used in my Northumbrian, Mercian days
> Before I became a Haslam or a Borges. . . .
> Praised be the infinite
> Mesh of the effect and causes
> Which, before it shows me the mirror
> In which I shall see no one or I shall see
> another,
> Grants me now this contemplation pure
> Of a language of the dawn.

"Before I became a Borges." There is in Borges' penetration of different cultures a secret of literal metamorphosis. In "Deutsches Requiem," the narrator becomes, *is*, Otto Dietrich zu Linde, condemned Nazi war criminal. Vincent Moon's confession, "The Shape of the Sword," is a classic in the ample literature of the Irish troubles. Elsewhere, Borges assumes the mask of Dr. Yu Tsun, former professor of English at the *Hochschule* at Tsingtao, or of Averroes, the great Islamic commentator on Aristotle. Each quick-change brings with it its own persuasive aura, yet all are Borges. He delights in extending this sense of the unhoused, of the mysteriously conglomerate, to his own past: "I may have Jewish ancestors, but I can't tell. My mother's name is Acevedo: Acevedo may be a name for a Portuguese Jew, but again it may not. . . . The word *acevedo*, of course, means a kind of tree; the word is not especially Jewish, though many Jews are called Acevedo. I can't tell." As Borges sees it, other masters may derive their strength from a similar stance of strangeness: "I don't know why, but I always feel something Italian, something Jewish about Shakespeare, and perhaps Englishmen admire him because of that, because it's so unlike them." It is not the specific doubt or fantastication that counts. It is the central notion of the writer as a guest, as a human being whose job it is to stay vulnerable to manifold strange presences, who must keep the doors of his momentary lodging open to all winds:

> I know little — or nothing — of my own forebears;
> The Borges back in Portugal; vague folk
> That in my flesh, obscurely, still evoke
> Their customs, and their firmnesses and fears.
> As slight as if they'd never lived in the sun
> And free from any trafficking with art,
> They form an indecipherable part
> Of time, of earth, and of oblivion.

This universality and disdain of anchor is directly reflected in Borges' fabled erudition. Whether or not it is "merely put there as a kind of private joke," the fabric of bibliographical allusions, philosophic tags, literary citations, kabbalistic references, mathematical and philological acrostics which crowd Borges' stories and poems is, obviously, crucial to the way he experiences reality. A perceptive French critic has argued that in an age of deepening illiteracy, when even the educated have only a smattering of classical or theological knowledge, erudition is of itself a kind of fantasy, a surrealistic construct. Moving, with muted omniscience, from eleventh-century heretical fragments to baroque algebra and multi-tomed Victorian *oeuvres* on the fauna of the Aral Sea, Borges builds an anti-world, a perfectly coherent space in which his mind can conjure at will. The fact that a good deal of the alleged source material and mosaic of allusion is a pure fabrication — a device which Borges shares with Nabokov and for which both may be indebted to Flaubert's *Bouvard et Pécuchet* — paradoxically strengthens the impression of solidity. Pierre Menard stands before us, instantaneously substantial and implausible, through the invented catalogue of his "visible works"; in turn, each arcane item in the catalogue points to the meaning of the parable. And who would doubt the veracity of the "Three Versions of Judas" once Borges has assured us that Nils Runeberg — note the runes in the name — published *Den hemlige Frälsaren* in 1909 but did not know a book by Euclides da Cunha (*Revolt in the Backlands*, exclaims the reader) in which it is affirmed that for the "heresiarch of Canudos, Antonio Conselheiro, virtue 'was almost an impiety' "?

Unquestionably, there is humor in this polymath montage. And there is, as in Pound, a deliberate enterprise of total recall, a graphic inventory of classical and Western civilization in a time in which much of the latter is forgot or vulgarized. Borges is a curator at heart, a treasurer of unconsidered trifles, an indexer of the antique truths and waste conjectures which throng the attic of history. All this arch learning has its comical and gently histrionic sides. But a much deeper meaning as well.

Borges holds, or, rather, makes precise imaginative use of, a kabbalistic image of the world, a master metaphor of existence, which he may have become familiar with as early as 1914, in Geneva, when reading Gustav Meyrink's novel *The Golem*, and when in close contact with the scholar Maurice Abramowicz. The metaphor goes something like this: the Universe is a great Book; each material and mental phenomenon in it carries meaning. The world is an immense alphabet. Physical reality, the facts of history, whatever men have created, are, as it were, syllables of a perpetual message. We are surrounded by a limitless network of significance, whose every thread carries a pulse of being and connects, ultimately, to what Borges, in an enigmatic tale of great power, calls the Aleph. The narrator sees this inexpressible pivot of the cosmos in the dusty corner of the cellar of the house of Carlos Argentino in Garay Street on an October afternoon. It is the space of all spaces, the kabbalistic sphere whose center is everywhere and whose circumference is nowhere, it is the wheel of Ezekiel's vision but also the quiet small bird of Sufi mysticism, which, in some manner, contains all birds: "I was dizzy and I wept, for mine eyes had beheld this secret and conjectural object, whose name is usurped by men, but which no man has looked upon: the inconceivable universe."

From the point of view of the writer, "the universe, which others call the Library," has several notable features. It embraces *all* books, not only those that have already been written, but every page of every tome that will be written in the future and, which matters more, that could conceivably be written. Re-grouped, the letters of all known or lost scripts and alphabets, as they have been set down in extant volumes, can produce every imaginable human thought, every line of verse or prose paragraph to the limits of time. The Library also contains all extant languages and those languages that either have perished or are yet to come. Plainly, Borges is fascinated by the notion, so prominent in the linguistic speculations of the Kabbala and of Jacob Boehme, that a secret primal speech, an *Ur-sprache* from before Babel, underlies the multitude of human tongues. If, as blind poets can, we pass our fingers along the living edge of words—Spanish words, Russian words, Aramaic words, the syllables of a singer in Cathay—we shall feel in them the subtle beat of a great current, pulsing from a common center, the final word made up of all letters and combinations of letters in all tongues that is the name of God.

Thus, Borges' universalism is a deeply felt imaginative strategy, a maneuver to be in touch with the great winds that blow from the heart of things. When he invents fictitious titles, imaginary cross-references, folios and writers that have never existed, Borges is simply re-grouping counters of reality into the shape of other possible worlds. When he moves, by word-play and echo, from language to language, he is turning the kaleidoscope, throwing the light on another patch of the wall. Like Emerson, whom he cites indefatigably, Borges is confident that this vision of a totally meshed, symbolic universe is a jubilation: "From the tireless labyrinth of dreams I returned as if to my home to the harsh prison. I blessed its dampness, I blessed its tiger, I blessed the crevice of light, I blessed my old, suffering body, I blessed the darkness and the stone." To Borges, as to the transcendentalists, no living thing or sound but contains a cipher of all.

This dream-logic-Borges often asks whether we ourselves, our dreams included, are not being dreamed from without—has generated some of the most witty, original short fiction in Western literature. "Pierre Menard," "The Library of Babel," "The Circular Ruins," "The Aleph," "Tlón, Uqbar, Orbis Tertius," "Averroes' Search" are laconic masterpieces. Their concise perfection, as that of a great poem, builds a world that is closed, with the reader inescapably inside it, yet open to the widest resonance. Some of the parables, scarcely a page long, such as "Ragnarök," "Everything and Nothing" or "Borges and I," stand beside Kafka's as the only successes in that notoriously labile form. Had he produced no more than the *Fictions* (1956), Borges would rank among the very few fresh dreamers since Poe and Baudelaire. He has, that being the mark of a truly major artist, deepened the landscape of our memories.

Nonetheless, despite its formal universality and the vertigo breadths of his allusive range, the fabric of Borges' art has severe gaps. Only once, in a story called "Emma Zunz," has Borges realized a credible woman. Throughout the rest of his work, women are the blurred objects of men's fantasies or recollections. Even among men, the lines of imaginative force in a Borges fiction are stringently simplified. The fundamental equation is that of a duel. Pacific encounters are cast in the mode of a collision between the "I" of the narrator and the more or less obtrusive shadow of "the other one." Where a third person turns up, his will be, almost invariably, a presence alluded to or remembered or perceived, unsteadily, at the very edge of the retina. The space of action in which a Borges figure moves is mythical but never social. Where a setting of locale or historical circumstance intrudes, it does so in free-floating bits, exactly as in a dream. Hence the weird, cool emptiness which breathes from many Borges texts as from a sudden window on the night. It is these lacunae, these intense specializations of awareness, which account, I think, for Borges' suspicions of the novel. He reverts frequently to the question. He says that a writer whom dimmed eyesight forces to compose mentally, and, as it were, at one go, must stick to very short narratives. And it is instructive that the first important fictions follow immediately on the grave accident which Borges suffered in December, 1938. He feels also that the novel, like the verse epic before it, is a transitory form: "the novel is a form that may pass, doubtless will pass; but I don't think the story will . . . It's so much older." It is the teller of tales on the highroad, the *skald*, the raconteur of the pampas, men whose blindness is often a statement of the brightness and crowding of life they have experienced, who incarnate Borges' notion of the writer. Homer is often invoked as a talisman. Granted. But it is as likely that the novel represents precisely the main dimensions lacking in Borges. The rounded presence of women, their relations to men, are of the essence of full-scale fiction. As is a matrix of society. Number theory and mathematical logic charm Borges (see his "Avatars of the Tortoise"). There has to be a good deal of engineering, of applied mathematics, in a novel.

The concentrated strangeness of Borges' repertoire makes for a certain preciousness, a rococo elaboration that can be spellbinding but also airless. More than once, the pale lights and ivory forms of his invention move away from the active disarray of life. Borges has declared that he regards English literature, including American, as "by far the richest in the world." He is admirably at home in it. But his personal anthology of English writers is a curious one. The figures who signify most to him, who serve very nearly as alternate masks to his own person, are De Quincey, Robert Louis Stevenson, G. K. Chesterton, and Rudyard Kipling. Undoubtedly, these are masters, but of a tangential kind. Borges is perfectly right to remind us of De Quincey's organ-pealing prose, and of the sheer control and economy of recital in Stevenson and Kipling. Chesterton is a very odd choice, though again one can make out what *The Man Who Was Thursday* has contributed to Borges' love of charade and high intellectual slapstick. But not one of these writers is among the natural springs of energy in the language or in the history of feeling. And when Borges affirms, teasingly perhaps, that Samuel Johnson "was a far more English writer than Shakespeare," one's sense of the willfully bizarre sharpens. Holding himself beautifully aloof from the bombast, the bullying, the strident ideological pretensions that characterize so much of current letters, Borges has built for himself a center that is, as in the mystical sphere of the Zohar, also a far-out place.

He himself seems conscious of the drawbacks. He has said, in more than one recent interview, that he is now aiming at extreme simplicity, at composing short tales of a flat, sinewy directness. The spare encounter of knife against knife has always fascinated Borges. Some of his earliest and best work derives from the legends of knifings in the Palermo quarter of Buenos Aires, and from the heroic razzias of gauchos and frontier soliders. He takes eloquent pride in his warring forebears: in his grandfather, Colonel Borges, who fought the Indians and died in a revolution; in Colonel Suarez, his great-grandfather, who led a Peruvian cavalry charge in one of the last great battles against the Spaniards; in a great-uncle who commanded the vanguard of San Martín's army: "My feet tread the shadows of the launches that spar for the kill. The taunts of my death, the horses, the horsemen, the horses' manes, tighten the ring around me. . . . Now the first blow, the lance's hard steel ripping my chest, and across my throat the intimate knife." "The Intruder," a very short story, illustrates Borges' present ideal. Two brothers share a young woman. One of them kills her so that their fraternity may again be whole. They now enjoy a new bond: "the obligation to forget her." Borges himself compares this vignette to Kipling's first tales. "The Intruder" is a slight thing, but flawless and strangely moving. It is as if Borges, after his rare voyage through languages, cultures, mythologies, had come home, and found the Aleph in the next patio.

In a wonderful poem, "In Praise of Darkness," which equivocates with amused irony on the fitness of a man nearly blind to know all books but to forget whichever he chooses, Borges numbers the road that have led him to his secret center:

> These roads were footsteps and echoes,
> women, men, agonies, rebirths,
> days and nights,
> falling asleep and dreams,
> each single moment of my yesterdays
> and of the world's yesterdays,
> the firm sword of the Dane and the moon of the Persians,
> the deeds of the dead,
> shared love, words,
> Emerson, and snow, and so many things.
> Now I can forget them. I reach my center,
> my mirror.
> Soon I shall know who I am.

It would be foolish to offer a simple paraphrase for that final core of meaning, for the encounter of perfect identity which takes place at the heart of the mirror. But it is related, vitally, to freedom. In an arch note, Borges has come out in defense of censorship. The true writer uses allusions and metaphors. Censorship compels him to sharpen, to handle more expertly the prime instruments of his trade. There is, implies Borges, no real freedom in the loud graffiti of erotic and political emancipation that currently pass for fiction and poetry. The liberating function of art lies in its singular capacity to "dream against the world," to structure worlds that are *otherwise*. The great writer is both anarchist and archi-tect, his dreams sap and rebuild the botched, provisional landscape of reality. In 1940, Borges called on the "certain ghost" of De Quincey to "Weave nightmare nets / as a bulwark for your island." His own work has woven nightmares in many tongues, but far more often dreams of wit and elegance. All these dreams are, inalienably, Borges'. But it is we who wake from them, increased.

[Review of *The Aleph and Other Stories 1933–1969*]

Geoffrey H. Hartman*

The reputation of Jorge Luis Borges in the United States is astonishing, and less than a decade old. "Labyrinths" and "Ficciones," the first substantial translations of his work, appeared in 1962, one year after he shared the International Publishers' Prize with Beckett; by then he was 63 and well known in his native Argentina and elsewhere in Latin America and Europe (though not in Great Britain). These two volumes were followed by "Dreamtigers" (1964) as well as collections of lesser note. Several books have now been devoted to him; his conversation is avidly taped and printed; he has served as a visiting professor on several American campuses; and the claim is sometimes heard that he ranks with Joyce and Kafka. This despite the fact that Borges has cultivated a methodical modesty and never departed from the minor genres of essay, story and short poem.

What can this new sampler tell us about the truth of his reputation? It is devoted mainly to the stories, and has a wide chronological range, taking us from 1933 to 1969. But it remains an incomplete gathering, since rights to retranslate some or the most famous pieces (such as "Tlön, Uqbar, Orbis Tertius") could not be obtained. It is irritating to have Borges divided this way by competing anthologies, but it may be a kind of justice since he is, in fact, a scattered Orpheus whose prose-parts lament a fading power. The inventor of the "Aleph," a miniaturized replica of all visionary experience, knows that human kind cannot bear much fantasy. The present volume, with its charming "Autobiographical Essay" and its chatty comments on the stories, is well adapted to readers who wish to be reminded of great art rather than to experience it. With Borges they can flee from too vivid an enchantment into a little wilderness.

There is an art which, like the sounds of a clavichord, provides a perfect setting for thought and conversation. The art of Borges is generally like that: cool, well-tempered, with a consciously easy pace. His questers delay, or are delayed; and even in the most dangerous or baffling situation they have time to look off at the trees, at a "sky broken into dark diamonds of red, green and yellow." Lönnrot, the trapped detective in "Death and the Compass," quietly offers his killer a mystico-mathematical reflection before being shot. What is most human—the "irrelevant texture" of ordinary life—escapes from a ruthless plot by running into such asides. Each story, however continues to demand its victim despite the intricate delay, the charm of detail.

The humanizing asides are felt even more in the stories about the gauchos of Argentina. Here Borges, a reporter of traditions, weaves his

*From the *New York Times Book Review*, 13 December 1970. Reprinted by permission of the author.

thoughts directly into the narrative. In his unusual blend of ballad bloodiness and familiar essay there is sometimes as much reflection as plot: the brutal knife-fight in "The Challenge," little more than a paragraph long, is swathed in asides. Its naked brevity is relaxed by the narrator's comment on the courage of the gauchos, their exact way of duelling, a canto from the "Inferno," "Moby Dick," and so on. While time comes to a point which is also a knife's point, the story swerves, a mental picaresque, from the pure moment of encounter.

No Borges story is without this pointed moment, this condensation of time; yet it tends to be undercut by a mock-realistic setting or a whimsical narrator. So the microcosmic Aleph is found in the cluttered cellar of a second-rate poet, the unsavory Carlos Argentino Daneri. The only way that Borges can conduct his narrative is, like so many symbolists before him, by viewing ordinary life as a needful distraction from some symbolic purity. His humorous realism — names, dates and nature-motifs formulaically introduced — is a pseudo-realism. Even the gaucho stories, for all their local color, are fantasies — knives *are* magical in them, and the knife-fighter's sense of invulnerability is like the eternity-experience recorded in so many of the "fantastic" stories.

The fatality of form, the humanity of the aside — these are the most obvious pleasures given by Borges. There is, in addition, a wealth of small invention, perfect handling of gradual disclosures, and an elegance that makes life appear sloppy. Mixing, with charming ruthlessness, fantasy and fact, Borges reverses that "decay of lying" which Oscar Wilde (one of his favorite authors) had already deplored.

Beyond all this we feel for the narrator, for *his* quest. He is clearly a man trying to get into his own stories, that is, wishing to discover himself rather than an image. Like the fire-priest in "The Circular Ruins" Borges sets out to dream a real man but seems unable to dream of more than an intruder. Thus in a great many stories a stranger or interloper comes onto the scene and is given a predetermined lease on life before being eliminated. This figure, whether person or magical agent, never effects a lasting change: having played out its role, or lived its bit of dream, it is "sacrificed" like the woman in the late story actually called "The Intruder" (1966) or the upstart gaucho in "The Dead Man" (1946).

Surely, Borges himself, as artist, is that intruder. He comes to art belated — deeply conscious of traditions that both anticipate him and will survive his bluff. He is their victim, a dreamer who finds he is dreamt by a larger than personal symbolism — the formal world of legend and archetype with which he must merge. He may think he has mastered the magical instruments called symbols but they have their own will. "I began to wonder," he writes of a strange knife-fight in "The Meeting" "whether it was Maneco Uriarte who killed Duncan or whether in some uncanny way it could have been the weapons, not the men, which fought."

This living sacrifice of person to myth, of the individual to magic instrument, haunts Borges and is a source of his peculiar pathos. "I live," he says in "Borges and Myself," "I let myself live so that Borges can weave his tales and poems, and those tales and poems are my justification." We are not far, after all, from Mallarmé's remark that the world was meant to become a book. The symbols that purify us also trap us in the end. Symbolism may be nothing more than the religion of over-cultured men; and Borges—curious bibliophile, ardent comparatist—its perfected priest.

Meeting Borges   Alfred Kazin*

Meeting Borges is like reading him; to meet Borges *is* to read him. He talks mostly about literature or the life he has led in literature, and in shapely clever English sentences he says things about himself that you have to read or will read in his essays, stories, legends, lampoons—so many of which deal with the life he has led in literature, with the favorite late-19th-century English authors from whom he regularly takes off, with the blindness that regularly steals up on members of his family. Now near-blind ("I can see that there are windows there but I cannot see your face"), his gentlemanliness even more pronounced than his gentleness, his tremulous but controlled sensibility (which seems located in the large flaring nostrils turned up to receive the outside world, in the uplifted attentively *humble* face of the blind), the face he presents is that of a writer writing.

I see him, meet him, only as a mind—visibly in the process of composition. One reason for this, of course, is the formality of his upper-class Latin Americanness—very formal, rather studied people to the south of us! And blind writers do have to compose in their heads. Borges says his poetry has taken to regular metres again, easier to keep in the head. But it is also a fact that Borges, no doubt just because he is Borges, is as strange in the flesh as he is on the page. There is no one remotely like him.

One can have one's doubts about various things in Borges's work; one can understand the young specialists in Latin America at the Hebrew University who have protested the forthcoming "City of Jerusalem" award to Borges on the ground that it should have been given to Gabriel García Marquez for the extraordinary "One Hundred Years of Solitude," a novel certainly in the van of contemporary literature and at the heart of Latin America situation. But what one cannot doubt, what constitutes the distinct presence of Borges on every page, is the fascination of *his* 70 years of solitude.

He is a thoroughly original creative being who is confessedly strange to the Spanish tradition, and probably so even to the Latin America

*From the *New York Times Book Review*, 2 May 1971. Reprinted by permission of the author.

tradition. But though he is mad about the English literary imagination, and still works at Anglo-Saxon and Old Norse every weekend, there is something about his intellectual solitude, and the form that his essay-tales take, that reminds me of 19th-century Americans having to make up their own literature from the ground up.

So let me talk about my strange fancy that Borges really grew up with Poe, Emerson, Melville, Thoreau. He strikes me as a man who literally had to make up a world he could live in; he has gone far enough to please his imagination. One has the sense, confronting his shut-in state, of some immense need that *is* satisfiable, of some primary personal effort at renewal—through the word alone—that one associates with poets, fantasists, alchemists before the age of the novel and "realism."

Perhaps it is this that makes Borges's necessary originality, the innocent newness to the world that he gives off even at past 70, the need to make even a planet of his own (in "Tlön, Uqbar, Orbis Tertius") so hauntingly reminiscent to an American writer. There are knife fights in the growing dusk on the pampas, but the fights are never between enemies but between a man and his courage—which is a little like Melville—and many Westerns.

No doubt it is as South American as it is North American for a writer to be steeped in a tradition but not able to use it. There is in Borges's work a loneliness in regard to space and time that probably springs not just from the anomaly of his upbringing—his father was an academic with an immense library of English books, he learned his letters in English and he spent even more of his school years in Europe than did Henry James—but from an inability to use that affected construct of "culture" so dear to the old Latin American élites, with their idolatry of Paris, their ostentatious manners and their empty superiority to their own people.

Of course Borges himself is upper class and very, very bookish—the very product, you might think, of English cultural imperialism and what we in this country used to decry as the colonial complex. But a point about Borges is his constant transmutation and extension—often as parody—of his father's library. He is in fact "English" only in the sense that some American writer in Texas or Wyoming, some Wallace Stevens in Hartford who absorbed and mimicked French poetry without going to France—can be called "French." Borges has built his work—and, I suspect, his life itself—out of the same dogged effort to make himself a home in his own mind.

For the "American" writer there has never really been a "world" except the one he creates. That is why Borges reminds me not of contemporaries, not of any novelists, but of Poe and Melville even to their "immaturity"—the childlike fantasists, the lonely builders of dreams in the wilderness, the writers who like Emerson and Thoreau always wrote "pieces," journals, essays, fragments of one great truth. For Borges, too, the "imagination" he constantly celebrates—and works in—is God.

Borges is a "romancer," a teller of tales, a bit of a magician and puzzle-artist, a virtuoso of the symbol-tale, the legend told and retold from many an old manse, the quest. He is a writer fascinated and appalled by the empty space that broods over his stories like a curse. In the great story "The Intruder," of the brothers who lived with the same girl until she got in the way of their love for each other, we read—"Without any explanation, they lifted her onto the oxcart and set out on a long, tiresome, and silent journey. It had rained, the roads were heavy with mud and it was nearly daybreak before they reached Moron. There they sold her to the woman who ran the whorehouse."

Though the brothers are more luminous than the empty plains, they seem burdened, like the solitary figures in so much American fiction, by the incongruence of their existence in an unfathomable land. Over and again one finds in Borges's stories that "American" obsession with the labyrinth, the cipher, the frustrating passageway, the longing for the universal secret, the magic elixir—along with the dreamlike impersonal violence that remind one more of Poe than of the Chesterton and Stevenson from whom Borges learned to say "Gentlemen, let-me-weave-you-a-tale!"

For all I can tell from his stories, Borges is not even Catholic, and is as much an amateur of Oriental religions as Emerson-Thoreau. The absence of institutions in Borges is as marked as the old-fashioned American ability to make one's own God out of the fancies of the human brain. And along with this interest in beliefs, not belief, goes the absence of a felt literary community, the absence of literature as a "career" that those worldly failures Thoreau and Melville would have recognized. (Borges's present fame in the English-speaking world is due to the deterioration of many conventional modes of fiction, which is why Borges now regularly appears in The New Yorker when so many of its old standbys do not.)

But along with this personal and very American unconventionality is the sense we get in Borges of a wholly and obsessively mental world, of a lack of great experiences, of any deep sexual concern. There is in Borges, as in so many 19th-century American writers, a fundamental propriety of outlook that permits, indeed fosters, "cosmic" invention, a love of ambiguity, shadows of a dream that accompanies us on our farthest journey into the personal. Over sexual conflict and emotion—except in that great story "The Intruder," of the two brothers sharing the same girl—is as rare in Borges as it is in many, a New Englander of the last century.

What is different about Borges the *Americano* is his view of place. In 19th-century American literature the place is always there, in the center of our mind, but unoccupied. Borges's Buenos Aires, which is his whole world, is ineffably far-flung, a multitude, yet strangely empty of everything except place names, anecdotes, and a few friends. The great city seems as vague as the endless pampas. But this may have something to do with Borges's sight. He certainly does not put us in close touch with his own country. His Argentina remains a place of dreams. Borges's mind is the realest thing in it.

The Reality of Borges   Robert Scholes*

"Fame is a form of incomprehension, perhaps the worst."
                                                        —J. L. B.

My argument here is simple. I submit that we have missed the reality of Borges because we have misunderstood his view of reality and of the relationship between words and the world. All too often he has been taken for an extreme formalist, where it would be much more appropriate to see him as a kind of fallibilist in fiction. It will be proper, then, to consider what he has had to say about the fact / fiction relationship, beginning in a very humble way by considering some of the instances of the word "reality" in his texts. Our first set of illustrations will be taken from his essays on other writers collected in *Other Inquisitions*, where he takes up this problem on many occasions, with different emphases that are often quite illuminating.

Writing of Quevedo, Borges introduces a persistent theme in his critical work. He says of one sonnet, "I shall not say that it is a transcription of reality, for reality is not verbal. . . ." This opposition between language and reality, the unbridgeable gap between them, is fundamental to the Borgesian vision, and to much of modern epistemology and poetic theory. In particular, the notion of a lack of contact between language and world is a characteristic of those schools of critical thought that are usually called "formalist." In its extreme form, this view is highly vulnerable to attacks such as that made by Fredric Jameson in *The Prison-House of Language*, for language is seen in this view as cutting man off from authentic experience by its artificialities and evasions. It is frequently assumed that Borges is a typical formalist, who holds that language is self-contained and self-sufficient — self-referential, in fact. But this is simply not the case. Let us return to that statement about the Quevedo poem. In presenting it the first time I actually cut it off in mid-sentence. Here is the whole thing: "I shall not say that it is a transcription of reality, for reality is not verbal, but I can say that the words are less important than the scene they evoke or the virile accent that seems to inform them" (*Other Inquisitions*, p. 40).

Poems are made of words, and reality is not; yet there is something here between the words and the reality which is important. In this case

---

*From *Fabulation and Metafiction* (Champaign: University of Illinois Press, 1979). Reprinted by permission of the publisher.

there are actually two things: a "scene" evoked by the words, and an "accent" that seems to inform them. This scene and this accent, then, are mediations between language and world. Born of words, they have nevertheless moved beyond words toward experiences. The words suggest a speaker with a virile accent; they imply a human being of an order of reality greater than their own. They also present a scene which is more real than language, though it falls short of reality. These fictions or inventions, then, move language *toward* reality, not away from it. Artful writing offers a key that can open the doors of the prison-house of language.

Borges develops this idea further in his philosophic discussion, "Avatars of the Tortoise": "It is hazardous to think that a coordination of words (philosophies are nothing else) can have much resemblance to the universe. It is also hazardous to think that one of those famous coordinations does not resemble it a little more than the others, if only in an infinitesimal way" (p. 114). The term "coordination of words," of course, applies equally well to philosophies and stories. They are all fictions because they are verbal and the universe is not. But again comes the qualifying notion. Some of these coordinations catch more of the universe than others. And Borges adds that, of those he has considered in this context, the only one in which he recognizes "some vestige of the universe" is Schopenhauer's. Reading this, we are permitted, or even obliged, to ask by what faculty Borges or anyone else is capable of recognizing vestiges of the universe in a mere coordination of words. I don't want to pause and consider this question here. Or you might say I can't. But Borges's statement seems to imply that we are in touch with reality in some way, either through valid perceptions or through intuitions which are non-verbal. Considering this further would lead us into philosophical labyrinths darker than the ones Borges himself constructs, so let us avoid them and pick up the thread of his thought.

Twice, when turning to the question of the relationship between language — especially the language of fiction — and reality, Borges has recourse to the same quotation from Chesterton. Summarizing Chesterton's view, he writes, "He reasons that reality is interminably rich and that the language of men does not exhaust that vertiginous treasure" (p. 50). This position is very close to the others we have been considering, but here the solution is a bit more explicit. In both cases the quotation from Chesterton leads to a discussion of allegory, and in both cases Borges is cautious about revealing his own views — or perhaps he is simply uncertain of them. But he clearly entertains the possibility that a certain kind of allegory may serve as the vehicle that links the verbal cosmos with the greater reality. In one discussion he reports that Chesterton considered allegories capable of "somehow" corresponding to "ungraspable reality" (p. 50). And in the other he develops the same notion somewhat more thoroughly, suggesting that allegory may be a useful mediator between language and reality because "it is made up of words but it is not a language of language, a sign of other signs" (p. 155). And he adds, following Chesterton, that Dante's Beatrice, for example, "is not a sign of the word *faith*; she is a sign of the active virtue and the secret illuminations that this word indicates — a more precise sign, a richer and happier sign than the monosyllable *faith*" (p. 155).

In both these discussions of allegory, Borges suggests that allegory fails when its fictions are reducible back to single word-concepts, but succeeds when its fictions function as complex signs moving away from simple concepts toward the "ungraspable reality." For Borges, the language's tendency toward logic is a movement away from reality. The more precise and fixed the terminology, the more inadequate it must become. Thus allegory, at its best, is thinking in images, intuitive and open to truth. Whereas logic is a kind of game, often admirable, but not likely to catch much of the universe in its play. An allegory like Nathaniel Hawthorne's, which at its best is "refractory, so to speak, to reason," may indeed approach the ungraspable. But Borges reproaches Hawthorne for a tendency toward reducing his own allegorical intuitions to mere moral fables. The pointing of a moral at the end of a tale is, of course, an attempt to reduce the complex to the simple, to substitute a concept for an image, and hence is a move away from the possibility of truth. "Better," he says, "are those pure fantasies that do not look for a justification or moral and that seem to have no other substance than an obscure terror" (p. 51).

In discussing the writer to whom he is most justly generous, he elaborates this notion further, making his illustrations concrete and specific. Having discussed the excellence of H. G. Wells as a storyteller, and having recounted with amusement the reaction of Jules Verne to Wells's *The First Men in the Moon* (Verne "exclaimed indignantly, *'Il invente!'* "), Borges suggests that Wells's achievement rests on something even more important than ingenuity:

> In my opinion, the excellence of Wells's first novels — *The Island of Dr. Moreau*, for example, or *The Invisible Man* — has a deeper origin. Not only do they tell an ingenious story; but they tell a story symbolic of processes that are somehow inherent in all human destinies. The harassed invisible man who has to sleep as though his eyes were wide open because his eyelids do not exclude light is our solitude and our terror; the conventicle of seated monsters who mouth a servile creed in their night is the Vatican and is Lhasa. Work that endures is always capable of an infinite and plastic ambiguity; it is all things to all men, like the Apostle; it is a mirror that reflects the reader's own features and it is also a map of the world. And it must be ambiguous in an evanescent and modest way, almost in spite of the author; he must appear to be ignorant of all symbolism. Wells displayed that lucid innocence in his first fantastic exercises, which are to me the most admirable part of his admirable work. [p. 87]

This is one of the most perceptive and succinct paragraphs of literary criticism that I have encountered, and it takes us to the heart of Borges's notion of literary reality. Wells's work is a *"mirror* that reflects the reader's own features and it is also a *map* of the world." I wish to suggest that the two images employed here were not chosen lightly. Mirrors and maps are two highly different ways of imaging the world around us. They are also images that Borges returns to again and again in his own fiction. They are, of course, pointedly non-verbal signs of reality, and they are signs of different sorts. Mapping is based on a sign system that is highly arbitrary in its symbols but aspires toward an exact iconicity in its proportions. Mirrors, on the other hand, are superbly iconic in their reflections of reality, but patently artificial in at least three respects. They reduce three dimensions to a plane surface of two, they double distance and reduce size (our face in a mirror is only half its true size), and, most significantly, they reverse right and left.

The distortions of maps and mirrors, because they are visible and comparable with the reality they image, are obvious. With language, however, the distortions are less obvious and therefore more sinister. Thus fiction, which gives us images of human situations and actions, is superior to philosophy, which tries to capture these things in more abstract coordinations of words. Like Sidney, Shelley, and other apologists for literature, Borges is answering Plato's charge that poets falsify the universe. But this is a more total answer, and a stronger one, for two reasons. Unlike the others, it does not weaken itself by accepting the Platonic premise. Borges does *not* argue that literature points toward some eternal realm of perfect ideas. His argument concerns a complex human reality. Furthermore, he uses this complexity as the ground for an attack on philosophy itself. He denies it a privileged position from which to judge the value of literature. His very praise of philosophy robs it of its power of evaluation. Philosophy, he says, "dissolves reality," giving it "a kind of haziness." "I think that people who have no philosophy live a poor kind of life, no? People who are too sure about reality and about themselves. . . . I think that philosophy may give the world a kind of haziness, but that haziness is all to the good" (*Conversations with Borges*, p. 156).

Returning now to the passage on Wells, there is yet another aspect of it that must be considered. The notion that art is a mirror is not a new one. We are all familiar with the classical view that art is a mirror held up to nature, and with Stendhal's more pointed version of this notion — a mirror being carried down a roadway, reflecting the mud below and the sky above. But Borges's mirror is more modest, and does only what ordinary mirrors do. We see in it not nature or the world, but only ourselves: "it is a mirror that reflects the reader's own features." Of the world, art is merely a map, but it is a map that points accurately to things that are there in reality. In Wells's image of the invisible man we recognize "our own solitude and our terror"; and in the "conventicle of seated monsters who mouth a servile creed in their night" we see an image of "the Vatican" and "Lhasa." Such mirroring and such mapping take us deeply into reality, though the images are obviously fabulations rather than transcriptions. And this is a major point. Reality is too subtle for realism to catch it. It cannot be transcribed directly. But by invention, by fabulation, we may open a way toward reality, that will come as close to it as human ingenuity may come. We rely on maps and mirrors precisely because we know their limitations and know how to allow for them. But fiction functions as both map and mirror at the same time. Its images are fixed, as the configurations of a map are fixed, and perpetually various, like the features reflected by a mirror, which never gives the same image to the same person. "Work that endures," says Borges, "is capable of an infinite and plastic ambiguity."

The world that Borges maps for us in his own fiction seems at first to be as strange an image of reality as the work of a medieval cartographer. It is a world populated mainly by gauchos and librarians, men of mindless brutality and others of lettered inactivity. These extremes meet, of course, in the figure of the detective, who both acts and ratiocinates. But for the most part the extremes are what Borges chooses to present to us. His map of the world excludes much of the middle ground of life. He concentrates on the fringes, where heroes and monsters, warriors and demigods, meet and interact. And his map abounds in cartographers, busily making their own maps and titling them "Reality." For Borges, the ultimate futility is that of the creature in "The Circular Ruins" who hopes to "dream a man . . . with a minute integrity and insert him into reality"—only to discover that he is himself a fiction in someone else's dream world, and not in "reality" at all. This vertiginous notion that the world may be a dream is perhaps what most people think of when they hear the name Borges. But I am trying to suggest that this notion is not a value held by him, but a fictitious position assumed by him to provoke reality into showing itself. Unlike the figure in "The Circular Ruins," Borges is in reality himself and knows it. The fires of time are consuming him, even as they are consuming us and all we perceive: "Time is the substance I am made of. Time is a river which sweeps me along, but I am the river; it is a tiger which destroys me but I am the tiger; it is a fire which consumes me, but I am the fire. The world, alas, is real; I, alas, am Borges" (*Labyrinths*, p. 234; *Other Inquisitions*, p. 187).

The world in all its awful reality is finally inescapable. When asked whether the writer has a responsibility to the world which he must discharge by writing fiction that is "engaged in the political and social issues of the times," Borges has not answered simply, "No," with formalist disdain, but has spoken as follows:

I think it is engaged all the time. We don't have to worry about that. Being contemporaries, we have to write in the style and mode of our times. If I write a story — even about the man in the moon — it would be an Argentine story, because I'm an Argentine; and it would fall back on Western civilization because that's the civilization I belong to. I don't think we have to be conscious about it. Let's take Flaubert's novel *Salammbô* as an example. He called it a Carthaginian novel, but anyone can see that it was written by a nineteenth-century French realist. I don't suppose a real Carthaginian would make anything out of it; for all I know, he might consider it a bad joke. I don't think you should try to be loyal to your century or your opinions, because you are being loyal to them all the time. You have a certain voice, a certain kind of face, a certain way of writing, and you can't run away from them, even if you want to. So why bother to be modern or contemporary, since you can't be anything else? [*Borges on Writing*, p. 51]

The problem for the writer is not to "represent" his own time. This he cannot help but do. The problem is to be like the apostle, all things to all men. To reach beyond reality to truth, beyond the immediate and contemporary to those aspects of the real which will endure and recur. No dream tiger ever becomes a real tiger, but the image of a man of letters struggling to capture the tiger's reality is an image that may still be valid when both men and tigers are extinct and replaced by other forms of life. The writer seeks this kind of durability for his work — against great odds: "There is no exercise of the intellect which is not, in the final analysis, useless. A philosophical doctrine begins as a plausible description of the universe; with the passage of the years it becomes a mere chapter — if not a paragraph or a name — in the history of philosophy. In literature this eventual caducity is even more notorious" (*Labyrinths*, p. 43).

These are the views of Pierre Menard, author of the *Quixote*, who is in one sense Borges's greatest hero and in another his greatest fool. By acting on the feelings of futility expressed in this passage, Menard has refused the possibilities of literary creation. He has sought to defy time by plunging backward through it toward seventeenth-century Spain. But his work, because it is *his* and to the extent that it is *his*, must be read as that of a *fin de siècle* Frenchman affecting an archaic style. He is as tied to his time as Flaubert, even though he sought to avoid the curse of temporality by hiding in the past and assuming the voice of Cervantes. Either he has no reality and is absorbed into the voice of the dead Spaniard, or he has his own, that of a contemporary of William James and the friend of Valéry. Readers will see him as "brazenly pragmatic" or hopelessly relativistic. Borges is reminding us in this tale that there is no meaning without a meaner. Language itself always assumes a larger context. It can never be self-referential, because in order to interpret it we must locate it in a frame of reference which is ineluctably temporal and cultural. The world is real and Menard, alas, is Menard.

There is a further paradox here, which I have only hinted at so far, but which Borges himself has clearly articulated. Reality itself is real, is in time and is subject to the same consuming fires as the creatures and things which constitute it. He has expressed this exquisitely in his "Parable of Cervantes and the Quixote," from which I quote:

> Vanquished by reality, by Spain, Don Quixote died in his native village in the year 1614. He was survived but a short time by Miguel de Cervantes.
>
> For both of them, for the dreamer and the dreamed one, the whole scheme of the work consisted in the opposition of two worlds; the Unreal world of the books of chivalry, the ordinary everyday world of the seventeenth century.
>
> They did not suspect that the years would finally smooth away that discord, they did not suspect that La Mancha and Montiel and their knight's lean figure would be, for posterity, no less poetic than the episodes of Sinbad or the vast geographies of Ariosto.
>
> For in the beginning of literature is the myth, and in the end as well. [p. 242]

Thus reality itself is a thing which fades into mythology with the passage of time. Or rather, most of reality fades into obscurity, and what endures is transformed into mythology. Truth vanishes. Fiction endures if it partakes of that reality beyond reality, which enables it to survive as myth. The real reality is that which has not yet happened but is to come. In one of his finest essays, "The Modesty of History," Borges encourages us to consider this situation. He begins by remarking on the way governments try to manufacture or simulate historical occasions with an "abundance of preconditioning propaganda followed by relentless publicity" (*Other Inquisitions*, p. 167). But behind this fraudulent façade there is a "real history," which is "more modest," he suggests, with "essential dates that may be, for a long time, secret." He cites as one instance an occasion which passed with no chronological marker but certainly altered the world of letters—the date when Aeschylus is said to have changed the shape of drama by introducing a second actor upon the scene. Where only the chorus and a single speaker had appeared, on some "remote spring day, in that honey-colored theater" a second figure took up a position on stage, and with this event "came the dialogue and the infinite possibilities of the reaction of some characters to others. A prophetic spectator would have seen that multitudes of future appearances accompanied him: Hamlet and Faust and Segismundo and Macbeth and Peer Gynt and others our eyes cannot yet discern" (p. 168).

This was a truly historic occasion because the future ratified it and made it such. In the same essay Borges then speaks of another occasion, this one not in the world of letters but in that of heroic action. When the Vikings invaded England in the eleventh century, led by Harald Sigurdarson and Tostig, the brother of England's Saxon King Harold, there occurred a confrontation in which the English king spoke words of great valor and followed them with deeds that led to the death of the two invading chieftains and a great victory for the Saxons. As recorded almost two centuries later by the Icelandic historian Snorri Sturluson, this confrontation has what Borges calls "the fundamental flavor of the heroic," which he considers a value in itself. But he adds,

> Only one thing is more admirable than the admirable reply of the Saxon King: that an Icelander, a man of the lineage of the vanquished, has perpetuated the reply. It is as if a Carthaginian had bequeathed to us the memory of the exploit of Regulus. Saxo Grammaticus wrote with justification in his *Gesta Danorum*: "The men of Thule [Iceland] are very fond of learning and of recording the history of all peoples and they are equally pleased to reveal the excellences of others or of themselves."
>
> Not the day when the Saxon said the words, but the day when an enemy perpetuated them, was the historic date. A date that is a prophecy of something still in the future: the day when races and nations will be cast into oblivion, and the solidarity of all mankind will be established. The offer owes its virtue to the concept of a fatherland. By relating it, Snorri surmounts and transcends that concept. [pp. 169–70]

Thus politics, wars, exchanges of words and sword thrusts, are saved from oblivion by the historian who turns them into instances of heroic myth, and by doing so offers us a glimpse of a humanity beyond nationalistic pride. The men of heroic action need the men of letters if they and their deeds are to survive. And the men of letters need the heroic actors in order to keep their letters alive. The gaucho on the pampas and the librarian in Buenos Aires are parts of a mythical beast, a kind of centaur, each needing the other for completion.

History, for Borges, is a matter of witnessing as much as a matter of doing. The forms of the past are preserved in frail human vessels which are themselves destined to die—and these deaths, too, are historic, though unrecorded. In his parable of "The Witness" Borges writes, "In time there was a day that extinguished the last eyes to see Christ; the battle of Junín and the love of Helen died with the death of a man. What will die with me when I die, what pathetic or fragile form will the world lose? The voice of Macedonio Fernándes, the image of a red horse in the vacant lot at Serrano and Charcas, a bar of sulphur in the drawer of a mahogany desk? (*Labyrinths*, p. 243). Here, in accents reminiscent of Pater, Borges reminds us not of the intractability of reality but of the fragility of it. How it resides in little things as well as great, and how they pass away, and how finally even those who have seen them pass away as well. And though Borges can mention the voice of Macedonio Fernándes, his words will never capture that voice. What they will convey, however, is something even more fragile: his feeling about the voice. This, too, is a kind of reality, and not the least kind.

Approaching the end of an essay or a lecture, one's thoughts turn toward conclusions. Speaker and spectator glance surreptitiously at clocks and watches, both, perhaps looking forward to release from the rigidity of their roles. Still, there is a painful dimension to conclusions; it has animated one of Borges's finest poems, "Límites," which (like much of his literary work) is about something very real indeed. Speaking of that poem to Richard Burgin, he observed,

> It's quite easy to write an original poem, let's say, with original thoughts or surprising thoughts. I mean, if you think, that's what the metaphysical poets did in England, no? But in the case of "Límites," I have had the great luck to write a poem about something that everybody has felt or may feel. For example, what I am feeling today in Cambridge—I am going tomorrow to New York and won't be back until Wednesday or Tuesday and I feel that I am doing things for the last time.
>
> And yet, I mean that most common feelings, most human feelings, have found their way into poetry and been worked over and over again, as they should have been for the last thousand years. But here I've been very lucky, because having a long literary past, I mean, having read in many literatures, I seem to have found a subject that is fairly new and yet a subject that is not thought extravagant. Because when I say, especially at a certain age, that we are doing many things for the last time and may not be aware of it—for all I know I may be looking out of this window for the last time, or there are books that I shall never read, books that I have already read for the last time—I think that I have opened, let's say, the door, to a feeling that all men have. [*Conversations with Borges*, pp. 90–91]

The value of the poem is seen by Borges as less in its originality than in its universality: "something that everybody has felt, or may feel"—a sentiment that brings Borges very close to Samuel Johnson. There is a reality of shared human experiences, then, that justifies poems and fictions by their encompassing it. Far from being self-referential or a labyrinthine cul-de-sac, poem and story exist to bridge the gap between people and things—and between one person and another. In this connection it is interesting to observe that Borges's poem bears a startling resemblance to a brief meditation written by Johnson himself—*Idler* 103, the closing paper in the *Idler* series, in which he speculates on the phenomenon of finality:

> Though the Idler and his readers have contracted no close friendship, they are perhaps both unwilling to part. There are few things not purely evil, of which we can say, without some emotion of uneasiness, *this is the last*. Those who never could agree together, shed tears when mutual discontent has determined them to final separation; of a place which has been frequently visited, though without pleasure, the last look is taken with heaviness of heart; and the Idler, with all his chillness of tranquility, is not wholly unaffected by the thought that his last essay is now before him.

> This secret horror of the last is inseparable from a thinking being,
> whose life is limited, and to whom death is dreadful.

I do not mean to suggest that Borges, like Pierre Menard, has been trying to rewrite Dr. Johnson. Quite the opposite. For, though their subjects are quite similar, they are each irrevocably of their time, in style and emphasis, and in those unspoken values that inform style and emphasis. What links them despite these differences is reality itself, and in particular the human condition of that reality. And Johnson, I am sure, would applaud Borges's most succinct statement of his position in this matter. Literature, he has said, "is not a mere juggling of words" (*Borges on Writing*, p. 164). It requires that a writer have what Chesterton called "everything." A notion which Borges glosses in the following way: "To a writer this everything is more than an encompassing word: it is literal. It stands for the chief, for the essential, human experiences. For example, a writer needs loneliness, and he gets his share of it. He needs love, and he gets shared and also unshared love. He needs friendship. In fact, he needs the universe" (p. 163). And the universe — the universe of men and women, at any rate — needs the writer. We need him to say the big things, of course, but also the little ones: things like "Perhaps a bird was singing and I felt for him a small, birdlike affection" (*Other Inquisitions*, p. 180). And when I say "the writer" I mean specifically the one who is called Jorge Luis Borges, for whom many people in many lands feel a strong human affection, and of whom it is very appropriate to speak in precisely the same language in which he spoke of H. G. Wells. Referring to Wells's early scientific romances, Borges, wrote: "I think they will be incorporated, like the fables of Theseus or Ahasuerus, into the general memory of the species and even transcend the fame of their creator or the extinction of the language in which they were written" (p. 88).

Certain fictions, like the fabulations of Wells and Borges, endure because they continue to function for human beings as signs of some unattainable reality, and as emblems of the human struggle to imagine that reality. They are, as Peirce would say, "real dreams."

COMPARATIVE ESSAYS

The Flaunting of Artifice in Vladimir Nabokov and Jorge Luis Borges

Patricia Merivale*

Vladimir Nabokov never lets his readers forget that he is the conjuror, the illusionist, the stage-manager, to whom his characters owe their existence; this flaunting of artifice, not merely as technique but also as theme, can perhaps be elucidated by a closer examination of one type of Nabokovian device, the book that, in whole or in part, explicitly imitates another book: a "discovered manuscript," a fictitious confession, a book about imaginary books, or a book that parodies such an already conventionalized structure as the detective story, the scholarly commentary, or the literary biography. Of the large number of contemporary writers employing such devices, Jorge Luis Borges, the Argentine poet, essayist, and author of disturbingly effective philosophical-fantastic tales, offers the closest and most illuminating parallels with Nabokov. Yet the similarity of their forms and structures brings into focus a fundamental difference in their premises about the relationship of art and reality.

Both Borges and Nabokov could be called "modern mannerists";[1] Borges, who said that "la irrealidad es condición del arte"[2] ("unreality is the necessary condition of art"), has often been called "baroque" as well, a term that reminds us that *Don Quixote* is the father of the book-conscious-of-its-bookness. Both Borges and Nabokov exploit, for their own thematic purposes, all the narrative tricks and devices of the Gothic fantasy writers of the last two centuries, and they blend mannerism and Gothicism together in their single most important parodic pattern, the metaphysical detective story.

Borges' tales, rational and horrid, in the manner of Poe, yet paradoxical and philosophically teasing, in the manner of G. K. Chesterton, blend paradox, wonder and fear in a way that has often been compared with the nightmare logic of Kafka; the comparison is both obvious and justified. Both men see the world as a labyrinth of passages, a series of unopened doors, a thwarted or negated quest, a pointless wait separating the hero from a doubtfully existent Law, from a somehow menacing Judgment.

*From *Wisconsin Studies in Contemporary Literature* 8, no. 2 (1967). Reprinted by permission of the author.

Both authors are masters of the short poetic parable with much paradox and riddling in it, a form hovering somewhere between "fiction" and philosophic or even mythic tale-telling. But Borges, motivated by a passionate, highly intellectual curiosity, seeks to know what, if anything, is true; Kafka, motivated by a deep anxiety, seeks to know where, if anywhere, he belongs; the distortions of "laconicas pesadillas"[3] seem more relevant to his quest than do the distortions of self-conscious and explicit artifice that charm both Borges and Nabokov. Even Nabokov's *Invitation to a Beheading*, so Kafkaesque in structure and effect, if not in intention,[4] seems rather to lead back towards a world of the sane and normal, where something could perhaps be both real and beautiful at once.

The logical extrapolation of Borges' brief tales into novel form would be not *Das Schloss* or *Der Prozess*, but a real metaphysical detective story like Alain Robbe-Grillet's *Les Gommes* (1953), where the detective hero himself becomes, by "accident" or by "destiny," the murderer he has been seeking. Wallas, Robbe-Grillet's stoical hero, lives out not only the rigid, deliberately conventional fiction of a *roman policier*, following the web of clues to a "surprise" ending, but also through a labyrinthine city, he re-enacts the search of his literary predecessor, the detective Oedipus, who likewise pitted an ironic ignorance and the power of reason against the riddling clues to his own guilt and walked into the trap of his own accord. Wallas' victim, like Oedipus', is his "father," rather than, as in the Borgesian pattern, his own self or his anti-self; otherwise for both authors the "solution" — truth and identity — is found in violence and annihilation at the center of the labyrinth. The fatal gunshots that climax or conclude five of Nabokov's major fictions and the sudden deaths that end two others serve a less readily definable purpose; at times is appears that, in a very serious and complex Nabokovian sense, "Death often is the point of life's joke."[5]

While Nabokov seems, in actuality, to have preferred the patterns of Mayne Reid's Wild Westerns[6] to detective stories per se, Borges has always admired and enjoyed detective stories, and indeed translated, anthologized and parodied them.[7] In his own volume of detective stories, pointedly entitled *Seis problemas para don Isidro Parodi* (Six Problems for Isidro Parodi, 1942), the detective's purity of ratiocination, of armchair detection, is guaranteed by his being in jail the whole time. But the Chestertonian tricks of Parodi, presented without deep thematic purpose, fall flat in comparison with those in, for instance, "Abenjacán el Bojarí, muerto en su laberinto" ("Abenjacán el Bojarí, Dead in his Labyrinth"). This tale retains the device of the uninvolved detective, reasoning out, from the evidence presented in the apparent story, the real story, or "solution," an elaborately Chestertonian paradox: the labyrinth was not the refuge where the king was hiding, but instead the trap where the slave was waiting to rob the king of life and, thematically more important, of identity as well.

Justly the most famous of the detective stories is "La muerte y la brújula" ["Death and the Compass"], where Borges' detective-reasoner is, like Robbe-Grillet's, also the active follower of clues. The detective, Lönnrot, using clues from the Jewish cabbalistic tradition of the four letters of the mystic name of God, works out with map and compass where a fourth murder will take place, extrapolating from the locations of the first three. At the point where the structure is logically completed, a solitary, labyrinthine building, he discovers, again like Robbe-Grillet's Wallas, that he is not a mere investigator but a chief participant — in fact, the victim. The villain now plays the detective's role of explaining the true story. The clues were planted, so that Lönnrot could build from them his own four-sided labyrinth, or trap, and then walk into it. The real labyrinth was, paradoxically, merely a simple straight line from starting-point to doom. After the explanation, the fourth murder occurs.[8]

Not only the opportunities but also the limitations of the detective story form suit Borges's purposes. It has been said that he builds "a world of shadows" in his fiction;[9] perhaps a better term would be "abstractions." Though the more intellectual emotions of curiosity and awe at the marvellous are abundant, the less intellectual ones of sexuality, love, and the entanglements of human relationships are replaced by a little hate and fear and, a quality not unlike that of a Conrad hero, the strange, free honor of the solitary man.

While none of Nabokov's heroes are, strictly speaking, detectives, many of them follow out clues to self-discovery according to the structure of the metaphysical detective story. Indeed, the author Sebastian Knight has written just such a story, *The Prismatic Bezel*, where, as in Borges or Robbe-Grillet, the alleged victim turns up alive — in this case, by the simple, farcical device of removing his false beard.[10] More important, Knight's brother has embarked on the detective-like quest of the literary biographer, to find out what his brother's "Real Life" was, and perhaps what his own life is. The hero of *The Eye* is a voyeur rather than a detective, but Nabokov describes his quest in these terms: "The texture of the tale mimics that of detective fiction . . . the pursuit of an investigation which leads the protagonist through a hell of mirrors and ends in the merging of twin images. . . . The stress is not on the mystery but on the pattern."[11] But the quest of Smurov, a "superfluous man," to discover, from the mere reflections of himself in other people, whether he really exists or not, is but a pale prefiguration of the detective quests that pattern three of Nabokov's major novels: *Despair, Pale Fire* and *Lolita*.

Despair is the clearest and the least interesting. The narrator (Hermann), impassioned by creativity as well as greed, murders his own double, and, failing both as criminal and as artist, is caught at once when no one perceives any resemblance between them. Hermann is the weakest of the three heroes, as his fancies do not rise as far above the flat and hackneyed as he supposes; he merely wishes to turn his life into a good detective story, by slaying some necessary but imagined externalization of himself. The last third of *Lolita* is a sequence of stalkings and pursuits, including a "cryptogrammic paper chase" (Chapter 23) of puns and allusions, which ends with Humbert's slaughter, in a rather Gothic house, of Quilty, the man who resembles him in quasi-artistic perversity and who shares the guilt of Lolita's corruption. In effect, Humbert is, like Hermann, killing "himself," his sin externalized in the form of Quilty, and will shortly die for doing so.[12] *Pale Fire*, an amazingly complex book, again includes the slow approach of an assassin through a maze of words and inventions to slay the narrator's "double," the poet whose name is "Shade." But, as in *Despair*, a very ordinary, squalid murder is made into a metaphysical detective story by the imagination of the narrator. An escaped lunatic, a criminal who has come to kill his judge and executioner (compare the vengeance of Borges' gangster upon the detective Lönnrot), is turned into an invented "agent" journeying through the labyrinths of the poem's lines, of geography, and of the clues the narrator plants in his way. Gradus kills a "double," to be sure — among Nabokov's well-hidden clues is one indicating the close physical resemblance of John Shade, the poet, to his absent neighbor, the Judge — but not the narrator's double, for that, by refusing to write Kinbote's poem of Zembla,[13] John Shade has steadfastly refused to be. Ironically the mad Kinbote is right in thinking that Shade is his true friend, for only Shade, of all those who know him to be mad, has pity and some understanding for him: "One should not apply [the word "mad"] to a person who deliberately peels off a drab and unhappy past and replaces it with a brilliant invention. That's merely turning a new leaf with the left hand." (p. 238)

Nabokov's novelistic method of characterization stresses the individual personality, whose separateness will be marked by whims, quirks, eccentricity, perversion, and insanity, and whose complete fictional existence will be filled out by the fictional dimensions of memory, nostalgic nuance, and the pieced-together events of a whole life, thus implicitly denying the very possibility of the "doubles" whose supposed existence means so much to his narrators. Shade, Hermann's vagrant, and Quilty are all reluctant doubles, refusing to acknowledge the alleged resemblance.[14]

In Nabokov's work true doubles only occur as unreal grotesques, like the director and the lawyer in *Invitation to a Beheading* (p. 207) or the doubled spies of *Bend Sinister*, who might even be "Rosenstern and Guildenkranz, those gentle interchangeable twins" (p. 100). But again and again characters give an effect of double-ness by looking at themselves from the outside, vividly imagining the actions of, for instance, "the other Cincinnatus"; Hermann makes a fetish of self-voyeurism (pp. 37–39); *The Eye* depends upon the division the hero imagines in himself to render the complexity of his personality.

On the other hand, Borges, the *conteur philosophique*, is concerned not with personality, but only with identity, which is a definition of self, archetypal, abstract, inexplicable, to be sure, and yet in a way very simple. By a binary moral arithmetic, Borges strips down his characters to victim and executioner, slave and monarch, coward and hero, and distinguishes between the polar opposites in terms of a single moment of unequivocal symbolic action. In the story called "La otra muerte," for example, the question is whether the protagonist has run away or has fought and died bravely; a writer of realistic war fiction would insist that it is not so easy to say. The writer of philosophic parable can simply describe "la noche en que por fin vio su propia cara, la noche en que por fin escuchó su nombre" ("the night when he finally saw his own face, the night in which he finally heard his name"), asserting that "cualquier destino, por largo y complicado que sea, consta en realidad *de un solo momento*: el momento en que el hombre sabe para siempre quién es"[15] ("any destiny, however long and complicated, consists, in reality, of a *single moment*: the moment when a man knows once and for all who he is"). The protagonist then knows himself to be hero or coward, or both together, or discovers himself to be identical with someone else in past or future or dream, or perhaps with all men at once, or perhaps with no one at all. Nabokov is never more Borgesian than in the concluding lines of *The Real Life of Sebastian Knight*: "Sebastian's mask clings to my face, the likeness will not be washed off. I am Sebastian, or Sebastian is I, or perhaps we both are someone whom neither of us knows."

Borges' "La forma de la espada" ["The Shape of the Sword"] is a well-made story in which, like the pistols in a "well-made play," the crescent-shaped scimitar on the wall at the beginning will be used by the end. But, oddly, though John Vincent Moon bears the scimitar-shaped scar of guilt, the Mark of Cain, his brother's slayer, and is at the same time Judas, the informer, we see that he has in a way achieved what, in "Abenjacán el Bojarí," the lackey only attempted: pretending to the identity of the brave man as he tells his own story, Moon has attained that identity, along with the strength and purpose of his victim — exchanged it for his former self, the trembling, cowardly fugitive. Hero and betrayer have become the same. Likewise, in "Los teólogos" ["The Theologians"], driven by the subtler violence of an obsessive life-long hatred, the two theologians battle to death at the stake, only to discover that in the eye of God there is no difference between the two abstrusely intellectual heresies that had made them enemies, or indeed between the two men themselves. They are now indistinguishable, "una sola persona," doubles of each other after all.

There are numerous possibilities in this Borgesian concept of identity, yet all the permutations of character are virtually reducible to a formula of "fire" and "algebra" in a way in which Nabokov's Humbert Humbert, or Kinbote, or even the rather stiffly contrived Hermann are not. Nabokov's characters are "real," even while following out the apparently patterned destiny, shaped by artifice, which they have created or imagined for themselves.

The stylized, patterned, cliché properties of the detective story, its very nature as a labyrinthine exercise of ingenuity, make it, or its parody, an especially valuable form for a book conscious of its bookness, whether it is used alone or is gracefully combined with some other artifices of bookness which have had a long literary history. There is, for instance, that manuscript, not to be published until after its author's death, edited by a fictitious editor, the confession of that arraigned criminal, Humbert Humbert. It is, in effect, a Manuscript Found in a Bottle, a Gothic device, like such notable works as the story found in the trunk in the Inn in *Don Quixote*, or the papers in the ebony cabinet in *Northanger Abbey*, or the dusty, charred and, unfortunately, torn and fragmentary manuscripts found in, say, *Melmoth the Wanderer*, which always break off at the point of greatest suspense. From Charles Maturin to Arthur Machen and beyond, any author of fantastic fiction is likely to employ the device: we think of Ambrose Bierce, H. G. Wells, M. P. Shiel, and of course Poe, author of the story called "MS found in a Bottle." Less perfunctory and more integral to the theme, the device is a staple of narrative technique in such more characteristically modern authors as François Mauriac, Hermann Hesse, Junichiro Tanizaki, Max Frisch, John Barth, Lawrence Durrell and Abram Tertz. It is a device of pseudo-realism, "giving an air of verisimilitude to an otherwise bald and unconvincing narrative," distancing, relieving the alleged author or editor of responsibility for what is said. It is especially useful in making possible the first-hand story of an Arthur Gordon Pym, a man distant or dead. The Manuscript Found in a Bottle comes to shore, like an inky Ishmael: "And I only am escaped alone to tell thee. . . ."

The device, originated for fantastic fictions, became available for fictionalized philosophies, whence the elaborate interplay of pseudonym, persona and editor in Kierkegaard's *Either / Or* and in Carlyle's *Sartor Resartus*, from both of which Borges has learned that the line between fiction and philosophy may be a blurred one. If "la metafísica es una rama de la literatura fantástica" ("metaphysics is a branch of fantastic literature," "Tlön, Uqbar, Orbis Tertius," *F*, p. 23), then Gothic devices can be parodied for the purposes of metaphysics. At least half of Borges' tales are what he calls "notas sobre libros imaginarios" ("notes on imaginary books," Prologue to *F*, p. 12), having inner books as a major structural element: for instance, the imaginary Herbert Quain's imaginary detective story, *The God of the Labyrinth*, and the other Quain story from which Borges claims to have derived an actual story of his own (see "Examen de la obra de Herbert Quain" ["An Examination of the Work of Herbert Quain"]). The manuscript of the story of Marcus Flaminius Rufus, the Immortal, is found in a copy of Pope's *Homer*, and part of the imaginary encyclopedia of Tlön, describing the imaginary literature of that realm, is found in (among other places) a set of the *Anglo-American Cyclopedia*, a good instance of the "imagined" taking up residence in the world of the "actual."

Nabokov's *Pale Fire* contains, of course, the most notable of his many invented manuscripts, John Shade's own poem called "Pale Fire"; Nabokov's novel consists of Shade's poem plus Kinbote's lengthy scholarly commentary upon it.[16] Kinbote, the editor, "finds" the manuscript, or rather snatches it away from the dying poet. But when, in the scholarly prose of the commentary, he tries to turn the domestic New England realism of John Shade's verse into the romantic fantasy of his own exile from his kingdom of Zembla, he inevitably fails. The externally verified artifact, the Manuscript Found, maintains a stubborn life of its own and it is the Commentary that becomes Kinbote's subjective, solipsist confession (like Humbert's and Hermann's), where deliberate self-justification and unconscious self-revelation throw into the sea an encoded message that may never be unraveled. The reader will find himself frustrated indeed when he tries to find the Zemblan Crown Jewels concealed somewhere in Kinbote's Index to his Commentary.

Borges' Hladik, in "El milagro secreto" ["The Secret Miracle"], lives and is condemned to death in a simpler, a more nearly solipsist world than Kinbote's. His miraculous reprieve of a year's imaginary life in the instant between the aiming and the firing of the guns suffices for him to complete his masterpiece, the work which justifies his life; it is a play about an action taking place outside of time. The last word needed to complete the play comes to him just before the bullets hit. Just as Sebastian Knight and his brother come closest to being "doubles" in the Borgesian sense, so Sebastian's own book, *The Doubtful Asphodel*, comes closest to being a true inner parallel in the Borgesian manner. Sebastian writes about a man dying while he himself is dying. His brother says of the work: "The man is the book; the book itself is heaving and dying. . . . We feel that we are on the brink of some absolute truth. . . . And the word, the meaning which appears is astounding in its simplicity" (pp. 175, 178–179). But of course the inner hero dies before this word can be uttered; of course Sebastian dies before his brother can thread the infuriating labyrinth that separates him from Sebastian's death-bed, and before he can receive from Sebastian's own lips the answer to the puzzle of both their lives.[17]

In Nabokov's *Bend Sinister* the most important inner artifact (among so many) is a distorted reflection, the "bend sinister," of Shakespeare's *Hamlet*. The central parodies, of cinematic, pedantic, and especially of totalitarian interpretations of the play are evident enough, as are the numerous specific allusions throughout the book, for instance, to a Protean Shakespeare "composed of two left arms and a mask" (p. 94); the forthcoming production would have constituted a play within the "play." But simmering below the distorted surface, where the tyrant Paduk (nicknamed "the Toad") sees himself as the redeemer Fortinbras, is a shadowy *Hamlet* structure extending through the book (like the Oedipus structure of *Les Gommes*), in which Krug and the reader know Paduk to be Claudius: "A toad . . . on the late king's favourite garden seat." (p. 99) The bereaved and grieving hero, an image of integrity, stands aloof and disdainful in the first "court" scene where the academics rally around the new regime; he rejects the bribes and wooings of his old school enemy, Paduk, so anxious for his support; he escapes into philosophy and meditates upon death when he should be escaping to another country; and in a "court" that reeks of a coy sexual corruption, he is constantly spied upon by, among others, an "Ophelia" sent to discover his secrets by seducing him. "Osric and Fortinbras have acquired a tremendous ascendancy over the rest of the cast" (p. 95); the first of death's summoners is grotesquely foppish. In the final "court" scene, the themes of madness and revenge coalesce at last, but Nabokov, the stage-manager, breaks off our heightened involvement in the "tragedy" of the logical ending: "Death is but a question of style, a mere literary device, a musical resolution. . . . And Krug ran towards him, and just a fraction of an instant before another and better bullet hit him, he shouted again: You, you — and the wall vanished, like a rapidly withdrawn slide, and I stretched myself and got up from among the chaos of written and rewritten pages. . ." (pp. xvii, 216). We have had some hints throughout that Nabokov is staging a play in which Krug dreams of a world even less real than he is himself, from which Nabokov must rescue him first by "blessed madness," and then by dismissing him, along with the rest of the cast, his other inventions, his "whims and megrims."[18]

Invitation to a Beheading, and that much slighter work, *The Waltz Invention*, being comic versions of the nightmare-reality situation, require only an act of heroic will by one of the characters to break the illusion; Nabokov's direct intervention is not needed. In *The Waltz Invention*, the mad inventor's dream of holding the whole world up to ransom becomes the world's nightmare, until at a touch of defiance from the actual, the nightmare villain collapses back into seedy nothingness. In *Invitation to a Beheading*, we are given, from beginning to end, clues that Cincinnatus is "realer" (more "opaque") than the grotesques around him, whom he himself is dreaming into existence, and that his prison is an artifice, a stage-set. At the end, with the prison collapsing like a house of cards, he realizes that he need not wait for the nightmare axe to fall; he simply gets up and walks towards "where, to judge by the voices, stood beings akin to him." (p. 223)

Both Borges and Nabokov like to make an appearance from time to time as characters within their own stories. Borges is the stage-manager of "La busca de Averroes" ["Averroes' Search"], whose hero disappears the moment Borges ceases to believe in him. "Borges" as a character appears in "Tlón, Uqbar, Orbis Tertius," "La forma de la espada" ["The Shape of the

Sword"], and elsewhere, much as Nabokov appears in the guise of the Russian émigré author to whom Hermann will send his manuscript, or of the Russian émigré lecturer who is coming to take over Pnin's job, or the Russian writer in exile of whom Kinbote thinks at the very end of *Pale Fire*, or the "I" who cannot possibly be any of the characters, yet who often helps to narrate a third-person novel. But Borges goes further and contemplates a world in which this "I" too is dreamed, a book in which he too is written. The Rabbi of Prague created a Golem, a stupid, clumsy creature who mimicked the Rabbi's pious gestures in a somehow frightening way; but "¿Quién nos dirá las cosas que sentía / Dios al mirar a su rabino en Praga?"[19] ("Who can tell us the things God felt while looking at His rabbi in Prague?") In "Las ruinas circulares" ["The Circular Ruins"], the hero, with great suffering and effort, dreams into existence a man who can live independently of his creator. But the creator discovers that, in turn, someone has been dreaming *him* into existence. Again and again it seems as characteristic for Borges to use the devices of artifice to trap us and himself in infinite regression—in an exitless labyrinth, a hall of mirrors, a dream within a dream—as it does for Nabokov to prick the richly iridescent bubble of artifice with a tiny touch from a world more actual.

Nabokov, writing fiction, asserts the primacy of "reality" over insane fantasy: Hermann, Humbert, and Kinbote are defeated as they attempt to impose their imagined structures—the perfect crime, the romantic kingdom, or the quintessence of ideal passion—on an unwilling world.[20] The walking-stick is left at the scene of the crime, when Hermann should have known that, by the rules of the literary genre, the "perfect criminal" always overlooks something. The real nature and needs of the person, Lolita, will not be denied. John Shade refuses to play "double" to Kinbote. In each case reality disrupts fantasy as a mode of action. The heroes are left only with the books they have written, their self-created artifices, for only a lunatic would behave as if the world were his own work of art, would try to make the world book-shaped.

But for Borges the world *is* book-shaped. Consider the complex series of "Chinese boxes," of story within story, in his tale "El jardín de senderos que se bifurcan" ["The Garden of Forking Paths"]. The tale is a fragmentary manuscript—we are told that the first two pages are missing—found and anonymously edited. It tells a story which must be placed in the context of historical events as given in a real book, Captain Liddell Hart's history of the First World War. It is the deposition or confession of an arraigned criminal, and its main action is that of a metaphysical detective story: a complex double pursuit—detective-assassin-victim—through a labyrinth to truth and violent death. And within these frames is an invented book, called, of course, *El jardín de senderos que se bifurcan*, written by an ancestor of the assassin. It is a novel structured upon a labyrinth, forking in time, showing the endlessly bifurcating possibilities of choice; it is very like the actual labyrinth-Garden, forking in space, which seemed to the assassin as he wound his way through it to be as large as the world. The victim, in effect supplying a commentary upon this invented book, explains that it is "una imagen, incompleta, pero no falsa" ("an image, incomplete, but not false," F, p. 109) of its author's universe, where every future possibility, including those of this very encounter, may be actualized.[21] Two of these possibilities are diametrically opposed: the two men will understand each other and be friends, or one will come as an enemy to kill the other. Both, of course, are true. But, as in "La muerte y la brújula," actuality draws a straight line through the labyrinths of possibility; all this occurs within a frame where the spy must kill the victim and in turn be captured, in order that a message, in the world of history, may be delivered. But "reality," if the spy story is any realer than the metaphysical novel it contains or than what the spy has imagined about the novel, does not negate fantasy for Borges; "reality" is simply another frame of the structure of artifice. The world can be seen as a labyrinth, and transcribed as a detective story which can be subsumed into an absolute Book, like Mallarmé's,[22] which perhaps can explain the world.

In the parable of the "La biblioteca de Babel" ["The Library of Babel"], where man is "el imperfecto bibliotecario" ("the imperfect librarian," F, p. 87), we have an ironic variant of the familiar topos of the World as God's second sacred book.[23] "La biblioteca total," the universe, is "la vasta Biblioteca contradictoria, cuyos desiertos verticales de libros corren el incesante albur de cambiarse en otros y que todo lo afirman, lo niegan y lo confunden como una divinidad que delira."[24] ("The vast contradictory library whose vertical deserts of books run the never ending risk of changing themselves into others, and which affirm all, deny all, and confuse all like a divinity in the midst of delirium.") The library contains every conceivable combination of twenty-five symbols, and will thus yield, eventually, the unwritten chapters of Edwin Drood, the song the Sirens sang, the autobiographies of the archangels, the true catalog of the Library, thousands of false catalogs, and even Borges' own story; but mainly, stretching out perhaps to the size of the Universe itself, perhaps to infinity, there will be shelf after shelf of nonsense. If the parable is serious, we are compelled either to search hopelessly for the true book through the endless nightmare of the Library, or else to mimic the Absolute book by means of dream, or magic, or art, to make a human sub-creation, obedient to human rules rather than to the non- or in-human rules of the Library. And of course Borges, though not in this despairing parable, has chosen the latter: art, with its imperfect, merely provisory reality, which may well be futile. Poetry can dream into existence only tigers stuffed or flimsy like the Golem; yet Borges must continue "esta aventura indefinida / Insensata y antigua"[25] ("this indefinite, senseless and ancient adventure") the search for the real tiger who escapes art, since Artifice, the realest thing we can know, is the only thing that can make reality endurable. With this Nabokov would agree. Thus Borges, "desde los laberintos de cartón pintado del truco" ("from the painted pasteboard labyrinths of the card-trick") from the artifices and devices of his literary tradition, feels that "nos hemos acercado a la metafísica: unica justificación y finalidad de todos los temas"[26] ("we have approached metaphysics: the sole justification and end of all themes"). With this, perhaps, Nabokov would not agree: insofar as he is asking at all the question "what is true?" he is giving a commonsense, empirical answer, to counterpoint against what is beautifully or horribly imagined. Borges, the stoic artificer, tries to make his book mirror the world, however feebly, and yet "poco antes de morir, descubre que ese paciente laberinto de líneas traza la imagen de su cara"[27] ("just before dying, he discovers that the patient labyrinth of lines traces [only] the image of his [own] face"). He has only written his own Confession; he has only added one object or artifact more to the world. For Nabokov, the comic artificer, however, "the lunatic, the lover and the poet" (and Nabokov's heroes are generally all three at once)[28] will go on projecting fantasies simply because they must, and Nabokov will go on writing about them for the aesthetic conjuror's fun of it. And, as for identity, about which Borges has to be metaphysically solemn, if richly ironic and paradoxical, perhaps Kinbote of *Pale Fire*, handsome, bearded, Zemblan, wretched, crazy and incurably pederastic, will turn up "on another campus" (in another book?) as an "old, happy, healthy, heterosexual Russian, a writer in exile . . . sans anything but his art." (p. 301)

These Prosperos, the poet-conjurors of our own day, flaunt the complex artifices of their revels with equal skill; but while Nabokov usually dismisses his actors "into thin air" and returns us to the real world, Borges takes the argument to its conclusion, and perpetually reminds us that both author and reader "are such stuff / As dreams are made on."

Notes

1. For Borges and "Manierismus," see Gustav Hocke, *Manicrismus in der Literatur* (Hamburg, 1959), pp. 22–23, and Marianne Kesting, *Vermessung des Labyrinths* (Frankfurt am Main, 1965), pp. 50–56. See also John Updike's excellent article on Borges, "The Author as Librarian," *The New Yorker* (October 30, 1965), pp. 223–246.

2. Borges, "El milagro secreto" ["The Secret Miracle"], *Ficciones*, in *Obras Completas* (Buenos Aires, 1956), V, 162. Further references to tales in this edition will be given in the text, using the abbreviation *F*. Where English translations are readily available, either in *Ficciones*, ed. Anthony Kerrigan (New York, 1962), or in *Labyrinths: Selected Stories and Other Writings*, ed. Donald A. Yates and James E. Irby (New York, 1962), the English titles will be given in the text in square brackets. English translations have been supplied, in parentheses, for all quotations, and for the titles of stories not found in these editions.

3. (Laconic nightmares.) See Borges' introduction to his translation of nine Kafka stories, *La metamorfosis* (Buenos Aires, 1938), p. 7.

4. See Nabokov's Foreword to *Invitation to a Beheading* (New York, 1965), p. 6, where he firmly denies the possibility of a "Kafkaesque" strain, as he had read no Kafka at the time he wrote the book.

5. *Laughter in the Dark* (New York, 1938), p. 182.

6. *Conclusive Evidence: A Memoir* (New York, 1951), p. 137.

7. Wilkie Collins, Chesterton, Agatha Christie and Ellery Queen are among the many authors represented in his anthology *Los mejores cuentos policiales*, 2d series (Buenos Aires, 1951). See also his *Antología de la literatura fantástica* (Buenos Aires, 1940).

8. In numerous other stories ("El Sur" ["The South"], or "Hombre de la esquina rosada," for instance), where the hero follows a devious route to his doom, Borges leaves to the reader the detective's function of reasoning from clues, of supplying the missing scene or the true explanation. Detective-story structure is still there; "story" still equals "puzzle," but some of its paraphernalia has dropped away.

9. Ana María Barrenechea, *Borges the Labyrinth Maker*, ed. and tr. Robert Lima (New York, 1965), p. 22.

10. *The Real Life of Sebastian Knight* (Norfolk, 1959), pp. 91–95.

11. *The Eye* (New York, 1965), pp. 9–10.

12. This idea is interestingly corroborated in Martin Green's valuable article, "The Morality of *Lolita*," *Kenyon Review*, XXVIII:3 (June 1966), 357. The Quilty-Humbert-Lolita triangle is foreshadowd in many ways by the Rex-Albinus-Margot triangle in *Laughter in the Dark* (New York, 1938), with Rex a phonier, more corrupt Albinus ("Rex was Albinus' shadow," p. 208), and Albinus a feebler, but equally possessive and unwanted Humbert, seeking a blind man's revenge upon his fickle mistress by stalking her, horribly, in the "dark."

13. New York, 1962. See Kinbote's Foreword, p. 26, and Commentary on lines 47–48, p. 83. For Gradus' labyrinth, see especially p. 78 (Commentary on lines 17 and 29). Shade's Zembla is merely his own unshaven face in the mirror (ll. 937–8). But cf. Swift, scattering innuendoes for Rosicrucian commentators (as Nabokov plants clues for his Freudian interpreters), and the elaborate artifices of *The Battle of the Books*: "a malignant Deity, call'd *Criticism* . . . dwelt on the Top of a snowy Mountain in *Nova Zembla.*"

14. Even Pnin, in the novel which has perhaps less "flaunting of artifice" than any of the others, insists that his colleague, Wynn, has a "double," a "T. Wyn."

15. "Biografía de Tadeo Isidoro Cruz (1829–1874)," *El Aleph* (Buenos Aires, 1962), p. 66. See also "El espejo de tinta," in *Historia universal de la infamia* (Buenos Aires, 1935), for a good example of the paradoxical identity of victim and executioner. The theme of mirrors runs through the whole work of both authors, and along with their other images of artifice — chess and card games, maps, juggling and conjuring, masks and disguises, invented languages, and so on — it deserves to be discussed at length.

16. Life imitates art; see Edward J. Brown, "Nabokov and Pushkin," *Slavic Review* (December, 1965), 688 ff., for a discussion of Nabokov's real scholarly commentary on a real poem as an extension of the techniques of *Pale Fire*.

17. Again there is a false double; Sebastian is already dead, and the brother sits all night by the side of the wrong man. Nabokov's numerous books-within-books more often provide a mocking contrast to the outer book, as in the false life of Sebastian which his brother must explicitly refute by writing "the real life" (a Cervantean touch), and as in *Pale Fire* itself. But cf. Cincinnatus' Journal, Krug's writings on philosophy, the literary biography within *The Gift* and especially the elaborate concept (*Band Sinister*, p. 73) of inventing the works of Shakespeare as a hoax, and making all the interpolations in subsequent books that are needed to certify to the existence of the plays. This hoax is remarkably like the composition of the Encyclopedia of Tlön, which got away from its makers and became real, or like Pierre Menard's re-writing *Don Quixote* word for word. Cf. "La escritura del Dios," for the phrase that solves everything, the phrase of magic power.

18. *Bend Sinister* (New York, 1964). See especially Nabokov's introduction (1963), pp. xii, xiv, xviii, the whole of chapter 7 and p. 116.

19. "El Golem," *Poemas 1923–1958* (O.C. II), p. 173. See also the conclusion of

"magias parciales del *Quijote*" ["Partial Enchantments of the *Quixote*"] for the key image of infinite regression, the perfect map which must contain a map of itself within it, which must in turn contain . . . and for the propositon that the metaphysical significance of plays within plays is simply that it reminds us that "if the characters in a story can be readers or spectators, then we, their readers or spectators, can be ficticious [also]." *Other Inquisitions*, tr. Ruth L.C. Simms (Austin, 1964), p. 46.

20. As, in a different way, Luzhin (*The Defense*) turns life into the pattern of a chess-game and the world into a giant chess-board: a dangerous trifling with the actual from which only death can release him.

21. See not only Olaf Stapledon's *Starmaker* (1939) for a source of these ideas, but also the selection from *Starmaker* that Borges translated and included in his *Antología de la literatura fantástica*. (p. 182)

22. See Jacques Scherer's commentary, *Le "Livre" de Mallarmé* (Paris, 1957). Cf. Shade's lines 939–40: "*Man's life as commentary to abstruse / Unfinished poem*. Note for further use," and Kinbote's paraphrase of them. (p. 272)

23. Ernst Curtius, *European Literature and the Latin Middle Ages* (New York, 1963), gives some interesting early examples of "The Book as Symbol," pp. 302–347. See also Borges' "Del culto de los libros" ["On the Cult of Books"], *Otros Inquisiciones*, where he gives a brief yet detailed history of the topos of the Absolute Book, with references to Carlyle, Léon Bloy, Sir Thomas Browne, Sir Francis Bacon, and the *Koran*, among others. Marianne Kestner summarizes Borges' relation to the baroque world-theatre or world-book as follows: "aber immerhin noch Gott die Fäden in den Händen halten liess, während hinter Borges Metaphern sich das unendliche Nichts verbirgt." (*Vermessung*, p. 54)

24. "La biblioteca total," *Sur* LIX: 59 (August 1939), p. 16. A case of a pure essay giving literary antecedents and historical facts, later to be turned into the "fiction," or philosophical parable, of "La biblioteca de Babel," where this quotation, slightly altered, is used again, along with a similar list of hypothetical books.

25. "El otro tigre" ['The Other Tiger"], and also the prose poem "Dreamtigers," both in *El Hacedor* (Buenos Aires, 1960), pp. 76, 12. Translated in *Dreamtigers* (Austin, 1964).

26. "El truco," *El idioma de los argentinos* (Buenos Aires, 1928), p. 34.

27. "Epílogo" ["Epilogue"], and "Una rosa amarilla" ["A Yellow Rose"], *El hacedor*, p. 109, pp. 31–32.

28. Humbert, for instance, calls himself "an artist and a madman, a creature of infinite melancholy," and then identifies himself with "poets and lovers," *Lolita* (New York, 1959), p. 19 and p. 50.

Borges and Thomas De Quincey   Ronald Christ*

An imaginary still-life composed of two principal objects can, by his own choice, represent De Quincey's spirit and evoke his presence: marking the visual horizon, the arm of an easy chair nudges a small table top where, in the foreground, we see the ingredients of De Quincey's spiritual communion — a large decanter of red laudanum and an open book of German metaphysics. Placed side by side, these iconographical objects

*From *The Narrow Act: Borges's Art of Allusion* (New York: New York University Press, 1969). Reprinted by permission of the author.

will, De Quincey tells us, "sufficiently attest my being in the neighbor-hood" (II, 418). Both instruments of imagination and high fancy, the bottle and the book, nevertheless, exhibit two strains of mental activity in De Quincey. On the one hand, the container of laudanum represents the personal and subjective, the internal scene of nightmare and dream, the activated individual memory creating unending corridors, vast ruins, and dramas of frustrated search from its own store of images; in a word, the psychologically *autobiographical*, which in De Quincey always takes us back to what he called "the dream-theatre of my childhood" (XIII, 340). On the other hand the book may stand for his externalized intellect fixing on studies and occupations which support and extend, nurture and develop that private world. If the former is childlike and fanciful, a form of mental play—terrifying—yielding image and scene, the latter is adult and learned, a mode of employment—necessary and inevitable—produc-ing information and argument. The laudanum expresses the *vates*, the book tokens the *gramaticus* (that it is a book of *German* metaphysics may be a sufficient indication of *doctus*); but only in conjunction—it *is* a book of metaphysics after all—do they typify that writer who, in so many ways, is the prototype of the curious combination we find in Borges.

Borges first read De Quincey around 1917. He was about eighteen, and the effect, apparently, was immediate, while the affect, certainly, has been chronic. De Quincey, of course, is famous for two things: first, an elaborate style, and second, descriptions of opiate, visionary experience—the respective signs of *gramaticus* and *vates*. Although it may have been that famous style alone which first attracted Borges, there can be no doubt that it is the metaphysical, and thus, for Borges, concomitant erudite quality in De Quincey's works, which have held Borges's attention and issued in his writings. Here as almost everywhere, Borges's concern with the mystic or metaphysical takes precedence, total or final, over the writer's value as stylist, as *literato*. So when we come to describing the actual influence, or more accurately, the real presence of De Quincey in Borges, we are by and large able to pass over stylistic influence and concentrate on two phases of what may be called, with Borgesean license, mysticism—the learned, symbolized by the book, and the personal, symbolized by the decanter.

ERUDITION

Dividing his writings according to subject into the matter of autobi-ography and the matter of literature (far from an exact division), one finds that the latter accounts for the bulk and the former for the best of De Quincey's work. His writing is largely the product of reviewing and explaining, translating and editing, abridging and reworking other people's books, so that Albert Goldman, who probably knows more about the question that anyone else, is convinced "that De Quincey's dependence on printed sources is the key to his literary career."[1] We could say the same thing of Borges and reapply Bioy Casares' phrase by noting that De Quincey's essays, like all of Borges' prose, are "a literature of literature," adding with emphasis Casares' next phrase: "and of thought,"[2] for De Quincey, like Borges, chiefly pursues poetry, history, philosophy, and theology. Both men contemplate vast synthesizing projects — *History of Eternity*, "Prolegomena to all Future Systems of Political Economy" — and write essays which digest the enormous breadth of their reading. In fact De Quincey's peculiar use of the essay form may have served to determine Borges' own. Both employ the essay in the way David Masson ascribes to De Quincey:

> An "Essay," in his definition of it (which, however, may not be univer-
> sally accepted), is a paper addressed purely or primarily to the under-
> standing as an insulated faculty, — *i.e.* distinguished from other papers
> by containing a good deal of the speculative element. It does not merely
> give information by presenting in a compact shape all the existing
> knowledge on any subject; nor is its main object that of delight to the
> reader by dreams and pictures of the poetical kind; nor does it seek
> merely to rouse and stimulate the feelings for active exertion of some
> sort; but, without any of these aims, or while perhaps studying one or
> other of them to some extent, it has in view always the solution of some
> problem, the investigation of some question, so as to effect a modifica-
> tion or advance of the existing doctrine on the subject. (VI, 1–2)

Both share an intense interest in the written past which enters their works in many ways, none more persistent or revelatory of their bookishness than the etymologies which trail along the bottom of De Quincey's pages and tense Borges' prose. The hallmark of this bookishness in De Quincey, the footnote, carried to its baroque extreme of footnoting footnotes,[3] is also stamped on Borges' work. De Quincey's comprehensive and idiosyncratic scholarship, matched by Borges' own peculiar erudition, is a continuing source of discovery for Borges, who writes: "The work which endures is always capable of an infinite and plastic ambiguity; it is everything for everyone, like the Apostle; it is a mirror which manifests the traits of the reader and it is also a map of the world" (*OI*, 126–27). This is precisely the effect of De Quincey's *Works* — infinite and encyclopedic, but precise and individual as well. In a word, an *Aleph*, as Borges' works strive for alefdom. De Quincey is himself a mirror of the world, a collection of possibilities for essays, stories, poems, quotations. His work is a seeming *Brittanica* which implies and substantiates a world of literature and thought; De Quincey the writer is reader and dreamer.

In De Quincey, as in Borges, the metaphysical and the erudite are seldom separated; they are, in fact, aspects of each other, since books of abstruse doctrine are after all abstruse themselves. De Quincey recognizes this when he describes his reading: "I will assert finally that, after having read for thirty years in the same track as Coleridge — that track in which few of any age will ever follow us, such as German metaphysicians, Latin schoolmen, thaumaturgia, Platonists, religious Mystics . . ." (II, 147). The Coleridgean series proposed by De Quincey prophetically includes Borges as a subsequent term, if not as the terminus itself; but there is this difference: Borges self-consciously exploits this train of reading to elicit the fantastic undercurrent in life. Abstruseness is a positive value in his writing. Working, as he usually does, on the explicit or implicit equation of life and literature, the world and a library, Borges asserts the possibility of a hidden key (like the volume searched for in "The Library of Babel") which necessarily must exist in a remote place. Literature, like life, is a mystery and a dream; they are both fundamentally recondite, and the purpose of his work, the procedure of his mind, is always to pierce to that secret meaning: "Epictetus ("Remember the essential: the door is open") and Schopenhauer ("Is Hamlet's monologue the meditation of a criminal?") have vindicated suicide with a multitude of pages; the prior certainty that those defenders are right makes us read negligently. That is what happened to me with the *Biathanatos* until I perceived, or believed that I perceived, an implicit or esoteric argument beneath the notorious argument" (*OI*, 130). The negligence of our acceptance of these arguments is the same negligence with which we accept the surface of literature (the point, remember, of "The Approach"); it is, in fact, the same negligence which leads to our acceptance of apparential reality: we receive life itself with "previous certitude." Borges shocks us with the weird and marvellous from his fund of knowledge in order to destroy that easy negligence and force our attention to an awareness of our existence which he discovers or imagines ("I perceived, or thought I perceived"), one which is both intrinsic and esoteric. The uncommon, the supernatural, the fantastic all serve his end: to demonstrate the esoteric, he depends on the esoteric. Hence the Coleridgean strain which works its way into his text is intended to give us the content of that mystery, and a key or kind of solution, just as it is in De Quincey; while the means of its entry, in allusions to obscure authors or to little-known passages of well-known ones, is intended to give us a real *sense* of discovering the inherently occult nature of literature and life itself. Borges cultivates fantastic literature because life is fantastic; he is erudite, similarly, because "meaning" is erudite. What, then, is the implicit quality or character of De Quincey's writing becomes the very point of Borges.

FORMS OF INTERCHANGE

De Quincey's polymathic writing suggest Borges' fictions and essays; Borges' writings discover De Quincey's compositions: the commutual relationship is carefully and consciously elaborated by Borges for personal reasons and esthetic ends. The interchange assumes various forms, of which I want to consider four: the documented debt, the congenerous story or essay, the method of construction, and the fundamental image or symbol.

Emblematic of the first form is the opening sentence of Borges' essay on Donne's "Biathanatos": "To De Quincey (to whom my debt is so vast that to specify one part seems to repudiate or to silence the others) I owe my first awareness of the *Biathanatos*," (*OI*, 129). The debt acknowledged here is one of information, perhaps knowledge, and it is almost always for surprising thought or stimulating information that Borges cites De Quincey. Unlike Wells, who is recognized in the epilogue of *El Aleph* (*A*, 172) to have impressed the central, inspiring images of two stories on Borges' imagination, De Quincey is usually recognized, most often with unusual specificity of volume and page number, to have supplied material from what David Masson, De Quincey's editor, calls "his budget of carefully acquired erudition, often most curious and out of the way" (VI, 3). Therefore it is not strange to find De Quincey referred to only a few times in the stories, many times in the discursive writings. In "The Immortal" he is credited with having contributed a descriptive passage (*A*, 26), and more typically in "Three Versions of Judas" (*F*, 170) he is quoted for a theory about Judas. But even more usual expressions of the one writer's thought working through the other occur in terse references like the epigraph to *Evaristo Carriego*; the anecdote in *Discussion* about a pastor who swore from the pulpit by the *Iliad* and *Odyssey* (*D*, 145); a footnote to "The 'Biathanatos'" (*OI*, 132); a passing reference in "From Alegories to Novels" (*OI*, 211); or the brief reminder of De Quincey's own reminder that ". . . the true name of Rome was secret . . ." (*OI*, 224). De Quincey appears, overtly at least, in Borges' works as an item in the stock of erudition, much as many authors figure in De Quincey's own essays, and it would seem that the major appeal of De Quincey for Borges is the way in which his works (*both* their works, to be sure) proceed from "libraries that stretch into infinity, like the armies of Xerxes . . ." (VI, 295). But the references to De Quincey are only clues to the profound connection between their imaginations. What Borges got from De Quincey in the way of useful information — useful to him, that is — he could have gotten finally from numerous other sources, from De Quincey's own sources. A case in point is the theme of Achilles and the tortoise, which Borges presents in "The Perpetual Race of Achilles and the Tortoise," and in "Avatars of the Tortoise," briefly returns to in "Kafka and His Precursors," and mentions, in a slightly different form, in "The Lottery in Babylon." Borges must know De Quincey's treatment of the same conundrum in the biographical sketch of Sir William Hamilton (V, 330–32), and he cannot be unfamiliar with De Quincey's proffered solution, yet De Quincey is never mentioned in either of Borges' essays on the subject, where authors from Artistotle to Lewis Carroll are cited. The two men travel the same rivers of knowledge, right to their sources, so that the many referential allusions to De Quincey in Borges' writing really takes us very little of the way toward appreciating what Borges ultimately found in De Quincey.

There is this to be learned from the explicit references to De Quincey: Borges' referential allusions, especially those which indicate a borrowing or a "debt," seldom tell the whole story. They point us in the right direction, but as to real information, they are apt to ignore more than they avow. A good example occurs in the reference to De Quincey in "The Immortal," which I cited in the preceding paragraph. As we shall see later, the description of the ruinous city which Borges admits borrowing from De Quincey, is by no means the whole of his obligation nor even the most important part. There is, then, in addition to the strikingly explicit quality of Borges' listing the sources for his fiction, a secret property: the appearance of scrupulous, almost scholarly acknowledgment does not correspond to the real basis in other writings. If nothing else, a recognition of this property should guide the reader to a sense of these references as selected, controlled statements rather than as expressions of literary *politesse* or pedantry.

The case of "The Perpetual Race of Achilles and the Tortoise" is typical in that Borges often makes no reference to De Quincey's essays, even when he is writing on a theme which De Quincey develops at length. In my first chapter I mentioned "The Cult of the Phoenix"; other examples are "The Secret Miracle" and "The Immortal." To *prove* that Borges actually found his inspiration in De Quincey's essay "Secret Societies" for the first story and in the essay called "Miracles as Subject of Testimony" for the second story may indeed be possible, while the case for his having lifted his theme for the third from De Quincey's "Homer and the Homeridae" is circumstantially, at least, beyond a doubt. But, especially in the first two examples, I have neither sufficient evidence nor the inclination to make such an ascription, and prefer instead to look at these similarities in another way, namely under the heading of congeners. By "congeners" I mean to describe the parallel or sibling status of the works in question rather than the origin-outcome status which is so often the conclusion in studies of influence. This heading is legitimate, because in each case what Borges finds in De Quincey is information, perhaps even first knowledge, but knowledge which itself is funneled from immense reading, which in turn becomes or already is part of Borges' own vast store. The debt therefore is not so much *to* De Quincey as *through* De Quincey, to previous and even subsequent sources. De Quincey, like Sir Thomas Browne and Pliny, is a repository of erudition to which Borges returns again and again, only to be sent out to the same and other quarries from which these writers gathered their supplies of matter. In turn, Borges' own work becomes a new repository, more selective, more concentrated, more synthetic, but fundamentally the same.

Borges' story "The Cult of the Phoenix" is a brief, non-narrative fiction in the form of an unstated riddle—still another indication of Borges' sense of mystery. The story describes a sect or secret society and refers to an enigmatic rite which guarantees immortality to the sect's members. By claiming that the mysterious rite "does not require description" (*F*, 183) Borges leaves the reader with a puzzle. Those readers I have talked with all suggest that the answer is propagation by sexual intercourse, a way of guaranteeing the immortality of species rather than of individuals. At first this seems a properly Borgesean interpretation, but it finally is unacceptable and explicitly denied by "The Nightingale of Keats" which argues that "the individual is in some way the species . . ." (*OI*, 167), and is supported by Emerson's essay "Nominalist and Realist," to which Borges alludes on several occasions, which states that "We fancy men are individuals; so are pumpkins; but every pumpkin in the field goes through every point of pumpkin history."[4] Then there are those perplexing ingredients of cork, wax, gum arabic and, sometimes, slime or mud. One chooses to stop short of seeing a sexual implication in those. I think Borges has a rather more typically metaphysical answer in mind. The rite which is celebrated by the sect of the Phoenix is the last rite, that of death. We die in order to be reborn, a point illustrated by "The Immortal"; and as for the sect's emblem, Sir Thomas Browne says about the Phoenix in *Pseudodoxia Epidemica*: "So have holy men made use hereof as far as thereby to confirm the Resurrection. . . ."[5] I must admit, however, that I owe my solution of the puzzle to a reading of De Quincey's essay "Secret Societies" which could well have inspired Borges' story.[6]

In "Secret Societies" De Quincey speaks of those he has read about and offers several bits of information which are appropriate to Borges' story. De Quincey's startling point about the most famous of secret societies—the Eleusinian Mysteries and Freemasonry—is that they have no secret: the rite they guard is nonexistent or vulgarly commonplace and therefore cannot be revealed because no one would believe it to be a mystery. In this account, one can see an impetus for the form of "The Cult of the Phoenix." The second fact is that most such societies are concerned with immortality. On the one hand we have the frauds, whom De Quincey sarcastically whips: "He (Bishop Warburton) knew, he could circumstantially reveal, what was taught in the Eleusinian shows. Was the Bishop ever there? No; but what of that? He could read through a milestone. And Vergil, in his 6th Aeneid, had given the world a poetic account of the *Teletai*, which the Bishop kindly translated and expanded into the truth of absolute prose. The doctrine of immortality, he insisted, was the chief secret revealed in the mysteries" (VII, 198). But, in contrast, De Quincey had read of societies which meet ". . . in secret chambers at the noontide of night, to shelter, by muffling with their own persons interposed, and at their own risk, some solitary lamp of truth—sheltering it from the carelessness of the world and its stormy ignorance; *that* would soon have blown it out—sheltering it from the hatred of the world; *that* would soon have made war upon its life: all this was superhumanly sublime" (VII, 181). De Quincey goes on to describe the immortality of such societies and specifically to introduce the Phoenix: "But another feature of sublimity, which it surprises me to see so many irreflective men unaware of, lies in the self-perpetuation and phoenix-like defiance to mortality of such societies. . . . Often and often have men of finer minds felt this secret spell of grandeur, and laboured to embody it in external form" (VII, 182). One of these "men of finer minds" was De Quincey; another is Borges, whose story is precisely a response to this "secret spell of grandeur," and whose imagination seems to have been stirred by De Quincey's history of such societies:

> There was a Phoenix Club once in Oxford (up and down Europe there have been several), that by its constitution grasped not only at the sort of immortality aspired after by Phoenix insurance offices— . . . far more faithful, literal, intense, was the realization in this Oxford case of undying life. Such a condition as a "sede vacante," which is a condition expressed in the constitution of all other societies, was impossible in this for any office whatever. That great case was realised which has since been described by Chateaubriand as governing the throne of France and its successions. "His Majesty is dead!" shouts a voice; and this seems to argue at least a moment's interregnum. Not at all—not a moment's: the thing is impossible. Simultaneous (and not successive) is the breath that ejaculates "May the King live for ever!" The birth and death, the rising and the setting, synchronise by a metaphysical nicety of neck-and-neck, inconceivable to the bookkeepers of earth. . . . Now this Oxford club arose on these sublime principles: no disease like intermitting pulse was known *there*. No fire but vestal fire was used for boiling the teakettle. The rule was that, if once entered upon the *matricula* of this amaranthine club, thence-forwards, come from what zone of earth you would . . . instantly you are shown in to the sublime presence. You were not limited to any particular century. Nay, by the rigour of the theory, you had your own choice of millennium. (VII, 182–83)

The secret of the society at Oxford is not the same as that of Borges' sect, but the underlying principle surely is. In fact this underlying principle is the theme and goal of Borges' thought and imagination: "The same principle in man's nature, the everlasting instinct for glorifying the everlasting, the impulse for petrifying the fugitive and arresting the transitory, which shows itself in ten thousand forms, has also, in this field of secret confederations, assumed many grander forms. To strive after a conquest over Time the conqueror, to confound the grim confounder is already great, in whatsoever direction" (VII, 184). We can imagine the response such passages, with their refutations of space, time, and individuality evoked in the mind of Borges. We can point with confidence to these same passages and declare them the source or origin of his conundrum, but just a brief look at the manuscript page reproduced in *The Paris Review*[7] will indicate the broader base of Borges' information.

The important thing to remember is the foundation in reading for both De Quincey and Borges. The one begins, in the section I quoted: "But in Barruel I had heard only of Secret Societies that were consciously formed for mischievous ends. . . . Soon I read of other societies, even more secret . . ." (VII, 181). And the other: "Those who write that the Sect of the Phoenix had its origin in Heliopolis and derive it from the religious restoration which followed the death of the reformer Amenophis IV, allege texts from Herodotus, Tacitus, and the Egyptian monuments, but they are ignorant of the fact that the denomination by the Phoenix is not anterior to Hrabano Mauro and that the oldest sources (the *Saturnalia* or Flavius Joseph, let us say) only speak of the People of the Custom or of the People of the Secret" (F, 181). Borges' sources are apparently wider than De Quincey's—in one point they are definitely more inclusive in that De Quincey himself figures—but both the essay and the story derive from other works and are developed according to each author's individual intentions. The manuscript page confirms what his notes, prefaces, and epilogues assert: Borges writes by a process of accretion. Certainly this is the obvious practice of his essays which add reference to reference and summary to summary in a sequential order which seems to reflect the final organization of a complex note-taking system. De Quincey's system is different, but no less contingent on other books.

Much recent study of De Quincey, culminating in Albert Goldman's book, *The Mine and the Mint*, emphasizes this aspect of De Quincey's work. *Rifacimento* is what Goldman appropriately labels the procedure, and while that is not Borges' method, one explanation Goldman offers for De Quincey's adopting this method is curiously similar to an aspect of Borges I described earlier:

> For it is one of the peculiar traits of De Quincey's character that he must invariably work as though behind a mask; and even when he has expended the most enormous effort in recasting some wretched piece of historiography or biography, he must perforce claim that his original and highly imaginative work is an authentic and scholarly document. This strange and perverse passion for truth—or at least for an appearance of truthfulness—can be ascribed . . . either to his practical sense that a romanticized version of historical fact would not be acceptable to his English readers, or else to some deep peculiarity in his nature which made the act of creation something secret and furtive, something that must never be openly avowed.[8]

De Quincey's claim is the fictional basis of "Pierre Menard," of "The Approach," and of portions of other Borges' stories; and De Quincey's "deep peculiarity" may correspond to Borges' timidity about writing fiction in the first place. It is entirely possible that Borges is familiar with De Quincey's literary methods (after all Goldman tells us nothing really new about De Quincey; he merely documents the extent of what De Quincey himself alerts us to). On the other hand it may be the principle

Borges announced in "Kafka and His Precursors" which leads us to see a Borgesean quality in De Quincey's deceptions. I shall offer two examples to support respectively and simultaneously my alternative surmises.

The *Walladmore* hoax is one of the minor, forgotten scandals of literary history.[9] A German writer, taking advantage of Sir Walter Scott's popularity, wrote an imitation Waverly novel which he claimed only to have translated from English. De Quincey translated sections of the book and summarized the rest in an abusive review which also laid bare the imposture, but he ended by translating the novel, in abridged form, into English. The title page of De Quincey's English translation of the German translation of a nonexistent novel epitomizes an authentic Borgesean artifice-within-artifice revealing a central nullity which is the source of all: " 'Freely translated into German from the English of Walter Scott' and now Freely Translated from the German into English." Did Borges take the cue for some of his literary high jinks from De Quincey's behavior? I do not know, but there is a good chance that a less startling bluff of De Quincey's, but a no less metaphysically potent one, did come to his attention. Goldman summarizes nicely:

> At first sight there would not appear to be any need to demonstrate a source for De Quincey's series of papers on the Homeric question "Homer and the Homeridae." The reason for this is that in his introductory remarks in the first of these three articles, De Quincey states quite frankly that he intends to seat himself in the chair of the foremost German authority on this subject, a certain Nitzsch, and expound the views of that scholar, which are inaccessible to most readers, locked up as they are in the remote fastness of an enormous German encyclopedia bearing the forbidding title *Allgemeine Encyklopadie der Wissenschaften und Kunste*. This unaccustomed show of ingenuousness, however, proves to be a blind, for when one consults the dusty volumes of the *Universal Encyclopedia*, one finds that the article entitled "Homeros" was not written by Nitzsch, who is in fact the author of a well-known commentary on the *Odyssey*, but by an obscure person named Grotefend; and there is no reason to believe De Quincey consulted this article.[10]

We know that Borges follows De Quincey's leads—reads the books De Quincey names; we know that Borges reads German encyclopedias for pleasure; we know that he wrote a story entitled "The Immortal" which deals with Homer, fulfills suggestions made by De Quincey, and even explicitly cites De Quincey as a source; but if we lacked all this information, we could be fairly certain that Borges, a man who reacts to the fascinating strangeness of the name Yarmolinsky, could not possibly pass by the temptation of that monosyllable—*Nitzsch* (especially since De Quincey quips: "Nitzsch's name is against him. It is intolerable to see such a thicket of consonants with but one little bit of a vowel amongst them; it is like the proportions between Falstaff's bread and his sack" [VI, 16]. But all such speculation aside, the fact remains, even if the motive and methods are different, that Borges and De Quincey fabricate their writings from other writings and often free themselves of obligations to factual accuracy by disguised and distorted references. The similarity is unquestionable, the difference indicative: Borges has seen a metaphysical possibility where none seemed to exist. Whether he learned the procedure of building literature out of literature from De Quincey or not, and whether he hit upon his special device of the phantom book within a book from De Quincey or not, the opportunities to do so were there, so that if we choose not to see De Quincey as the source of Borges' inspiration on these points, we must see, even more inevitably as a consequence, a kinship of mind and intellectual disposition which is perhaps more important than any specific influence could have been.

After these similarities of intellectual content and artistic strategy and form have been suggested, we are in a position to approach what from my point of view is the most significant aspect of Borges' relationship to De Quincey—the sharing of a common world view expressed in a common imagery. As we read through the diffusive volumes of De Quincey's *Works* after the trenchant brevity of Borges' essays and stories, the thing which strikes us first is the frequency with which we encounter, not only the same idea, but twin formulations in striking images. We are, given the situation I have set up, attuned to Borges' imagery and therefore supersensitive to any similarities in De Quincey; that is, we are apt to notice things which would not have struck us previously—the tiger or the mirror, for example—but as these resemblances mount and intensify we are unable to ignore them.

I mentioned the tiger—I mentioned the mirror too, but a discussion of that would not be complete without extensive mention of other writers, Chesterton, for example, and that would take me too far from my appointed subject. The tiger, then, is one of Borges' favorite animals, and the subject of a two-paragraph autobiographical piece called "*Dreamtigers*," where he explains how as a child the ferocious Asian tiger captured his imagination and how it still haunts his dreams. He returns to the tiger in "The Writing of God," in "The Circular Ruins," and particularly to Blake's tiger (that the title "*Dreamtigers*" is in English matters) in *Evaristo Carriego* and again in *Other Inquisitions*: ". . . the infinite nightingale has sung in British literature; Chaucer and Shakespeare, Milton and Matthew Arnold celebrate it, but to John Keats we inevitably link its image, as to Blake that of the tiger" (*OI*, 169). It must have been with some satisfaction, therefore, that he encountered passages like the following in De Quincey:

. . . with eyes glaring like a tiger's . . . (XII, 247)

Now, terror there may be, but how can there be any pity for one tiger destroyed by another tiger? (XIII, 47)

. . . the tiger's heart was masked by the insinuating and snaky refinement . . . (XIII, 78)

The tiger that slept in Catalina wakened at once. (XIII, 182)

. . . Death the crowned phantom, with all the equipage of his terrors and the tiger roar of his voice. (XIII, 318)

. . . bounding with tiger's leaps . . . (XIII, 368)

A very small point of correspondence, surely, but I think it sufficient to show that as well as providing a stock of metaphysical topics and information which activate and nourish Borges' mind, De Quincey provides images or concretions of metaphysical intuitions, which no less meaningfully stimulate Borges' imagination and corroborate his own responses; and as long as we are talking of these two men as writers, there can be little more important than the verbal pictures they have in common.

Notes

1. *The Mine and the Mint* (Carbondale and Edwardsville, Illinois, 1965), p. 154.
2. *Sur*, 92 (May, 1942), 60.
3. See VI, 338, 358, 359 for examples.
4. *Complete Essays*, p. 446.
5. *The Works of Sir Thomas Browne*, ed. Charles Sayle (Edinburgh, 1912), III, 7.

6. I am wrong—and right—as I learned after writing this. When Borges was in New York in 1968, I asked him if he ever revealed the answer to the riddle. "Yes, sometimes." Would he tell me? And I knew, at once, my error: he turned and looked at his wife for a moment and then said, "Not now; tomorrow, I'd like to keep you guessing for one more day." The following day at a reception I reminded him of his promise. He leaned over and whispered into my ear so that no one else could hear: "Well, the act is what Whitman says 'the divine husband knows, from the work of fatherhood.'—When I first heard about this act, when I was a boy, I was shocked, shocked to think that my mother, my father had performed it. It is an amazing discovery, no? But then too it is an act of immortality, a rite of immortality, isn't it?"

Borges' sense of decorum further explains the form of the story while his childhood shock helps explain the appearance of dirt in the rite itself. For the source of his Whitman-esque euphemism, see "From Pent-Up Aching Rivers" in the "Children of Adam" section of *Leaves of Grass* (*Complete Poetry*, p. 70).

7. No. 40 (Winter–Spring, 1967) pp. 152–53.

8. *The Mine and the Mint*, p. 10.

9. For a detailed account of the hoax and the sources of my information see De Quincey's note to "Walladmore, a Pseudo-Waverly Novel" (XIV, 132–45) and *The Mine and the Mint*, pp. 92–97.

10. *The Mine and the Mint*, p. 64.

Borges and American Fiction
1950–1970
Tony Tanner*

"The fear of the crassly infinite, of mere space, of mere matter, touched Averroes for an instant. He looked at the symmetrical garden. . . ." The implied opposition here between the man-made symmetry and mere space and matter is analogous to the feeling I have been trying to point to in Nabokov's work. It comes however, from a story by Jorge Luis Borges, a writer whom Nabokov admires and with whom he has much in common (even in possible influences—they both greatly admire Lewis Carroll, James Joyce, of course, and Robert Louis Stevenson, and it seems that both of them were struck by Carlyle's idea in *Sartor Resartus* of writing a commentary on an imaginary work of literature). Borges is a Latin American writer whose work has had a significant influence on recent American writers. Some of the recurrent furniture of his stories is like Nabokov's—mirrors, chess, games, labyrinths, doubles; they both share an awe for man's fiction-making powers, and help to remind us that we live in fictions anyway, that the dividing line between dream and reality is not so easily drawn. In an interview Borges rejected any idea that his work was tendentious—"I have no intentions"—and referred to it as "a kind of juggling," a juggling of "just words."[1] He also said, "Really, nobody knows whether the world is realistic or fantastic, that is to say, whether the world is a natural process or whether it is a kind of dream, a dream that we may or may not share with others." This feeling is partly responsible for the strange, haunting atmosphere of his short elusive parables whose ontological status often seems to be in doubt. By this I mean that most of them are offered as bits of impeccable, if arcane, erudition, but erudition conducted in such remote areas of knowledge that it is impossible for the reader to tell where erudition ends and invention begins, and he enters a realm of twilight or penumbral knowledge. From strange depths in the stories we are suddenly brought back to the surface and do not know quite what it is we have read. It may be a dream or a game or a fantasy, but why then did it move us so much?

It is the constructional power of the human mind that moves and amazes Borges. His stories are full of the strangest architecture—the Library of Babel, the City of the Immortals, the Garden of Forking Paths, as well as examples of the endless variety of lexical architecture to which man throughout history has devoted his time—philosophical theories, theological disputes, encyclopaedias, religious beliefs, critical interpretations, novels, and books of all kinds. There are also a large number of plots referred to in his stories (cosmic and criminal), and there is a comparable amount of that counter-plotting called detection. All these are ways in

*From *City of Words: American Fiction 1950–1970* (New York: Harper & Row, 1971). Reprinted by permission of the publisher.

which man has introduced shapes into that "mere space, mere matter" which touched the heart of his ancient philosopher with dread.

The imperatives of pattern-making, of "building," are very clear to Borges, as are their own very equivocal results, and that is one reason why his short parables are so remote from any of the conventions of European naturalism. He admires Henry James, but prefers the stories to the novels, and the situations to the characters: it would seem that he prefers to aim for an almost diagrammatic clarity, aware that such clarity can make for the most intense sense of mystery and enigma. One of his stories, "Funes, the Memorious," is about a young man who after an accident is able to perceive every detail of everything going on around him. In addition to this hypersensitivity of perception he is unable to forget a single perceptual or imaginary experience. This sets him the task of trying to invent new ways of classifying the constantly growing heaps of his perceptions: yet he is aware that the job is both interminable and useless. The moral would seem to point to the possible thraldom of detail.

> He was the solitary and lucid spectator of a multiform world which was instantaneously and almost intolerably exact. . . . It was very difficult for him to sleep. To sleep is to be abstracted from the world . . . I suspect, nevertheless, that he was not very capable of thought. To think is to forget a difference, to generalize, to abstract. In the overly replete world of Funes there were nothing but details, almost contiguous details.

Funes dies of pulmonary congestion. This sense of the need for abstractions to secure some removal from the welter of experience can be found in a number of the American novelists we will be discussing.

While having a deep feeling for the shaping and abstracting powers of man's mind, Borges has at the same time a profound sense of how nightmarish the resultant structures might become. The library at Babel is referred to by the narrator as the "universe" and one can take it as a metaphysical parable of all the difficulties of deciphering man's encounters in existence. On the other hand Babel remains the most famous example of the madness in man's rage for architecture, and books are only another form of building. In this library every possible combination of letters and words is to be found, with the result that there are fragments of sense separated by "leagues of insensate cacophony, of verbal farragos and incoherencies." Most books are "mere labyrinths of letters." Since everything that language can do and express is somewhere in the library, "the clarification of the basic mysteries of humanity . . . was also expected." The "necessary vocabularies and grammars" must be discoverable in this lexical totality. But "it is now four centuries since men have been wearying the hexagons . . ."; the story is full of the sadness, sickness and madness of the pathetic figures who roam around the library as around a vast prison.

There is a touching little story called "The House of Asterion" in which a voice describes with some defensiveness the house it lives in, denying that it is a prison. "The house is the same size as the world; or rather, it is the world." At the end we realize that the voice is that of the Minotaur describing the strange architecture of his labyrinth, and the imaginary distractions with which he fills his solitude. I don't think the point is simply that existence itself is labyrinthine (although Borges in praising Henry James and Kafka suggests that "they both thought of the world as being at the same time complex and meaningless . . . I think they both lived in a kind of maze"); the suggestion is rather that the labyrinths man builds are his varying attempts to make a statement about the labyrinths he lives in. A good example of this is what is perhaps the most haunting and odd architecture in all of Borges, the city built by the Immortals. When the narrator finally manages to find a way into the city his reaction comes in three successive responses. "This palace is a fabrication of the gods . . . The gods who built it have died . . . The gods who built it were mad." Empty and unthreatening, it is yet in some way a distillation of the dreadful. What the narrator subsequently finds out is that the troglodytes who live in miserable holes outside the city are in fact the Immortals. They built the mad city as a last symbol — an "inversion and also temple of the irrational gods who govern the world." Then, resolving to live in pure thought, they abandoned their final structure and took to the caves. They have receded almost completely from perception of the external world. That the last concrete work of the Immortal artists should be a mad city, which is at once intended as a parody and an image of the irrational gods felt to control the world, carries a moral which reflects on all the lesser structures which man builds or puts together in Borges's work.

The labyrinth with its multiplication of possible paths and choices is also for Borges an image of the possible proliferation of varying realities in time, as well as in space. In "The Garden of Forking Paths" we read of a man, Ts'ui Pên, who set out to make a book and a labyrinth. His family supposed these to be two separate activities and, ignoring the chaotic manuscripts he left, they search for "the garden of forking paths" in the outside world. Only the narrator discovers the secret. The *book* is the labyrinth. In it time keeps forking and bifurcating so that various possible futures are envisaged. The narrator realizes that this was an image of the universe as the author conceived it. "This web of time . . . embraces *every* possibility. We do not exist in most of them. In some you exist and not I, while in others, I do, and you do not, and in yet others both of us exist." Elsewhere Borges imagines a similar phenomenon in spatial terms. "I thought that Argos and I participated in different universes; I thought that our perceptions were the same, but that he combined them in another way and made other objects of them." A part of the appeal that Borges has for American writers is his sense that "reality" is an infinitely plural affair, that there are many different worlds and that the intersection points might not be so fixed as some people think, that the established ways in which we classify and order reality are as much "fictions" as his stories. Like his imaginary writer Herbert Quain he affirms "that of the various pleasures offered by literature, the greatest is invention." To elevate invention over more conventional modes of "imitation" is to demonstrate how the mind can liberate itself from its own circumstances in a way which has much more appeal for young American than young English writers. (Why this should be so is a matter to be taken up later in the book: see especially Chapter Six.)

Of particular importance in this connection is Borges's story called "Tlön, Uqbar, Orbis Tertius" which is about the invention of a world (it is perhaps worth noting in passing the quite amazing popularity of Tolkien's *The Lord of the Rings* in America — another invented world, or worlds). The story starts with the sentence "I owe the discovery of Uqbar to the conjunction of a mirror and an encyclopaedia," clearly relating those physically unlocatable spaces created by those two primary reflectors of reality, mirrors and words. In its more economic way the story is as much a book of mirrors as *Pale Fire*. The narrator and his friends come across a reference to an undocumented country named Uqbar in an encyclopaedia. No other references outside this entry can be found elsewhere. In that entry the language and literature section has one notable characteristic: "it remarked that the literature of Uqbar was fantastic in character, and that its epics and legends never referred to reality, but to the two imaginary regions of Mlejnas and Tlön." The fantastic literature of a country which itself seems to be unreal — already the mind is beginning to lose its hold on these receding planes. Borges's stories are often like those drawings of impossible objects which seem to abrogate the dimensions of customary perception so that they are both visible yet impossible to "read" in the ordinary way.

The narrator later comes across *A First Encyclopaedia of Tlön* which contains the inscription ORBIS TERTIUS, so he now has "a substantial fragment of the complete history of an unknown planet, with its architecture and playing cards" and all the other details of its philosophies, games and taxonomies. From a study of this book, the narrator and his friends conclude that this "brave new world" was "the work of a secret society" of specialists of all disciplines in all the spheres of human knowledge, each contributing his share. And, rather like Ts'ui Pên's book, what seems at first to be a random mess turns out to be a coherent structure, a complete cosmos with carefully formulated, "albeit provisional," laws. What is notable about the language of Tlön is that it is purely idealistic, and has no nouns. "For them, the world is not a concurrence of objects in space, but a heterogeneous series of independent acts." A conception of the world which does not employ nouns is rather like a story which portrays a situation without using characters: in both cases you have the idea of a diagram of energies and qualities which has dispensed with the usual separation of people and things into clearly defined identities. It is another example of freedom from accepted reality pictures. And the metaphysicians of this country are like artists—Borgesian artists. They are not after truth, but "a kind of amazement"; they regard metaphysics as a type of fantastic literature. The geometry of the country embraces a belief which at a certain level Borges would accept as a truth about conditions of perception. "This system . . . states that, as man moves about, he alters the forms which surround him." In this world objects can be brought into being by suggestion and hope. Contrariwise things also tend "to lose their detail when people forget them." In this fantastic land it would seem that the potency of mind over matter is everywhere evident—perception precedes and determines reality, and those games of consciousness variously subsumed under imagination and dreams seem, like Nabokov's artistic electricity, to sustain the world.

All this is clearly very central to Borges's own thinking about his art. But the Postscript adds a dimension of considerable importance to the story. The mystery of Tlön is "cleared up entirely" as the narrator says with unconscious irony. It all started in Lucerne or London in the seventeenth century when "a benevolent secret society . . . came together to invent a country." Two centuries later this "persecuted brotherhood" turned up in America. An American millionaire who had joined them proposed "the invention of a whole planet" with the additional idea that the enormous project should be kept "a secret." What happens subsequently is that first of all the alphabet of Tlön is found on an object in this world—"Such was the first intrusion of the fantastic world into the real one"—and later, objects from Tlön also make their appearance. Suddenly a complete set of *The First Encyclopaedia of Tlön* turns up, probably as part of a deliberate plot which the narrator describes as "the plan of projecting a world which would not be too incompatible with the real world." As the planted evidence mounts up the world enthusiastically accepts Tlön: "reality gave ground on more than one point. The truth is that it hankered to give ground. Ten years ago, any symmetrical system whatsoever which gave the appearance of order—dialectical materialism, anti-Semitism, Nazism—was enough to fascinate men. Why not fall under the spell of Tlön and submit to the minute and vast evidence of an ordered planet." The superior attraction of Tlön to that of reality is that it is a human fabrication and therefore amenable to human deciphering. Since man made it, it makes sense to man. The narrator foresees a day when all the different languages will disappear and the whole world will be Tlön. He however vows that he will ignore this phenomenon. Instead he will shut himself up and work on a translation into Spanish of Sir Thomas Browne's *Urn Burial*.

What is important in this conclusion is the depth of Borges's vision. At the beginning Tlön seems like a delightful monument to man's power of invention and imagination, the work of a *benevolent* society. Yet the story shows how quickly a provisional system may impose its fantasy structure on the world and be taken for reality; any system, including Nazism. What at one stage might be a gesture of liberation may at a later stage become a monolithic imprisoning force, so that whole societies abandon themselves to the soothing simplicities of a construct of "reality" which is in origin simply a man-made coherent fantasy. We hear much of man's rage for order; what Borges makes clear is that the same yearning may be responsible for our most pleasing artefacts *and* our most grotesque and hideous ideologies. Very aware of the consolations afforded man by his patterning powers and capacity for abstractions, Borges is also well aware of the related danger that at any time man may accept one of his invented systems as the definitive model of reality—and go mad. In the story of Tlön the narrator hopes to keep himself free from the prevailing and usurping fantasy by shutting out the world, or Tlön, by working in a hotel room on a revision of a translation never to be published, perhaps thereby retaining a bit of freedom by moving quietly and self-effacingly around older lexical spaces. A modest resolution, perhaps, yet in his lonely determination to extrude an imposed system this figure has a great deal of relevance for contemporary American fiction.

The important thing is that he is aware of the possibilities of conspiracy. Borges shares this apprehension of powers which may be interfering with the given reality or imposing a world of their own. In "The Babylon Lottery" for instance he brings into focus man's suspicion or intuition that chance events are in fact all determined by secret decrees emanating from "the Company." Not that the Company can be identified—"nothing is so contaminated with fiction as the history of the Company"—but speculation about it is endless. Since the Company's agents are secret it is impossible to differentiate its orders from those of impostors. Some people think that the Company is eternal; others that it is omnipotent only in certain areas. One conjecture has it that the Company simply does not exist, while another argues that it is pointless to argue whether it exists or not since Babylon is simply an infinite game of chance. You could say that this is a parable about the origin of religious belief, or a parable about paranoia. But the way it touches on man's feelings of being controlled from without by the invisible agents of some unknown conspiracy, of having his "reality" quietly, yet constantly, tampered with, makes it a tale which seems to be echoed or paralleled by some of the more experimental writing in America today.

Borges knows that, as he puts it, "a system is nothing more than the subordination of all the aspects of the universe to some one of them" and that a system is like a fiction in that it selects and arranges its signs and symbols, quite aware that such a thing as a total statement about reality is impossible. If systems / fictions can result in Nazism as well as *Don Quixote* then the position of the writer himself as fiction-maker is always potentially equivocal since he is introducing Tlön into the reader's world.

But so far from wishing to impose any one fiction / system on to the reader, Borges keeps the fact of its fictitiousness well in the foreground. At the end of his stories we often find ourselves oddly released from the subject of the tale and returned to the spectacle of one of those enigmatic narrators inventing what he purports to be describing, making an intricate sequence of referential gestures which turn out to be "a diagram of his mental history." When the narrator is Borges himself the same observation holds true. By continuing to invent, he at least shows his ability to do so. This in itself is evidence that he has not been claimed or arrested by any of the other competing inventions which lay more or less subtle siege to the individual consciousness.

In this connection an article by Richard Poirier[2] is relevant, since he describes what he sees as the purpose of self-parody in modern literature, saying: "Self-parody in Borges, as in Joyce and Nabokov, goes beyond the mere questioning of the validity of any given invention by proposing the unimpeded opportunity for making new ones. Invention creates life in literature in the sense that invention is itself the act and evidence of life. It is a way of being present, in every sense of that word." And he concludes his article: "Nothing we have created, in politics or literature, is necessary — that is the central aspect of the literature of self-parody which humanly matters." This is a most rewarding way to regard this kind of literature and it gives some indication of how American writers of the present time are reading writers like Nabokov and Borges. Not that they aren't important writers by any standards, but it does seem as though they have a special appeal for the writer struggling within the American environment, trying to discover the significance and value of his own inventive power among the flowing, constantly metamorphosing fictions which make up contemporary American "reality."

In particular their example seems to have been an influential one for writers brought up in a period when Ortega y Gasset's idea of the death of the novel has been extended to embrace the notional mortality of language itself in Marshall McLuhan. Nabokov and Borges have shown that writers need not succumb to the exhaustion which is supposed to have afflicted the literature they are involved with. Whatever else they may be, they are great survivors, and a study of their particular techniques and approaches would reveal all manner of strategies for survival. John Barth is one American writer who has written enthusiastically about the work of Borges — "it illustrates how an artist may paradoxically turn the felt ultimacies of our time into material and means for his work."[3] He cites *Pale Fire* and *Labyrinths* as two exemplary ways of confronting the "felt ultimacy" of the exhaustion of narrative possibilities. Borges's work is also salutary: "When the characters in a work of fiction become readers or authors of the fiction they're in, we're reminded of the fictitious aspect of our own existence." Barth sees the labyrinth as a place which contains "all possibilities of choice." Most people get exhausted before they reach the heart of the labyrinth; it is only the hero, the "virtuoso," who, "confronted with baroque reality, baroque history, the baroque state of his art," has no need to explore all the possible paths in the labyrinth. "He need only be aware of their existence or possibility, acknowledge them, and go straight through the maze to the accomplishment of his own work." As Borges does.

The enthusiasm of McCarthy and Barth for the work of Nabokov and Borges is symptomatic of a more general admiration for their work, and what I have called their example, among American writers. I have tried to suggest some reasons for this and what there is in the achievement of these particular writers that younger American novelists might particularly value. At the same time one can fairly make the observation that one thing common to the work of both men is a certain attenuation of reality in the old sense of an empirically perceived environment. It is, as it were, distanced, or forced to recede as the author pre-empts the foreground for a display of his patterning powers. Nabokov's America is indeed at times fairly itemized, yet in such a way as to make it seem almost dreamlike and inert — secondary to the game he is playing and entirely dominated by it. As Nabokov has said of himself, he is absolute tyrant over his characters, and I think this extends to all his material. All good art necessarily requires the control of the artist; talk about characters runnings away from the writer is usually misleading. Still, one feels that there are shades and degrees in this matter, and Nabokov is quite willing to reduce his characters to playing cards to facilitate the impeccable progress of the perfectly conducted game. One novel is called *King, Queen, Knave*, and everywhere in his work characters are robbed of a certain dimension to fit into Nabokov's cherished patterning. As in Borges, the figures in the fictions move like chessmen — they are there mainly to reveal the brilliance of the chessplayer, and the rules of the game.

Borges seems to me the more profound writer of the two. He manages to convey a melancholy sense of the pathos of all man's makings in time — cities, beliefs, books, dreams — and distil a rare pity from the spectacle, which is kept marvellously clear by his metaphysical wit. Nabokov's cerebral conjurings are certainly extraordinarily clever, but occasionally he arouses suspicions of a fundamental hollowness under the diagrammatic brilliance of the surface. Be that as it may, in both writers the pattern of the game seems to be more important than the characters and material details serving to illustrate it. Both writers seem to have a need to elevate abstractions over perceptions; perhaps to avoid the paralysed congestion of "Funes the Memorious," perhaps in response to some deeper fear. In this connection Wilhelm Worringer's distinction between abstraction and empathy seems to me relevant.[4]

> Now what are the psychic presuppositions for the urge to abstraction? We must seek them in these peoples' feeling about the world, in their psychic attitude toward the cosmos. Whereas the precondition for the

urge to empathy is a happy pantheistic relationship of confidence between men and the phenomena of the external world, the urge to abstraction is the outcome of a great inner unrest inspired in man by the phenomena of the outside world; in a religious respect it corresponds to a strongly transcendental tinge to all notions. We might describe this state as an immense spiritual dread of space.

I have tried to suggest that just such a dread of space is discernible in works by both Nabokov and Borges, but more generally I think we can take up the suggestion that the urge toward abstraction betokens in some respects a defensive attitude towards the outer world; it points to the erection of invented shapes rather than the emulation of perceived ones. Again, from one point of view, all art necessarily participates in the urge to abstraction, but we are aware of differences of degree. It seems to me that if we can discern an unusually strong tendency towards the schematic, the visibly patterned, in much contemporary American fiction, we may see it as an attempt to evoke a personal stability and clarification as a result of a marked lack of confidence in the presence and pressures of the given environment. Certainly I do not imagine that any generation of American writers has felt so much "inner unrest inspired . . . by the phenomena of the outside world." It is against this background that I think we can begin to understand the attraction of the spectacle of Nabokov's and Borges's imperturable assurance on the terra firma of their lexical playfields.

Notes

1. This interview appeared in *Partisan Review*, Winter 1969.
2. "The Politics of Self-Parody" by Richard Poirier, *Partisan Review*, Summer 1968.
3. "The Literature of Exhaustion" by John Barth, *New Society*, May 16th, 1968.
4. *Abstraction and Empathy* by Wilhelm Worringer; translated by Michael Bullock (Routledge and Kegan Paul, London, 1963).

From Amhoretz to Exegete: The Swerve from Kafka by Borges   Margaret Boegeman*

Jorge Luis Borges is perhaps Kafka's most manifest disciple. The earliest evidence we have of his interest in Kafka is a Spanish translation he made of nine Kafka stories, published in 1938. Entitled *La metamorfosis*, the book included, besides the title story, the stories and sketches known in English as "The Great Wall of China," "A Hunger Artist," "First Grief," "A Sport," "The Vulture," "The City Coat of Arms," "Prometheus," and "An

*This essay is published here for the first time by permission of the author.

Everyday Confusion." Though the collection has no outstanding unifying features, several of the stories contain devices or themes that Borges was to implement extensively in his own fiction. "The Great Wall of China" is mentioned by a translator of Borges as his favorite story, and has been an especially rich source of inspiration for him.[1]

The timing of Borges's translation of Kafka's stories is interesting both from the perspective of what was happening to Kafka's work at that time and what was happening to Borges. Kafka's main works had appeared in German in the preceding decade, and three of his books had been translated into English by the Muirs in the thirties, but the collected edition in German was completed only shortly before Borges began his translation. This *Gesammelte Schriften* was the edition by Schocken Verlag, which ran into so much difficulty with the Nazi censors. Yet it is clear that the Schocken edition was the one Borges used as the basis for his translation. All of the stories in *La metamorfosis* were published in two volumes of the *Gesammelte Schriften*, 1 (1935) and 5 (1936), though it is true that many of them had also appeared in an earlier volume, *Beim Bau der Chinesischen Mauer* (1931). However, one of the stories, "Der Geier" ("The Vulture") had appeared nowhere other than in volume 5 of the *Gesammelte Schriften* when Borges made his translation. (Borges has himself confirmed this piece of logic in a conversation with me at UCLA on 22 March 1976. He even remembered buying the Schocken edition at the Goethe bookstore in Buenos Aires.) How the Schocken edition, which was supposedly confiscated by the Nazi Ministry of Culture, found its way to Buenos Aires within little over a year of its publication is a puzzle worthy of inclusion in a Borges story, but it is clear that we owe this small but courageous press yet another bow of recognition.

As for what of Kafka was then available in Spanish, only a few parables and sketches had appeared in *Sur*[2] in 1936, and two stories, "Der Verwandlung" and "Erstes Leid," had been translated earlier (1925 and 1932) in Ortega y Gasset's journal, *Revista de Occidente*. Kafka was relatively unknown in Spanish before 1938, and Borges began translating him just at the time when Kafka's name began to be widely recognized in that language, too. The same publisher for whom Borges worked, Editorial Losada, published a translation of *Der Prozess* the following year (1939); and another book of short stories and the novel *Amerika* were to be published in Buenos Aires shortly thereafter. Borges, like Auden and Muir, anticipated rather than responded to the wave of Kafka's popularity.

Now, what was happening to Borges at the time when he became interested in Kafka? Borges had been publishing poetry since 1923, but he began to attempt prose works only ten years later. His first story, "Street-corner Man" he now calls "the worst thing I ever wrote."[3] But of his second, "The Approach to Al-Mu'tasim," he says, "it now seems to me to foreshadow and even to set the pattern for those tales that were somehow awaiting me, and upon which my reputation as a storyteller was to be based."[4] We do not know the degree of Borges's exposure to Kafka when he wrote this second story in 1935; it could have been much or little. But by the time he wrote the other stories for his first volume of fiction, his Kafka translations had been published and his knowledge of that author must have been both extensive and intimate.

The stories for which Borges is best known were not written until after 1938. On Christmas Eve of that year he had an accident that resulted in a severe medical crisis that lasted for nearly a month. During that time he suffered fever and hallucinations, and even endured a loss of speech. After this illness, Borges feared for his mental capacities, and wondered whether he could still write. He says, "I thought that if I tried to write a review now and failed, I'd be all through intellectually, but that if I tried something I had never really done before and failed at that it wouldn't be so bad and might even prepare me for the final revelation. I decided I would try to write a story."[5] The result was "Pierre Menard, Author of the Quixote," published in Sur in May 1939. Encouraged by his success, he next tried something more ambitious—"Tlön, Uqbar, Orbis Tertius." The other familiar members of the Borges fictional family followed: "The Lottery in Babylon," "The Circular Ruins," "The Library of Babel." It is among these early stories that the Kafka influence appears most clearly.

These stories and a few others were gathered into the volume *El jardin de los senderos que se bifurcan*, and published in 1941. The eight stories of this collection were reprinted in a larger volume, *Ficciones*, in 1944, and later six of them became the lead stories in the English anthology *Labyrinths* (1962). They have become among the most widely known of Borges's works.

II

Borges is not in the least reluctant to admit influence from Kafka. He has said that in his early years, "I was aping Kafka. But Kafka was a genius, and I am only a man of letters. I couldn't go on being Kafka."[6] This admission of influence is consonant with Borges's oft-repeated ideas that "the 'I' does not exist," and "all authors are one author." But the admission of influence that welcomes all elements is virtually no admission at all. Borges's statement that "Kafka may still be working upon me; I don't know,"[7] is the gracious, but vague nod in the direction of a now established master, a flattering association with genius carefully diluted with a dash of humility. The tangible connection between the two authors remains to be made by the critic and can be substantiated only in the texts. To do this we must look primarily to Kafka's short fiction.

In the story of Kafka's literary reception, Borges is almost unique in being influenced by his short stories, whereas most other writers and critics have seen in the novel-fragments Kafka's greatest accomplishments. We may remember that Edwin Muir had hoped that his English translation of *The Great Wall of China* would serve to explain the paradoxical Kafkan mind to those readers who had been baffled by *The Castle*. The former collection, he said, "gives a more clear and general notion of Kafka's intentions as an artist and thinker than any of his other works."[8] But English readers did not heed his words. Like the Americans, they persisted in seeing the short story, the aphorism, the parable, and the sketch as "preliminary" forms, rating barely passing attention. Borges, on the other hand, has said about himself, "In a lifetime devoted chiefly to books, I have read but few novels, and in most cases, only a sense of duty has enabled me to find my way to their last page. At the same time, I have been a reader and rereader of short stories."[9]

He gives us a hint of the difference he sees between the two forms, and thus the inspiration he could draw from Kafka's stories to his own when he says, in his penetrating introduction to *La metamorfosis*.

> El argumento y el ambiente son lo esencial; no las evoluciones de la fábula ni la penetración psicológica. De ahí la primacía de sus cuentos sobre sus novelas; de ahí el derecho de afirmar que esta compilación de relatos nos da integramente la medida de tan singular escritor.[10]

> (The argument and the ambience are the essentials; not the way the plot is structured or the psychological penetration. Hence the primacy of his stories over his novels; hence the right to affirm that this compilation [of stories] gives integrally the measure of this singular writer.)

Nearly forty years later, he maintained the same distinction between short and long fiction: "Generally speaking, what I think is most important in a short story is the . . . situation, while in a novel what's important are the characters."[11] Upon reflection, it is clear that there are no "characters" in the literary sense in Borges's fiction, only shadows of characters, only automatons who act out their assigned fates as if drugged, or who comment on the lives of others with scholarly disinterest. Character in Kafka's stories is somewhat more conventional, but even when central, as for example, in "The Metamorphosis," it is curiously dimensionless, with little past or future and all attention concentrated on a material present. More often, we find the virtual absence of character in Kafka, such as the narrator who describes a situation in which he figures but peripherally, as in "The Great Wall of China," or the character who is but a symbol, as in "Prometheus" or "The Hunger Artist." In any case, especially in his short stories, the startling nature of the Kafkaesque situation overshadows whatever character may be necessary for furthering the plot.

So the parallels between, and the influence from, Kafka to Borges may be found in the situations they describe, and the metaphysical implications of those situations ("el argumento y el ambiente"). To some degree, Borges takes Kafka's enigmatic situations and turns them into philosophic reflections. He filters the immediacy and the pain of the Kafkaesque situation through the prism of the intellect, refining it, refracting it, splitting the dazzling white light of experience into a rainbow of postulates. He abstracts the paradox Kafka chose to leave embodied in the concrete event, and in so doing, substitutes the problem for the problematic.

For example, one theme that both authors treat extensively is the arbitrary nature of the most basic structures of meaning, upon which we depend unquestioningly, such as, measurements of time and space, causality, sequence. Tony Tanner notes that the "one thing common to the work of both men is a certain attenuation of reality in the old sense of an empirically perceived environment."[12] But this attenuation of reality is a parallel shared by many modern writers. Kafka's and Borges's attitudes toward this unreality differ, and this difference brings us closer to the heart of their fictions. In one sketch that Borges translated, "An Everyday Confusion," we find Kafka suspending the trusted conventions of time and space, but making no comment on this suspension. Neither do his characters. No one says "How strange!" or "How could this happen, that a journey which takes only ten minutes one day, takes ten hours the next, and but an instant to return?" The facts are given; no one questions them.

Borges, however, in a story like "Tlön," worries at each such suspension of logic, pursues its cause with a relentless curiosity. Where is Tlön? Who wrote its spurious entry in the Encyclopedia Britannica? What conspiracy constructed this fictional planet and its history? We have not so much a situation in Borges's story, as an investigation. We may recall here Borges's fondness for the detective story. In "Tlön," however, the mystery is never completely solved, leaving us with questions about the nature and limits of man's intelligence, questions that Kafka raises only indirectly. When a character in Kafka's fiction pursues the inexplicable, he is motivated by strength of will rather than strength of intellect. His power of determination is stronger than his power of analysis, whereas the reverse is true in Borges's characters.

Kafka's story "The Great Wall of China" is perhaps a more just comparison to "Tlön." In this story we have no such marvel as spaces that shrink or expand, merely the efforts of a community to build a wall, the purposes of which are obscured from the builders. The commission for the wall has been ordained by the high command, though that too remains unverifiable and inaccessible. Undeterred, the laborers pursue their assigned goal diligently, almost religiously, though at the same time, interminably:

> El infinito es múltiple: para detener el curso de ejercitos infinitamente lejanos, un emperador infinitamente remoto en el tiempo y en el espacio ordena que infinitas generaciones levanten enfinitamente un muro infinito que dé la vuelta de su imperio infinito.[13]

(The infinity is multiple: in order to detain the curse of armies infinitely distant, an emperor infinitely remote in time and space orders infinite generations to raise infinitely an infinite wall in order to restore his infinite empire.)

That in both "Tlön" and "The Great Wall," a monumental (if fragmentary) plan for a vast society is constructed by an unknown intelligence, constitutes a basis for the comparison.[14] Kafka's story is told from the viewpoint of a laborer who describes what he sees without understanding its raison d'être. He is a participant in this society, but only in an incidental way. The narrator of the Borges story, on the other hand, is an observer outside the (imaginary) society he describes, not only in time and space, but as the society is shown to be the product of a gigantic sham, even in its conception. Borges's narrator is the detective playing games with a clever deceiver. But his quest for a solution has no bearing on the conditions of his everyday existence. In short, the immediacy of the enigma is removed; it is a game.

Yet in the epilogue to "Tlön" the narrator suggests that the very pursuit of this imaginary world has made it real enough in fact to intrude upon his. First he cites the discovery of *hrönir*, those objects which can be imagined into existence. This is essentially what has happened to Tlön; its reality has been imagined into existence as a consequence of its (fictional) history. Second, the narrator observes that this fictional construct has found its way into the schools of the day and "the teaching of its harmonious history . . . has wiped out the one which governed in my childhood; already a fictitious past occupies in our memories the place of another, a past of which we know nothing with certainty — not even that is is false."[15] Borges projects that Tlön will eventually take over and supplant the structures of meaning we now use: "The world will be Tlön." So the system devised by "chess masters, not angels" has an effect and a reality that cannot be dispelled by the diligence and logic of the master detective (or scholar).

This paradox affects the narrator in a way he admits only obliquely. The last line in the story reads: "I pay no attention to all this and go on revising, in the still days at the Adrogué hotel, an uncertain Quevedian translation (which I do not intend to publish) of Browne's *Urn Burial.*"[16] Superficially, we read, "I do not intend to let these events which I cannot explain alter my daily habits of scholarship." But on another level, one could say that the narrator has retreated to the past to work within a system of order both obsolete and impractical, but at least under his own control. There is something both humorous and perverse in his choice of a seventeenth-century English pamphlet about the comparative practices of the underground preservation of human remains. Such an underground preservation, through scholarship, of human intellectual remains, seems the wistful objective of our (now slightly dotty) narrator.

There is, then, a mockery in the Borges story by the author of his character which Kafka did not allow. Like Kafka himself, Kafka's character faced the insoluble calmly and did not (could not?) retreat to the known and secure, even though he had to endure the vicissitudes of the unknown much more immediately than did Borges's narrator. Kafka's narrator concludes with a refusal to proceed with his inquiry about the nature of the confusing institutions that govern his life, for fear that further investigation "would mean undermining not only our consciences, but, what is far worse, our feet."[17] He accepts as necessary the limitations on man's quest for certainty. Borges's character refuses to face this necessity. When his quest for a "solution" is thwarted, he prefers to pretend that the inexplicable does not touch him.

Kafka describes paradoxes of behavior without claiming to uncover their source or to eradicate them. He notes the apparently perverse determination of the high command to build a wall by a means "makeshift and inexpedient," and the willingness of the people to believe in the system the more strongly, the further they are from the circumstances that occasion that belief, thus demonstrating irrelevance of fact to faith. There is a static, even a stoic quality to the Kafkaesque situation, an acceptance of inevitable confusions with their attendant pain and uncertainties. He warns, "Try with all your might to comprehend the decrees of the high command, but only up to a certain point: then avoid further meditation."[18]

Borges, on the other hand, has a certain delight in chasing down the causes and the consequences of puzzles like Tlön, and he leads one to believe that resolutions are within the possibility of human reason. He makes explicit the temptation with which Kafka's narrator struggles: the desire to find a rational and orderly system, contrary to all empirical evidence, and he carries this desire one step closer to our own fallibility. "Why not," he says, "fall under the spell of Tlön and submit to the minute and vast evidence of an ordered planet? Useless to reply that reality, too, is ordered. It may be so, but in accordance with divine laws — I translate: inhuman laws — which we will never completely perceive."[19] When, in his postscript, he suggests that the imaginary invades the real, and is beyond all rational systems of thought, we take this reversal lightly because the erudite language and slightly absurd reaction of the narrator distances us from his plight. There is none of the metaphysical tension that exists in the Kafka story; there is no immanence. Borges has domesticated Kafka by assimilating his terrors into the tomes of scholarship. As Paul de Man has said, "The stories that make up the bulk of Borges's literary work are *not moral fables* or parables like Kafka's, to which they are often misleadingly compared, even less attempts at psychological analysis."[20] There are no characters; there is no morality.

Borges has said that the effect he aimed for in these early stories was "amazement." Amazement is the residue left when the problematic is subtracted from religious awe. There are no choices to be made in "Tlön."

No soul has to decide the point at which his conscience would be undermined by further pursuit of the high command. The reader, too, may be passive. We may be dazzled by Borges, but we are not moved by him.

A second theme that figures largely in Borges's early fiction, the pattern of infinite regression, can also clearly be traced to Kafka's stories. This pattern, too, has implications of the moral dilemma in Kafka and of the intellectual game in Borges. The most famous example in Kafka is the parable of "Before the Law," which appears as a part of the novel *The Trial*. In this parable the doorkeeper says to the one who seeks admittance, "I am only the least of the doorkeepers. From hall to hall there is one doorkeeper after another, each more powerful than the last. The third doorkeeper is already so terrible that even I cannot bear to look at him."[21] The supplicant grows old before this impossible obstacle and as he is dying, asks the doorkeeper why no one else in all these long years has sought admittance. The doorkeeper responds, "No one else could ever be admitted here, since this gate was made only for you. I am now going to shut it."[22]

The same pattern is also evident in "The Great Wall." Here Kafka speaks of a message from the emperor, sent "to you alone," by a messenger who sets out immediately upon receiving the message, pushing his way through the throngs that crowd the courtyard:

> But . . . how vainly does he wear out his strength; still he is only making his way through the chambers of the innermost palace; never will he get to the end of them; and if he succeeded in that nothing would be gained; he must next fight his way down the stair; and if he succeeded in that nothing would be gained; the courts would still have to be crossed; and after the courts the second outer palace; and so on for thousands of years; and if at last he should burst through the outermost gate—but never, never can that happen—the imperial capital would lie before him, the center of the world, crammed to bursting with its own sediment. Nobody would fight his way through here even with a message from a dead man.[23]

In both cases the infinite regression obstructs the deliverance of some form of revelation; in both cases the revelation is intended only for the single individual in the story. Thus Kafka poses in this paradigm the impossibility of any form of revelation, or of salvation, for the designated individual: it can only be waited for, dreamt about.

Borges, however, proposes regressions that obstruct no one, that delay no revelation. There are only endless, arbitrary, and therefore meaningless choices, only infinitude, which finally cloys. These eternally forking paths are destined for no appointed individual; for no chosen people, is the denied consummation. Any and all persons meander through Borges's labyrinths; there is a leveling of gods and golems, of eras and of authorship, of fortuitous choices with abominations.

The clearest demonstration comes from a story called "The Immortal," in his 1949 collection *El Aleph*. A Roman military tribune seeks the City of the Immortals, drinks of the river of immortality, and is condemned to eternal life. From this perspective he reflects on such an existence:

> Indoctrinated by a practice of centuries, the republic of immortal men had attained the perfection of tolerance and almost that of indifference. They knew that in an infinite period of time, all things happen to all men. Because of his past or future virtues, every man is worthy of all goodness, but also of all perversity, because of his infamy in the past or future. Thus, just as in games of chance the odd and even numbers tend toward equilibrium, so also wit and stolidity cancel out and correct each other. . . . Seen in this manner, all our acts are just, but they are also indifferent. There are no moral or intellectual merits. Homer composed the *Odyssey*; if we postulate an infinite period of time, with infinite circumstances and changes, the impossible thing is not to compose the *Odyssey*, at least once. No one is anyone, one single immortal man is all men. Like Cornelius Agrippa, I am god, I am hero, I am philosopher, I am demon and I am world, which is a tedious way of saying that I do not exist.[24]

Stupefied by the prospect of infinite repetition, the Immortal seeks another river, which will rescind his immortality, so that his life once more may be "precious and pathetic."

The ennui of infinity is also clear in the earlier stories from *El jardin de los senderos que se bifurcan*. In "The Library of Babel," for example, Borges suggests that the Library may be "limitless and periodic," so that the finite combinations of letters in books may be repeated at some incredibly distant point in the labyrinth, ad infinitum. There being no "key" to the Library, and no end to it, none of the books tell the truth. The Word is rendered impotent. The Library exists to confound all languages, all knowledge and all ages alike. There is no message here "for you alone."

Another game with the infinite regress appears in the "Circular Ruins." Here Borges clearly mocks the idea of individual destiny or salvation. A god who dreams into existence a living being discovers that he himself is the creation of another dreamer, and an illusion no less than his own creation. He is therefore made ridiculous for presuming his powers and his role to be unique.

Again, in "The Garden of Forking Paths," the two participants, the murderer and the victim, are mere ploys in the course of a philosophical discussion on the infinitude of futures in time. The destiny of neither strikes us as crucial, seen as they are against a background of graceful civilities and the infinite recesses of time which gives opportunity for all alternatives: repetitions, reversals, negations. Urgency of individual destiny has vanished; immanence has been denied. The Pythagorean conception, the eternal return, has been substituted for the Hebrew belief in impending apocalypse.

Only slightly different from the idea of infinite regress in time, is the idea of an undetermined choice among alternatives, used again by both authors. Kafka plays with this idea in an attitude uncharacteristically light, in his parable of Prometheus.[25] He begins simply, "There are four legends concerning Prometheus." In the first legend, Prometheus was clamped to a rock for betraying the secrets of gods to men, while eagles fed on his liver; in the second, Prometheus pressed himself deep into the rock until he became one with it. In the third legend, his treachery was forgotten by everyone, by the gods, the eagles, himself. In the fourth legend, everyone grew weary of the meaningless affair, the wound closed wearily.

Kafka does not choose among the four legends, and they are alternative rather than synoptic versions. Thus the choice (or lack of choice) is forced upon the reader. Borges has adapted this same technique in his conjecture, called "A Problem," on how Don Quixote would react if he learned he killed a man. Borges lists four possibilities without choosing among them. Both authors refuse to arbitrate for the reader, but the endings of the two parables are somewhat different in emphasis. Kafka ends his four versions by saying "The legend tried to explain the inexplicable. As it came out of a substratum of truth, it had in turn to end in the inexplicable."[26] Borges ends his parable with a conjecture, which he calls: "alien to the Spanish orb and even to the orb of the Western world and requires a more ancient, more complex and more weary atmosphere. Don Quixote—who is no longer Don Quixote but a king of the cycles of Hindustan—senses, standing before the dead body of his enemy, that killing and engendering are divine or magical acts which notably transcend the human condition. He knows that the dead man is illusory, the same as the bloody sword weighing in his hand and himself and all his past life and the vast gods and the universe."[27]

This last conjecture has an inclusiveness that terminates conjecture and swallows the foregoing hypotheses in the infinitudes of the imagination. For Kafka it is the unassailability of the enigmatic that dominates; for Borges, the pointlessness of the choices, since all are illusory.

But if we confine our discussion only to Borges's first collection of fiction, we can see the same principle fascinating him from these early stages. For example, in "The Babylon Lottery," this preoccupation is most apparent. Chance in the form of the lottery governs the lives of everyone in the society, and while destinies are decided blindly, infinite alternatives are possible. Again moral considerations have been denied; the only interest in man's character arises from his renewed response when the danger of a mortal thrill is added to the lottery. But there is a strong suggestion that Borges is making an additional comment on Kafka here, and has for once drawn on a novel for his inspiration, in this case, *The*

Castle. Borges's lottery is executed by an anonymous and unreachable administration known as the Company, similar in its enigmatic character to Kafka's Castle:

> But it must be recalled that the individuals of the Company were and are all-powerful and astute as well. In many cases the knowledge that certain joys were the simple doing of chance might have detracted from their excellence; to avoid this inconvenience the Company's agents made use of suggestion and magic. Their moves, their management, were secret. In the investigation of people's intimate hopes and intimate terrors, they made use of astrologers and spies. There were certain stone lions, there was a sacred privy called Qaphqa [read phonetically], there were fissures in a dusty aqueduct which, according to general opinion, led to the Company: malign or benevolent people deposited accusations in these cracks [in order to influence the lottery].[28]

In suggesting that the people prefer mystery to chance, Borges implies that the lottery satisfies a psychological need of the people it serves: it both intensifies their responses to the fates they are allotted and it allows them the hope of influencing it. The people prefer the concept of the supernatural to a totally arbitrary concept of causality. In regard to Kafka, Borges seems to be saying that K's awe before the Castle was a product of his own psychological need, the need to revere what he could not understand. Borges eschews this need and mocks the mystery. As in "A Problem," he ends with a series of conjectures, each one rendering slightly more pointless the attempts of man to solve its enigma: the Company is eternal and will last until the annihilation of the cosmos; the Company is omnipotent, but it exerts its influence only in the most minute matters; the Company has never existed and never will; it is indifferently inconsequential to affirm or deny the reality of the shadowy corporation, because Babylon is nothing but an infinite game of chance. In this sequence, the illusory subsumes even the speculative. The latter is at least an ordered concept; the former, for Borges, dissolves in the endless and therefore the irrelevant.

Again in this story, Borges has removed the problem from the particular to the general. His lottery affects everyone; everyone is governed by this arbitrary system, not just the narrator. Everyone alike accepts his destiny as victim. Again the leveling process reduces the psychological tension that arches through all of Kafka, and eliminates his fascination with individual destiny. The dilemma of man is no longer pathetic, or unjust, but merely pointless. John Updike has said, "We move, with Borges, beyond psychology, beyond the human, and confront, in his work, the world atomized and vacant. Perhaps not since Lucretius has a poet so definitely felt men as incidents in space."[29]

The pointlessness of the multiple alternatives, whether in space or in time, and the uniformity with which they inform so much of Borges's early fiction, is clearly linked with the questionable nature of all structures of meaning, and of all knowledge. This is a third theme that the two authors share.

In Kafka's parable "Before the Law" and in his story "The Great Wall of China," the implication is that knowledge is simply not verifiable, that the messengers are perhaps suspect. In Kafka's fragment "The News of the Building of the Wall," when the messenger arrives from the emperor, the recipient of the message does not believe the news. In *The Trial*, when the parable of "Before the Law" is discussed by Joseph K. and the priest, the argument centers around whether the doorkeeper deceived the supplicant, or is himself deceived in his assumption of superiority and power. The argument ends as Joseph K. is still trying to discover the "truth," and the priest replies, " 'It is not necessary to accept everything as true, one must only accept it as necessary.' 'A melancholy conclusion,' said K. 'It turns lying into a universal principle.' "[30] In Kafka and in Borges both, uncertainty, if not lying, is a universal principle, but the implications of this principle differ.

Borges has said of his writing, "I think one should work into a story the idea of not being sure of all things, because that's the way reality is."[31] He repeatedly includes references in his texts to the unreliability of a narrator or an idea:

> "I myself, in making this hasty declaration, have falsified or invented some grandeur, some atrocity; perhaps, too, a certain mysterious monotony . . ." ("The Babylon Lottery")

> (of Pierre Menard, author of the *Quixote*) "his resigned or ironical habit of propagating ideas which are the strict reverse of those he preferred." ("Pierre Menard")

> "Bioy Casares . . . talked to us at length about a great scheme for writing a novel in the first person, using a narrator who omitted or corrupted what happened and who ran into various contradictions." ("Tlön")

> (Of the people of Tlön) "No one believes that nouns refer to an actual reality. . . . The mere act of giving it a name, that is of classifying it, implies a falsification of it." ("Tlön")[32]

If Kafka's narrator does not know the truth, if he struggles futilely with sorting out reliable information from unreliable, we can excuse his confusion by assuming that he is somehow on the outside of the privileged circle which has access to the truth. But Borges extends the principle of uncertainty and pointlessness to the entire universe; no one is exempt from it, not reader, not author, not future generations of characters. If one has the option of choosing any ending to "The Garden of Forking Paths," of reading any version of any absurdity in the library of Babel, including "the minute history of the future, the autobiographies of archangels, the faithful catalogue of the Library, thousands and thousands of false catalogues, a demonstration of the fallacy of the true catalogue,"[33] etc., then the universes which Borges constructs are wearying in the extreme, and hopeless beyond anything conceived by Kafka.

Though Kafka's narrator is always thwarted, always isolated, and always left in ignorance, his presence and his willpower hold together the fiction, by giving it a sense of direction, if not purpose. As Updike points out, "the fantastic realities of Kafka's fictions are projections of the narrator/hero's anxieties and have no communion, no interlocking structure without him."[34] Kafka's narrator never loses his determination nor his belief that there is an ultimate truth, or system or revelation, which may, in spite of his efforts rather than because of them, be revealed to him. And if not to him, then to another. In *The Castle*, for example, K. says to Pepi: "It is as if we had both striven too intensely, too noisily, too childishly, with too little experience, to get something that for instance with Frieda's calm and matter-of-factness can be got easily and without much ado. We have tried to get it by crying, by scratching, by tugging—just as a child tugs at the tablecloth, gaining nothing but only bringing all the splendid things down on the floor and putting them out of its reach forever."[35] If satisfaction is denied to K. and Pepi, in their quests for recognition or revelation, then it will be allowed Frieda, or another, who seeks not so clumsily. Uncertainty is a constant only for the outsider. Hope is not obliterated in Kafka's world, merely obstructed.

This leads us to the last theme shared by Kafka and Borges, which illuminates both Borges's dependence on Kafka, and his variance from him. This is the fascination in both authors with "the imminence of a revelation which is not produced,"[36] the paradigm of a hope unremittingly tantalized.

In an article called "The Enigmatic Predicament: Some Parables of Kafka and Borges," Ben Belitt argues that, "according to Borges, it is the purpose of fiction to render . . . ignorance *intimate* . . . to compel the heart to take up the 'burden of the Mystery,' each out of his own dream, and imagine the common dream of the world's knowledge."[37] Belitt says that Borges's habit of reworking of themes, of playing with multiple alternatives, of losing the reader in the infinities of the imagination, is, in fact, not a foundering on the "inexplicable mass of rock" as in Kafka, but an "incandescent" confrontation with the Unknown. "Only in a fictive complex of this nature can any 'man know who he is'; and only by these signs can his 'character' be absorbed into his collective humanity. Literature is greatest, 'truest,' most archetypal, when it is most enigmatic."[38] Belitt gives no examples of characters in Borges's stories finding "who they are," and I find none, though they are all certainly "absorbed into collective humanity" by the distancing and leveling devices I have discussed; narrators who dispassionately observe a multiplicity of enigmas without becoming involved in them; narrators who are involved in the action only to discover that their predicament is being endlessly repeated; repeated references to the untrustworthiness of all knowledge and the indifference toward distinguishing between truth and distortion; endless alternatives which dissolve in a dizzying pointlessness, etc. These devices lead, I believe, not to knowledge but to stupefaction, not to ecstasy but to ennui.

But Belitt asserts that "it is this exuberance of *unknowing*, the almost predatory gusto of his conjunction with the Beast of Enigma, which distinguishes the fictions of Borges from the fictions of Kafka. Presumably, both enact the anguish of ungratified ignorance and the malaise of the anomalous predicament. In the case of Borges, it is a vertigo whose circuitions lead to magical breakthroughs of the psyche."[39] At this point we must stop and examine a few of these magical breakthroughs.

I claimed that both Kafka and Borges repeatedly hint in their fictions of the imminence of a revelation that is not produced. However, Borges also sometimes produces the actual revelation, or a semblance of one. Belitt bases his comments about the "magical breakthroughs of the psyche," on a single short story, "The God's Script." In this story, a "magician of the pyramid," Tzinacan, suffers years in prison, waiting for the revelation he perceives as his destiny. After years of struggling to discern God's word among the scribble of the universe, Tzinacan has a dream of the endlessness of this task and its futility, and he resigns himself to the failure. Then, unexpectedly, comes the revelation: "Then there occurred what I cannot forget nor communicate. There occurred the union with the divinity, with the universe (I do not know whether these words differ in meaning.) Ecstasy does not repeat its symbols; God has been seen in a blazing light, in a sword or in the circles of a rose. I saw an exceedingly high Wheel, which was not before my eyes, nor behind me, nor to the sides, but every place at one time. That Wheel was made of water, but also of fire and it was (although the edge could be seen) infinite. Interlinked, all things that are, were, and shall be formed it, and I was one of the fibers of that total fabric."[40]

The vision is indeed a "magical breakthrough of the psyche," but the story does not end here, in "incandescence." We are allowed to see the consequences of the vision. They are nil. The magician gains neither power nor alleviation of his imprisoned state, though he *claims* he has such power, if only he wishes to exercise it. "A formula of fourteen random words . . . and to utter it in a loud voice would suffice to make me all powerful. . . . But I know I shall never say those words."[41] His reasoning seems somewhat specious: "Whoever has seen the universe, whoever has beheld the fiery designs of the universe, cannot think in terms of one man, of that man's trivial fortunes or misfortunes, though he be that very man. That man *has been he* and now matters no more to him. What is the life of that other to him, the nation of that other to him, if he, now, is no one. This is why I do not pronounce the formula, why, lying here in the darkness, I let the days obliterate me."[42] The "magical breakthrough of the psyche" has led, as many of Borges's stories seem to lead, to exhaustion. The magician has seen the infinite, but registers neither the awe of a Moses nor the grand passion of a Faust. Indeed, he has hardly the reaction of an enervated St. Anthony. It is as though St. Theresa yawned and took a nap after her heart was pierced with the arrow of God.

Borges plays much the same trick in another story, "The Aleph." The Aleph is "the only place on earth where all places are—seen from every angle, each standing clear, without any confusion or blending."[43] This vision is shared by two fictional Argentine writers, and the one, being jealous of the other, denies the reality of the vision, in order to lead the first writer into the suspicion that he is mad. The pattern in both stories is similar: a privileged person is given a revelation of infinity, which he passes on to us in brief description, in symbol, and in exclamations of rapture. When his vision passes, he refuses to use it in any way, whether for his own benefit or someone else's, whether in art or in magic. Characters in both stories "let the days obliterate [them]." Revelation, then, is not such a visitation that one would beg it twice. It changes nothing, and ends what anticipation there had been.

One is not sure if Borges makes this choice out of metaphysical considerations or formal ones, that is, whether he is making a comment on the limits of men in handling the limitless, and benefiting by it in any way, or on the limits of the writer to sustain such a tour de force as a mythological intrusion into the mundane world. But the earlier stories, in which he leaves the revelation *imminent*, as Kafka did, seem wiser choices from either view.

In the early story, which he explicitly admires, "The Approach to al-Mu'tasim," Borges not only suggests the attraction of such an imminent revelation, but also discusses its difficulties of presentation. The story is couched as a review of a book in which a student searches for years after the elusive and saintly al-Mu'tasim, who possesses a "clarity" that the student seeks. Borges says of the (fictional) novel, that "the successful execution of such an argument [as the search for an elusive saint] imposes two obligations upon the writer: one, the various invention of prophetic traits; the other, the obligation of seeing to it that the hero prefigured by these traits be no mere convention or phantom."[44] According to his own standards, Borges provides us with the anticipation, the invention of the "prophetic traits" but fails when he attempts to assure us that the revelation is "no mere convention or phantom," as he does in "The Aleph" and "The God's Script." We recognize the state of imminence in waiting for the prophet, or the revelation, the signs that hint at its coming. But we do not know its presence, and Borges's attempt to show us the actual prophet, or the actual transcendent vision does strike us as "mere convention or phantom," particularly because there is no consequence to the vision. Unless the revelation affects the character in some manner profound, or at least positive, we cannot accept its validity, and suppose it the hallucination of a weak mind. Perhaps this is the weakness in Borges's stories, that they remain ensconced in plot, and do not allow character to develop, even when plot dictates that it must. Borges himself has said, "The imminence of a revelation that is *not yet produced*, is perhaps *the* aesthetic reality."[45]

But Borges allows his revelations to remain imminent only in his earliest fiction, that most likely to have been influenced by Kafka. In "Tlön" and "The Approach to al-Mu'tasim," as in Kafka, the revelation is never consummated. Borges reduces the tension of expectation built up for the character and the reader through devices that distance: narrators who are not involved or affected by the imminence of the revelation; a retreat from its metaphysical significance through submersion in scholarship. The reader is left with the epistemological problem rather than the moral. Borges ignores the problem of individual as well as collective "right action," which so concerned Kafka. Neither action nor moral choice is a part of Borges's fictional interests. This attitude is consistent both in the early stories and in the later ones, where the revelation is produced. The latter is an even more emphatic rejection of the *pensum* of acting on one's knowledge. So the difference between these two sets of stories does not hinge on this principle.

Rather, it is that the early stories are much more successful in maintaining a belief in the inexplicable. A story such as "Tlön," leaves the reader dazzled but not disappointed. The origins of the imaginary Orbis Tertius are explained, but the consequences of its creation continue to plague and elude man's rational powers. The immanent (and the immi-nent) has been reduced to a son et lumière. "Tlön" and (probably) "The Approach to al-Mu'tasim" were both stories Borges was working on when his interest in Kafka was freshest. That these early stories were strikingly successful and remain not "early attempts by Borges," but the works for which he is best known, suggest the fruitful influence Kafka may have worked on his early fictional attempts.

III

In the four themes I have examined, however briefly, we see the marked difference between the two authors emerging as clearly as the marked influence. One could perhaps see the difference in terms of the figures of the insider vs. the outsider. Kafka, obviously, is the latter. The effect of the various kinds of biographical exclusions — religious, national, linguistic, social, familial, etc. — figure centrally and archetyp-ally in his fiction. The Kafka character, who changes little from fiction to fiction, has been fittingly described by Heinz Politzer as the *Amhoretz*, the man from the country, excluded from the urbanity and security of city life, excluded from the knowledge of The Law, either secular or sacred, caught in concrete practicalities and excluded from metaphysical abstractions.[46] Thus it is that he exists in a confusing welter of materiality, but knows vaguely that other forces control his life. He vainly tries to put himself in touch with these forces: The Law, The Court, or the Emperor, knowing all the while the futility of his efforts. It is this combination of stubbornness and hopelessness that most critics have been unable to reconcile, and that they, therefore, divide in order to throw away the half they choose to ignore. Kafka's characters are seen by critics as either determined *or* hopeless, rarely both.

But the confusion felt by the character in "The Great Wall of China," in being governed by a system whose existence he doubts and whose intentions he does not understand, cannot be avoided by retreating, for example, to Adrogué to dabble with an uncertain translation. Kafka's characters are never permitted retreat, or escape. They have not the luxury of "lying in the darkness, letting the days obliterate them." They have to deal with imminence *and* immanence. Once the machinery of the strange system has been set in motion, there is no escaping. The knock on the manor gate *will* be prosecuted in spite of the fact that "nowhere in the world would that be a reason for prosecution,"[47] and "a false alarm on the night bell once answered — it cannot be made good, not ever."[48]

Borges's characters labor under no such restrictions. They observe strange countries and customs, magic revelations, and yet may choose to pretend they never existed, or to engage in playful but not very active speculation on their causes and consequences. Imminence is an idea, not a presence. Likewise in the patterns of infinite regress and infinite choices among alternatives: regress in Kafka means denial, denial of a promised destiny "for you alone." In Borges, the infinite regress means acceptance, acceptance of all possibilities, for all places, ages, and stations. There is a fascination with the beauty of the pattern, the regularity of an infinite series of hexagons in the Library of Babel; there is challenge and excitement in the arbitrary rule of the lottery of Babylon, but finally, there is surfeit, ennui. The man who has become immortal desires only termination, so that his life does not repeat itself wearyingly forever. "Nothing can happen only once, nothing is preciously precarious. The elegiacal, the serious, the ceremonial, do not hold for the Immortals."[49] The insider, who has access to all knowledge, all times, and all places, finally tires, and says to himself what Kafka's character would never say, "Gibs auf!"

If choices are infinite and repetitions endless, the problem of verifying reality has been obviated. Borges slyly and playfully accepts, even welcomes, the incredibility factor; Kafka fights against it. Implicit in Kafka's stance is that there *is* an ultimate reality, however hidden, however inaccessible to our ineffectual efforts. Implicit in Borges's stance is that there is not. Perhaps this accounts for the effect of overintellectualization in the revelations that Borges does allow in his fictions. No revelation can be trusted on the basis of the skepticism and relativism that permeate his work. The aesthetic effect of such visions may be considered the terminus ad quem of Borges's characters. Kafka's characters reach for more than effect; they reach for consequence. They ask not for amazement, but for salvation, for a justification of their efforts.

Thus Borges, the insider, inheritor, and amalgamator of the vast Western literary tradition, has assimilated the radical chaos of Kafka's fictions into a mannered labyrinth, where the ultimate revelation is art, not religion. He has tamed Kafka's "No, In Thunder" for the literary establishment; he has made it speculative rather than problematic, intellectual rather than moral, erudite rather than terrifying. Borges plays a game whose rules he himself makes, while Kafka describes a game he does not understand and in which he is not even permitted to play. Borges toys with the archetypes of history and myth rather than stumbling among the shadows of the subconscious. His is a leveling, distancing process. It looks at the same problems that Kafka examined, only through the wrong end of the telescope. The problems are rendered small and safe. The exegete replaces the Amhoretz.

Notes

1. James E. Irby, introduction to Jorge Luis Borges, *Labyrinths* (New York, 1962), xix.
2. *Sur* is the influential Argentine literary journal founded in 1931 by Borges's friend Victoria Ocampo. Borges's own early work usually appeared first in this magazine.
3. Jorge Luis Borges, *Borges on Writing* (New York, 1973), 56.
4. Jorge Luis Borges, "An Autobiographical Essay," in *The Aleph* (New York, 1970), 168.
5. Ibid, 171.
6. Interview with the author, 22 March 1976.
7. Ibid.
8. Edwin Muir, introduction to *The Great Wall of China*, 10.
9. Borges, "Autobiographical Essay," 166.
10. Jorge Luis Borges, introduction to *La metamorfosis* (Buenos Aires, 1938), 11.
11. Borges, *Borges on Writing*, 46.
12. Tony Tanner, *City of Words* (New York, 1971), 47.
13. Borges, introduction to *La metamorfosis*, 10.
14. Borges's fascination with the laws and customs of imaginary societies is, like most of his famous themes, recurrent in his fiction. His much later story, "Dr. Brodie's Report" (1970), unapologetically leans on book 4 of Swift's *Gulliver*, but in its description of language and customs, is a rerun of "Tlön." Incidentally, it also calls forth Kafka's "Penal Colony," in which an outsider is called upon to understand and judge customs in a society that is strange to him. In "Dr. Brodie's Report," as in "Tlön," Borges reduces the moral obligation of the narrator, essential in both Swift and Kafka, to mere intellectual curiosity.
15. Jorge Luis Borges, "Tlön, Uqbar, Orbis Tertius," in *Ficciones* (New York, 1962), 34.
16. Ibid., 35.

17. Franz Kafka, "The Great Wall of China," in *Franz Kafka: The Complete Stories* (New York, 1972), 248.

18. Ibid., 240.

19. Borges, "Tlön," 34.

20. Paul de Man, "A Modern Master," *New York Review of Books* 3, no. 7 (19 November 1964):8 (my italics).

21. Kafka, "Before the Law," in *Complete Stories*, 3.

22. Ibid., 4.

23. Kafka, "An Imperial Message," in *Complete Stories*, 5.

24. Borges, "The Immortal," in *Labyrinths*, 114–15.

25. And less explicitly, in the alternate versions of numerous stories, among which he never decided. It can be argued with some justice that these story fragments are but working drafts, and that Kafka never chose among them because he was not yet finished working on them, which may certainly be true in the case of the two fragments of "The Hunter Graccus," or the several reworkings of "The Great Wall of China." But this is a claim that will not hold in the case of "Prometheus," which, while never published during Kafka's lifetime, has all indications of a completed sketch.

26. Kafka, "Prometheus," in *Complete Stories*, 432.

27. Borges, "A Problem," in *Labyrinths*, 244–45.

28. Borges, "The Babylon Lottery," in *Ficciones*, 68.

29. John Updike, "The Author as Librarian," *New Yorker*, 30 October 1965, 244–45.

30. Kafka, *The Trial* (New York, 1964), 276.

31. Borges, *Borges on Writing*, 45.

32. Borges, *Ficciones*, 71, 52, 17, 25.

33. Borges, "The Library of Babel," in *Ficciones*, 83.

34. Updike, "Author as Librarian," 244.

35. Kafka, *The Castle* (London, 1957), 293.

36. Borges, "The Wall and the Books," *Other Inquisitions* (Austin, 1964), 5.

37. Ben Belitt, "The Enigmatic Predicament: Some Parables of Kafka and Borges," *Triquarterly*, ser. 2, no. 25 (Fall 1972):286.

38. Ibid.

39. Ibid., 293.

40. Borges, "The God's Script," in *Labyrinths*, 172.

41. Ibid., 173.

42. Ibid.

43. Borges, "The Aleph," in *The Aleph*, 10–11.

44. Borges, "The Approach to Al Mu'tasim," in *Ficciones*, 41.

45. Borges, "The Wall and the Books," in *Other Inquisitions*, 5 (my italics).

46. Heinz Politzer, *Franz Kafka: Parable and Paradox* (Ithaca, 1962), 173ff.

47. Kafka, "A Knock at the Manor Gate," in *Complete Stories*, 418.

48. Kafka, "A Country Doctor," in *Complete Stories*, 225.

49. Borges, "The Immortal," in *Labyrinths*, 116.

SELECTED BIBLIOGRAPHY
OF WORKS IN ENGLISH

PRIMARY SOURCES

Labyrinths. Edited by Donald A. Yates and James E. Irby. New York: New Directions, 1962.

Ficciones. Translated by Anthony Kerrigan et al. New York: Grove Press, 1962.

Dreamtigers. Translated by Mildred Boyer and Harold Moreland. Austin: University of Texas Press, 1964.

Other Inquisitions 1937–52. Translated by Ruth L. C. Simms. Introduction by James F. Irby. Austin: University of Texas Press, 1964.

Fictions. Edited by Anthony Kerrigan. London: John Calder, 1965.

A Personal Anthology. Edited by Anthony Kerrigan. New York: Grove Press, 1967.

The Book of Imaginary Beings. In collaboration with Margarita Guerrero. Revised, enlarged, and translated by Norman Thomas di Giovanni in collaboration with the author. New York: Dutton, 1969.

The Aleph and Other Stories (1933–1969). Translated by Norman Thomas di Giovanni. New York: Dutton, 1970; London: Cape, 1971.

An Introduction to American Literature. In collaboration with Esther Zemborain de Torres. Translated and edited by L. Clark Keating and Robert O. Evans. Lexington: University of Kentucky Press, 1971.

Dr. Brodie's Report. Translated by Norman Thomas di Giovanni. New York: Dutton, 1972; London: Cape, 1974.

A Universal History of Infamy. Translated by Norman Thomas di Giovanni. New York: Dutton, 1972; London: Allen Lane, 1973.

Selected Poems 1923–1967. Translated by Norman Thomas di Giovanni et al. New York: Delta, 1973.

In Praise of Darkness. Translated by Norman Thomas di Giovanni. New York: Dutton, 1974.

Chronicles of Bustos Domecq. In collaboration with Adolfo Bioy Casares. Translated by Norman Thomas di Giovanni. New York: Dutton, 1976.

The Book of Sand. Translated by Norman Thomas di Giovanni. New York: Dutton, 1977.

The Gold of the Tigers. Translated by Alastair Reid. New York: Dutton, 1977.

SECONDARY SOURCES

Alazraki, Jaime. *Jorge Luis Borges*. New York: Columbia University Press, 1971.

Barnstone, Willis, ed. *Borges at Eighty: Conversations*. Bloomington: Indiana University Press, 1982.

Barrenechea, Ana María. *Borges the Labyrinth Maker*. New York: New York University Press, 1965.

Bell-Villada, Gene H. *Borges and His Fiction: A Guide to his Mind and Art*. Chapel Hill: University of North Carolina Press, 1981.

Burgin, Richard. *Conversations with J.L. Borges*. New York: Holt, Rinehart & Winston, 1969.

Christ, Ronald J. *The Narrow Act: Borges's Art of Allusion*. New York: New York University Press, 1969.

Cohen, J.M. *Jorge Luis Borges*. Edinburgh: Oliver & Boyd, 1973.

Cortínez, Carlos, ed. *Simply a Man of Letters; Papers of a Symposium on J.L.B.* Orono: University of Maine at Orono Press, 1982.

Cortínez, Carlos, ed. *Borges the Poet*. Fayetteville: University of Arkansas Press, 1986.

Crossan, John Dominic, *Raid On the Articulate: Comic Eschatology in Jesus and Borges*. New York: Harper & Row, 1976.

Dunham, Lowell, and Ivask, Ivar, eds. *The Cardinal Points of Borges*. Norman: University of Oklahoma Press, 1971.

Foster, David William. *J. L. Borges; An Annotated Primary and Secondary Bibliography*. New York and London: Garland Publishing, 1984.

McMurray, George R. *Jorge Luis Borges*. New York: Frederick Ungar Publishing Co., 1980.

Modern Fiction Studies 19, no. 3 (Autumn 1973). (Special issue devoted to Borges.) Purdue University.

Murillo, Luis A. *The Cyclical Night: Irony in James Joyce and Jorge Luis Borges*. Cambridge: Harvard University Press, 1968.

Newman, Charles, and Kinzie, Mary, eds. *Prose for Borges*. Evanston: Northwestern University Press, 1974.

Rodríguez Monegal, Emir. *Jorge Luis Borges: A Literary Biography*. New York: E. P. Dutton, 1978.

Running, Thorpe. *Borges's Ultraist Movement and Its Poets*. Michigan International Book Publishers, 1981.

Shaw, D. L. *Critical Guides to Spanish Texts: Borges's Ficciones*. London: Grant & Cutler, 1976.

Sorrentino, Fernando, *Seven Conversations with J. L. Borges*. Translated by Clark M. Zlotchew. New York: The Whitston Publishing Co., 1982.

Stabb, Martin S. *Jorge Luis Borges*. New York: Twayne Publishers, 1970.

Stark, John. *The Literature of Exhaustion: Borges, Nabokov, Barth*. Durham, N.C.: Duke University Press, 1974.

Sturrock, John. *Paper Tigers: The Ideal Fiction of Jorge Luis Borges*. London: Oxford University Press, 1977.

Wheelock, Carter. *The Mythmakers: A Study of Motif and Symbol in the Short Stories of J. L. Borges*. Austin: University of Texas Press, 1969.

INDEX

Acevedo, Isidoro (maternal grandfather), 24–25

Adrogué, 27–28, 42, 46, 70, 178

Alazraki, Jaime, 1–18

Allegories of Reading (de Man), 10

Allen, Woody, 15–16

Alonso, Amado, 2

Anglo-Saxon, 11, 50–51

Antioch Review, 9

Argentina, 1–3, 5, 6, 16

Argentine Diaries (Gombrowicz), 7

Ariosto, 13, 54

artifice, in fiction of Borges and Nabokov, 141–53

Ascasubi, 27–28, 39, 52

Ashbery, John, 15–16, 93–96

Atlantic Monthly, 9, 83

Austen, Jane, 38

"Author as Librarian, The" (Updike), 11, 62–77

baroque style, 2, 17

Barrenechea, Ana María, 14, 72, 92, 94

Barth, John, 13–14, 83–93, 98–108, 171–72

Beckett, Samuel, 8, 17, 52, 62, 83–93

Bénichou, Paul and Sylvia, 8

Biblioteca Nacional of Argentina, 8, 48–49

Bioy-Casares, Adolfo, 46–47, 117, 184; *See also* H. Bustos Domecq

"Boedo-Florida Polemic," 1, 2, 40–41

Borges and the New Generation (Prieto), 4

Borges: A Reader (eds. Monegal and Reid), 17–18

Borges, Colonel Francisco (paternal grandfather), 22–23, 25

Borges: Enigma and Clue (Tamayo and Díaz), 4

Borges, Jorge Guillermo (father), 22–23, 31, 41, 45

Borges, Jorge Luis: autobiography, 21–55; becomes director of national library, 48–49; birth, 21; blindness, 7, 49; career as lecturer, 46–47; childhood, 24–25; critical reaction to, 1–19; in South America, 5–7; in United States, 8–9, 11, 18, *165–73*; early reading, 25, 28–29; early style, 2; father's blindness, 27–28, 34; favorite reading, 42, 44–45; first poems, 30; infamy, as theme, 10–11; jobs, 43–44; libraries, importance of, 3, 11, 12, 24–25, 82, 121; life under Peron, 46; lives in Geneva, 27–30; moves to Europe, 27–28; moves to Spain, 30; place in Latin American literature, 3–7; prose style, 5, 12–13; reputation, 55, 62; return to Buenos Aires, 33; serious illness, 45; schooling, 26–28; travels in United States, 52–53; work at library, 44

WORKS—POETRY:

"Elegy," 1

"Embarking on the Study of Anglo-Saxon Grammar," 51, 119

"In Praise of Darkness," 124

"Límites," 138

"Mirrors," 70

"Muertes de Buenos Aires," 39

"Mythical Founding of Buenos Aires, The," 39

"Noche que en el Sur lo velaron, La," 39

"Plainness," 35

"Poem of the Gifts," 49, *69–70*

WORKS—PROSE:

Aleph and Other Stories, The, 8, 46, 125–27, 181

"Aleph, The," 60, 93, 125, 155, 187

"Approach to al-Mu'tasim, The," 43, 106, 161, 175–91

"Art of Insult," 43

"Autobiographical Essay," 3, 18, 21–33, 125
"Avatars of the Tortoise," 123, 131
"Averroes' Search," 122
Book of Imaginary Beings, The, 114
Book of Sand, The, 17
"Borges and I," 58, 68, 94, 127
"Challenge, The," 126
Chronicles of H. Bustos Domecq, 48
"Circular Ruins, The," 45, 77–83, 93, 122, 125–27, 134–39, 163, 181–93
"Comment on August 23, 1944, A," 63–64
Complete Works, 5–6
"Congress, The," 54
Cuaderno San Martín, 39
"Cult of the Phoenix, The," 158
"Dead Man, The," 126
"Death and the Compass," 45, 59, 77–83, 125–27, 143
Discusión, 3
Doctor Brodie's Report, 17, 54, 190n
Dreamtigers, 8, 11, 56–61, 67–72, 163
"Emma Zunz," 122
Evaristo Carriego, 39–40, 115n, 157
"Extent of My Hope, The," 1
Fervor de Buenos Aires, 34–35
Ficciones, 8, 11, 46, 58–61, 62–72, 74–77, 77–83
"Funes the Memorius," 60, 94, 172
Garden of the Forking Paths, The, 2, 3, 43, 46, 57–61, 62
Hacedor, El, 51, 67
History of Eternity, A, 8, 43
"Hombres pelearon," 38, 42
"House of Asterion, The," 166–67
"Immortal, The," 59, 162, 181
In Praise of Darkness, 54
Inquisitions, 2
"Intruder, The," 124, 126
"Investigations of a Dog," 69
"Kafka and His Precursors," 64–65, 157
Labyrinths, 56–61, 62–72, 77–83, 83–93, 94, 117, 134–39, 175–91
Language of Argentines, The, 2
"Library of Babel, The," 8, 11, 12, 45, 74–77, 77–83, 91–93, 94, 122, 150, 175–91
Los naipes del tahur, 33
"Lottery in Babylon, The," 8, 45, 77–83, 94, 122, 157, 170, 175–91
Luna de enfrente, 39
"Meeting, The," 126
"Metaphor, The," 13

"Modesty of History, The," 112
Other Inquisitions, 8, 63, 136–39
Others, The, 54
Personal Anthology, A, 16, 93–96, 115
"Pierre Ménard, Author of the Quixote," 14, 17, 45, 58, 77–83, 86–93, 95, 106, 112, 116, 134–39, 160, 175–91
"Ragnarök," 69
"Secret Miracle, The," 147, 158
"Shape of the Sword, The," 57–59, 80–81, 145
"Story of the Warrior and the Captive," 22
"Streetcorner Man," 42, 175–91
"Theme of the Traitor and the Hero," 59
"Theologians, The," 145
"Three Versions of Judas," 120
"Tlön, Uqbar, Orbis Tertius," 45, 57–59, 86–93, 94, 106, 122, 128, 146, 168–73, 175–91
Universal History of Infamy, 2, 8, 11, 42–43, 61
"Visera fatal, La," 26
"Waiting, The," 73–74
"Witness, The," 137
"Writing of God, The," 163, 186
"Zahir, The," 60
    with Adolfo Bioy-Casares:
    Six Problems for don Isidro, 47, 142,
    Model for Death, A, 47
    Two Memorable Fantasies, 47
Chronicles of H. Bustos Domecq, 47

Borges, Leonor Acevedo de (mother), 23–24, 48
Borges, Norah, 30, 33, 48
Borges the Labyrinth Maker (Barrenechea), 72, 92, 94
Borges y su pensamiento político (Orgambide), 5
Browne, Sir Thomas, 38, 61, 88, 169, 178
Buenos Aires, 1, 2, 8, 21, 28, 129

Cahiers de L' Herne, 8, 16–17, 62n, 80
Cahiers du Sud, 8
Caillois, Roger, 8, 51
Candelabro de los siete brazos, El (Cansinos-Assens), 32
Cansinos-Assens, Rafael, 31, 33, 35
Cardinal Points of Borges, The (eds. Dunham and Ivask), 16–17
Carriego, Evaristo, 21, 39, 108
Castle, The (Kafka), 12, 76, 184

Caudillo, The (Jorge Guillermo Borges), 25–26, 54–55
Cervantes, 10, 13, 58–61, 134–39
Chesterton, G. K., 12, 54, 64–66, 123, 131
City of Words: American 1950–1970 (Tanner), 14
compadritos, 21
Conti, Haroldo, 5
Cortázar, Julio, 6

de Man, Paul, 7–12, 55–62, 115n
de Quincey, Thomas, 153–64
de Torre, Guillermo, 33
dialectical materialism, 4
Díaz, Adolf Ruiz, 4
di Benedetto, Antonio, 5
Dickens, 6, 23
Dickstein, Morris, 17
"Dirty War," 5
Domecq, H. Bustos (pseudonym Borges and Adolfo Bioy-Casares), 9, 47, 117
Don Quixote, 10, 25, 43, 58–61, 170

Eliot, T.S., 12, 64–66
Encounter, 9
Esquire, 9
"exhaustion," 83–93
Expression of Irreality in Borge's Work (Barrenechea), 14

Fajardo, Saavedra, 38
Falklands War, 5
Fernández, Macedonio, 35–38, 70, 137
Fierro, Martín, 71
Figaro Litteraire, Le, 8
Finnegans Wake, 83–85, 99
Flaubert, 9, 85
Freud, 4
Fuentes, Carlos, 6–7

García Lorca, 30
García Márquez, Gabriel, 5–6, 13, 127
Gasset, Ortega y, 32–33, 171, 174
Gass, William, 15, 108–16
gauchos, 3
Giles Goat-Boy (Barth), 92, 99–108
Gobrowicz, Witold, 7
Gómez de la Serna, Ramón, 33
Grecia, 31, 32
Güiraldes, Ricardo, 40–41
Gutiérrez, Eduardo, 25

Hacia la Nada (Jorge Guillermo Borges), 26

Hakim, 10, 57–61
Hamlet, 10, 41, 156
Harper's Bazaar, 9
Harvard University, 8, 52
Haslam, Frances (paternal grandmother), 22–23
Human Comedy, The (Saroyan), 23
Hygiene des lettres, 8

Ibarra, Néstor, 35, 51
"Imaginary Borges and His Books" (Gass), 15, 108–16
infamy, as theme, 56–62
International Publishers' Prize, 8, 52, 62, 117

Johnson, Samuel, 138–39
Joyce, James, 83–85, 98–108, 125

Kafka, 11, 12, 16–17, 45, 54, 56–57, 62–77, 85, 90, 95, 117, 125, *173–91*
Kazin, Alfred, 16, 127–30

labyrinth, 3, 72–77, 77–83, 108–16, 149–50, 165–73
Lafinur, Juan Crisóstomo, 25
Latin America, 5–7; as part of Western culture, 5
Lettres Françaises, 8
Literature of Exhaustion: Borges, Nabokov, Barth, The (Stark), 14
Llosa, Mario Vargas, 5–6
Lorca, García; *See* García Lorca
Lugones, Leopoldo, 27, 30, 38–39, 52, 67

Macherey, Pierre, 18, 77–83
Mallarmé, 6
Márquez, Gabriel García; *See* García Márquez, Gabriel
Martín Fierro, 25
Marxism, 4
Megáforo, 1, 2
Ménard, Pierre, 10, 14, 58–61
mirror, as symbol, 71, 114, 116–24, 132–33
"Modern Master, A" (de Man), 9, 10, 55–62, 116n
Monde, Le, 8
Moyano, Daniel, 5

Nabokov, Vladimir, 14–17, 98–108, *141–52*, 168
New York (journal), 9
New Yorker, 9, 11, 13, 15, 18, 62

New York Review of Books, 9, 55n, 108n
New York Times Book Review, 17, 127n
Nosotros, 34, 37, 40
Nouvelle Revue Française, 8
Nouvelles Littéraires, Les, 8

Observateur, L', 8
Ocampo, Victoria, 2, 41, 45, 48–49
Old English, 7, 29, 50
Old Norse, 7, 25, 29, 50
One Thousand and One Nights, 10
On Heroes and Tombs (Sábato), 6
Orgambide, Pedro, 5

paradox, 1, 10, 15
Perón, Juan, 46, 48, 115
pop art, 83–85
Prieto, Adolfo, 4
psychoanalysis, 4

Quevedo, Francisco de, 11, 39, 63, 130

"Reality of Borges, The" (Scholes), 14
Remembrance of Things Past (Proust), 13,
   76
Revue Européenne, La, 8
romanticism, 4

Sábato, Ernesto, 3, 6, 10
Salmagundi, 9
Scholes, Robert, 14–15, 130–39
Schopenhauer, 29, 111–16
self-parody, 96–108, 171, 173n
Shakespeare, 13, 50
Stark, John, 14

Steiner, George, 8, 9, 15, 16, 116–24
Sur, 2, 8, 45, 49, 174
surrealism, 4

Tamayo, Marcial, 4
Tanner, Tony, 14, 17, 165–73, 177
Tel Quel, 8
Temps Modernes, Les, 8, 77n
Teste, Monsieur, 58
Texas, University of, 8, 117
Thackeray, 23
Times Literary Supplement, 9
Tolstoy, 6, 9
TriQuarterly, 9, 17
Twain, Mark, 38, 54

ultraism, 33, 113–16; beginnings, 34–35;
   early members, 40–41; revues, 40–41
Ulysses, 12
Updike, John, 11–13, 17, 52, 62–77, 183
Urondo, Paco, 5

Valéry, Paul, 3, 4, 36, 58–61, 66, 80, 108
Verdevoye, Paul, 8
Vogue, 9
Voltaire, 9, 10, 57

Walsh, Rodolfo, 5
Wells, H. G., 12, 23, 64–66, 108, 131–34
Wittgenstein, 15
World War I, 27
World War II, 7

Xul-Solar, Alejandro, 41

RITTER LIBRARY
BALDWIN-WALLACE COLLEGE